Good governance:
a practical guide for trustees, chairs and CEOs

| About this book

Chapters 1-10 © 2000-11 Dorothy Dalton
Chapter 11 by Tesse Akpeki edited by Dorothy Dalton
Contributions by Lindsay Driscoll, Robin Stephenson, Anne-Marie Piper, Julia Unwin and others.

ISBN 978-0-7199-0001-3

About the author

Dorothy Dalton is editor of *Governance: essential information for effective trustees*. She is a leading expert on governance and advises several national charities.

With a 'first' in mathematics, Dorothy, a former Headteacher, was chief executive of ACEVO, the association of chief executives of voluntary organisation from 1992 to 2000. From 2000 to 2003 she was a non-executive director of the Inland Revenue. She is a trustee of EveryChild and Grandparents Association, and governor of Northwood College where she chairs the Governance Committee. She has been chair of trustees of the Journey of a Lifetime Trust (JoLt), chairman of governors of Orley Farm School Trust, and trustee of several charities including Marie Curie Cancer Care. She is a fellow of the Leadership Trust Foundation and International Students House. She is on the Advisory Council of the Institute for Global Ethics UK Trust and of the Leadership Trust. She founded JoLt, the Network of Women Chairs, and *Groundbreakers: Voluntary sector women leaders*.

During her spare time, Dorothy has organised and led month-long challenging expeditions for disabled and disadvantaged teenagers to remote corners of the world as well as organising and participating in fundraising expeditions such as crossing the Jordanian Desert by camel or canoeing, kayaking and white-water rafting the Zambezi between Zimbabwe and Zambia.

Previous NCVO publications written by Dorothy:
- Recruiting a New Chief Executive: a guide for chairs and trustees
- The Board's Responsibility for Appraising the Chief Executive
- Good Governance: The Chair's Role
- Good Governance: The Chief Executive's Role

About the publication

This publication is primarily aimed at organisations with staff. Smaller organisations may benefit from the information outlined in this publication, but they are not the primary audience and as such may need to adapt the information for their circumstances.

This guide is written for chairs, chief executives and trustees. Chapter 5 is written specifically for the chair while the primary audience for chapter 6 is the chief executive. Nevertheless all trustees are advised to include both these chapters in their reading as it will give them a better understanding of the role of the chair and the chief executive in good governance.

| Contents

While all the chapters are useful to anyone with an interest in governance and can be used practically by chairs, CEOs and trustees, each chapter has been designed with a primary audience in mind. This primary audience is indicated on the edge of each page with the following key.

■ **Trustees** ■ **CEO** ■ Chairs

Acknowledgements

I am enormously grateful to Anne Moynihan, head of NCVO's Governance and Leadership team, for commissioning this publication and for her support and encouragement throughout. I am grateful to Crowe Clark Whitehill (CCW) for sponsoring this publication and especially to Sam Coutinho, partner at CCW, for her interest and enthusiasm for governance. I am grateful to the many contributors to this publication and especially to Tesse Akpeki who wrote one of the chapters (and put up with my editing!) and also to several other experts in the field including Lindsay Driscoll, Anne-Marie Piper, Robin Stephenson, Julia Unwin as well as various nonprofit governance specialists in the USA. Much of what I have learnt has come from them and from examples of good practice from a wide range of charities and their boards. The huge strength of the charity sector is its willingness to share good ideas and practice – long may this continue.

Finally, this publication is dedicated to my fantastic family: to Bill to whom I have been married for 40 years; our terrific sons, Mike and Tim; two fabulous daughter-in-laws, Emily and Casey; and four wonderful grandchildren Emma, Jacob, Kate and Beth. Without their support, encouragement, tolerance and the happiness they bring, none of my achievements would have been possible.

Introduction

Good governance on its own does not guarantee the success of a charity as strong governance cannot make up fully for weak management. Similarly, weak governance may not prevent a charity from being reasonably successful as outstanding management can carry a weak board. Good, strong governance balanced by good, strong management is a winning formula that creates opportunities and enhances the success of the organisation. Achieving this has to be the aim of every trustee, every chief executive and every chair of a professionally managed charity.

Although every board should aspire to delivering high quality governance, it is important to remember that perfect governance does not exist. Each of us can only make our own contribution to governance that is constantly evolving for the better and constantly improving. It is vital that each of us, each of our fellow trustees and our chief executive want to make governance of our charity as good as we can possibly make it.

I am a great believer in learning from others and adapting good practice in other charities to the needs of my 'own' charities. It also seems pointless to me to spend time reinventing the wheel. I have therefore tried to bring together in one publication lots of ideas and model documents that can be adapted easily to the needs of your charity. I hope you find them useful.

Good governance is all about team work and the willingness to learn and improve thereby being better able to achieve our vision and being of greater service to our charity's beneficiaries. It is a serious role that carries responsibilities and liabilities but should also be satisfying and fun. Thank you for all you do for your charity.

Chapter 1
Fundamentals of good governance

1.1 Introduction

Being a trustee should be enjoyable, satisfying and sometimes even challenging. As long as you are willing to use your skills, expertise, experience and good sense for the benefit of the charity, and as long as you are willing to learn, you will get a great deal from trusteeships. Delivering good governance isn't easy. Go into trusteeship with your eyes open. It is a serious role which does carry responsibilities and in certain rare occasions, personal liabilities.

To be an effective trustee, it is important to understand:
- who under charity law the trustees are
- what is expected of trustees
- the personal liabilities of trustees
- the role and duties of trustees, and
- what governance is and its relationship to management.

This chapter covers the first three bullet points. The next chapter covers the last two bullet points.

1.2 | Who are trustees?

In September 1992 the *On Trust* report (chaired by Lady Winifred Tumim), was published. It was the first major report on the governance of charities. The report came up with the amazing statistic that approximately two out of three trustees did not know they were trustees! I remember laughing out loud when I read this and wondered how it could be possible for trustees not to realise they were trustees – until it happened to me. I was a headteacher and was asked to serve on an advisory council of a youth club in central London. Having attended a couple of meetings, I was puzzled because we were being asked to rubber-stamp decisions which were clearly being made elsewhere instead of playing an advisory role. On being questioned further the chair admitted not being clear about our legal status. On taking legal advice he discovered that the members of the so-called 'advisory' council were in fact listed as trustees. In which case I was not prepared to rubber-stamp decisions being made elsewhere.

On the other hand, The Royal National Lifeboat Association (RNLI) used to have a council of 60, all of whom believed they were trustees. In line with other organisations with very large governing boards, RNLI set up a smaller committee which they called their trustee committee. This committee met more often and as the years went by, more and more was delegated to the trustee committee by council. Early in the 21st century, when carrying out their governance review, they discovered that because so much had been delegated to the trustees committee, the 60 council members who thought they were trustees, were in fact no longer trustees. Members of the trustee committee were trustees under charity law. This is because no matter what they are called, according to charity law, trustees are the

'persons having the general control and management of the administration of the charity'.

Many people are asked to serve on a local community committee, or to be a member of an executive committee without realising that by going onto these committees, they become trustees of a charity.

Because the law defines trustees as having control, they are legally responsible for the charity. Ultimate responsibility and ultimate authority lies collectively with the board of trustees. They can delegate some of their authority but can never delegate their responsibility.

If something goes wrong, the Charity Commission or the courts will look to see who are presenting themselves as trustees and who else might be a trustee under charity law because of the influence they have on major decision-making in the charity.

1.3 | Expectations of trustees

Trustees are expected:

- to act only in the best interests of the charity
- to be involved in major decisions and to take decisions jointly with other trustees
- not to benefit from their role as trustees and company directors.

To act only in the best interests of the charity

Conflicts of interest are almost inevitable. It is how they are handled that is important. Mishandling of conflicts can lead to adverse publicity and damage to the reputation of the charity and of some trustees. The key is openness.

Many charities have a register of trustees' interests. I find a register isn't particularly helpful. This is because, in my experience, it is impossible to get every trustee to fill in the register; the register soon becomes out of date and often trustees don't think of all potential conflicts of interest when filling in the register of conflicts.

It is far better to have:

- **a written conflict of interest policy and procedures, and**
- **very early in every agenda for board and committee meetings, an agenda item calling for trustees, chief executive and others present to declare any conflicts of interests with any items under consideration during the meeting.**

If there are no conflicts declared, this should be recorded in the minutes. If a conflict is declared, it should be noted in the minutes together with action taken in line with the trustees' conflict of interest policy, eg the conflict was so minor that the trustee concerned was allowed to stay in the room and take full part in the discussion and decision. Or, the trustee was allowed to remain in the room but take no part in the discussion or decision-making. Or the trustee was asked to leave the room throughout the agenda item. If the last of these situations occurs make sure that there is still a quorum for this part of the meeting – the trustee standing in the corridor cannot be counted as part of the quorum.

To be involved in major decisions and to take decisions jointly with other trustees

- **In order to be involved with major decisions, trustees need to attend meetings.**

When things start to go wrong, some trustees believe that by not attending meetings they cannot be blamed for the problems. This is not the case. The courts take the line that those trustees who did attend are, at least, making some attempt to address the issues whilst those who didn't bother are therefore more culpable. So it is in every trustee's interests to attend meetings.

If you serve on a board where attendance by some is poor, it helps to produce and circulate an annual register of attendance with percentage of meetings attended against each trustee's name. It is amazing how quickly trustee attendance will improve! Governing documents increasingly often include a clause which says that if a trustee does not attend trustees' meetings for a specified amount of time (eg six months or three consecutive meetings) the trustee automatically ceases to be a trustee. Sometimes this is included in a code of conduct for trustees instead.

- **The board should have the skills and expertise to make these major decisions.**

Base the skills needed on the board on what you hope the charity will achieve in the next five years or so (eg your strategic priorities), as well as skills needed for your particular area of work and more general skills, expertise and characteristics, eg knowledge of the voluntary sector, common sense. Identify gaps and tailor your trustee recruitment to filling these gaps. See also chapter 2 resource 2.6.

1.3 | Expectations of trustees continued

There is research to show that diverse, well-balanced boards make better decisions; diversity of age, gender, ethnicity etc, are important but so is diversity of personality. Try to avoid a board of clones.

Where and when they, ie when you do not have on the board the relevant professional expertise, trustees should seek professional advice (ideally in writing or if given in person, the key points of the advice should be recorded in the minutes).

- **Trustees must be fully aware that no one other than the board acting collectively has authority unless authority has been delegated by the board in writing to individuals (such as the chair) or committees.**

It is important to guard against an inner cabinet of senior or other trustees or small groups, such as the chair and chief executive or the chair on his/her own, taking over major decision-making and thus disempowering the board. Remember ultimate control must lie with the board.

- **Supporting democratically made decisions of the board**

When they leave the boardroom, trustees must publicly support decisions by the board even if they argued passionately against. If a trustee cannot publicly support decisions made by the board, the trustee should resign from his/her position as trustee (and company director).

Not to benefit from their role as trustees or company directors

- Trustees must not use their position as trustees or company directors of the charity to get preferential treatment for themselves, their families or other connected persons.
- Trustees must not use their position as trustees or company directors of the charity to gain work (eg provision of paid services) for themselves, for companies with which they have strong connections, for members of their family or for other 'connected' persons.
- Trustees cannot be paid for trustee duties unless the charity has the power to do so in their governing documents or is granted this power by the courts or the Charity Commission.
- Trustees need to be aware of the **'shared or common purse' rule** – ie that trustees are deemed to share a common purse with their spouses and any dependent adult members of their family. So any money going to a spouse or a dependent adult family member is deemed to go to the trustee.
- Trustees cannot be paid for **non-trustee services** unless the charity has the power to do so in their governing documents. Under certain circumstances it is possible for charities to give themselves the power to be paid for non trustee services. See CC11 Trustee Expenses and Payments from the Charity Commission website
  http://www.charity-commission.gov.uk/Publications/cc11.aspx
  In particular read section E part of which is printed here.

There are a number of conditions, all of which must be met before payment can be made validly. The conditions are that:
- *there is a written agreement between the charity and the trustee or connected person who is to be paid (see section E4)*
- *the agreement sets out the exact or maximum amount to be paid (see section E4)*
- *the trustee concerned may not take part in decisions made by the trustee board about the making of the agreement, or about the acceptability of the service provided (see sections E4 and E5)*
- *the payment is reasonable in relation to the service to be provided (see section E6)*
- *the trustees are satisfied that the payment is in the best interests of the charity (see section E7)*
- *the trustee board follows the 'duty of care' set out in the 2000 Act (see section E8)*
- *the total number of trustees who are either receiving payment or who are connected to someone receiving payment are in a minority (see section E9), and*
- *there is no prohibition against payment of a trustee (see section E10).*

- *It is also a condition that, before entering into this type of agreement, trustees must 'have regard to' Charity Commission guidance on the subject.*

We have used section E to provide this guidance and trustees must be able to show that:
- *they are aware of this guidance*
- *in making a decision where the guidance is relevant, they have taken it into account*
- *if they have decided to depart from the guidance, they have a good reason for doing so.*

I would advise charities to think very carefully before going down the route of paying trustees for non-trustee services. If things don't work out as they should, it can be a very painful process (especially for the chair of trustees) to deal with issues such as poor services or over-charging by a fellow trustee or his/her firm or his/her family member.

1.4 | Personal liability of trustees

Under charity law trustees will put themselves at risk of personal liability only if they

- *cause loss* to the charity by acting unlawfully, imprudently or outside the terms of the charity's governing documents or
- in the case of unincorporated charities, commit the charity to debts which amount to more than its assets; or, in the case of charitable companies, continue to operate when they know or ought to know that they cannot avoid insolvent liquidation.

Acting lawfully

Clearly trustees should ensure that the charity keeps within the law. Trustees with the executive have to work hard to keep up with new laws or changes to existing laws.

Acting within the governing documents

Trustees are personally liable if they act outside the charity's governing documents: for example, outside the charity's charitable objects or use powers that they do not have in their governing documents. Clearly governing documents are vitally important. Trustees will look to the chief executive and/or company secretary to inform them immediately if any proposal falls outside the charity's charitable objects or if the board wishes or needs to use powers that they do not have under the charity's governing documents.

| # Acting prudently

Little is said or written about the duty of prudence. Certainly the courts take into consideration that trustees are human and therefore can make mistakes. A test of reasonableness is therefore used – ie did trustees exercise 'reasonable care, skill and diligence, including such as would be exercised by a reasonably diligent person with the general knowledge, skill and experience of the particular director'. The courts also take into consideration that trustees are volunteers. A paid trustee would have a higher duty of care.

What does the Charity Commission say about prudence?

Trustees must:
- ensure that the charity is and will remain solvent
- use charitable funds and assets wisely, and only in furtherance of the charity's objects
- avoid undertaking activities that might place the charity's funds, endowments or other assets, or reputation, at undue risk and
- take special care when investing the funds of the charity, or borrowing funds for the charity to use.

What do the courts say about prudence?

- Do you have the power? (in the governing document or general law)
- Have you acted in good faith and only in the interests of the charity?
- Have you adequately informed yourself in order to make the decision in question?
- Have you taken into consideration any factors which it is not proper for you to take into account?
- Is the decision reasonable?

So what can trustees do to avoid acting imprudently and to prove that they acted prudently at the time the decision was made? They should record in the minutes **how major decisions are made** ie:
- check that any major proposal put to the board is within the charity's charitable objects and within powers given to the charity in its governing documents
- consider various options and the advantages, disadvantages and risks of each option
- consider whether any external professional advice is needed (get this in writing and make sure a copy is kept with the minutes of the meeting)
- make sure you act solely in the interests of the charity and check that you have not taken into account factors that would be inappropriate to take into account. For example, deciding not to sell to the highest bidder because some trustees think the person is rude
- if the proposal requires either the borrowing or lending of funds, ensure that this being done wisely and on the basis of a good business plan which has been fully scrutinised by the board. (Remember that loans to trading companies need to be considered as investments ie trustees must be confident that it is a wise investment and that the charity will get a good return on its investment in the trading company.)
- listen to the advice of the executive team and, as Lord Higgs said in his advice to non-executive directors, 'question intelligently, debate constructively, challenge rigorously and decide dispassionately'
- consider how risks attached to the chosen option are to be managed
- agree on how the success of the chosen option is going to be measured ie what are the key performance indicators
- decide whether the continuing feasibility of the project or proposal needs to be reviewed by trustees and, if necessary, fix dates for the feasibility reviews
- if new delegated authority from the board is required, make sure the authority is clear, recorded in writing and reviewed from time to time and
- ensure all the steps above are recorded succinctly in the minutes of the meeting.

1.6 | Insolvent liquidation

The most important things for trustees to know are:

- you need to ensure that restricted funds are only used for the purposes for which they were given. (If you have cash flow problems, you cannot under any circumstances 'borrow' from restricted funds to pay for activities that fall within unrestricted funds.)
- as soon as you think your charity might be insolvent or very near the point of insolvency, trustees must then act solely in the interest of the charity's creditors, You need to speak immediately to your auditors. Appoint an insolvency practitioner. The board must meet frequently and regularly. Careful minutes need to be kept of each meeting so that you can prove that the trustees were acting solely in the interests of creditors.

1.7 | Conduct

All trustees are expected to use their independent judgement on all matters and to follow advice from the Higgs Report for non-executive directors – ie to:
- question intelligently
- debate constructively
- challenge rigorously and
- decide dispassionately.

In addition all trustees are expected to adhere to Nolan's **seven principles of public life**:

Selflessness: Holders of public office should act solely in terms of the public interest. They should not do so in order to gain financial or other benefits for themselves, their family or their friends.

Integrity: Holders of public office should not place themselves under any financial or other obligation to outside individuals or organisations that might seek to influence them in the performance of their official duties.

Objectivity: In carrying out public business, including making public appointments, awarding contracts, or recommending individuals for rewards and benefits, holders of public office should make choices on merit.

Accountability: Holders of public office are accountable for their decisions and actions to the public and must submit themselves to whatever scrutiny is appropriate to their office.

Openness: Holders of public office should be as open as possible about all the decisions and actions that they take. They should give reasons for their decisions and restrict information only when the wider public interest clearly demands.

Honesty: Holders of public office have a duty to declare any private interests relating to their public duties and to take steps to resolve any conflicts arising in a way that protects the public interest.

Leadership: Holders of public office should promote and support these principles by leadership and example.

1.8 | Confidentiality

From time to time trustees will be involved in activities either at board meetings or on behalf of the board which call for tact, discretion and above all, confidentiality. Some of the more obvious examples of this include staff and employment issues or the appointment of new members of staff. The proceedings of all such meetings are confidential to those taking part. Breaches of such confidentiality cause distress to the individuals concerned. Any serious breach should be considered by the board with a view to considering whether the individual concerned should be asked to resign. See resource 1.3 for a model confidentiality policy.

Resources for Chapter 1

1.1 Sample conflict of interest policy: Marie Curie Cancer Care

Policy on management of conflicts of interest

Purpose of policy

This policy applies to all trustees of Marie Curie Cancer Care. Its purpose is to protect both the trustees and the charity from possible accusations of impropriety.

Trustees have a legal obligation to act in the best interests of the charity and, under the Companies Act 2006, a statutory duty to act in the way in which he/she considers in good faith would be most likely to achieve the charity's purposes. Conflicts of interest may arise where an individual's personal interests or loyalties to third parties conflict with the interests of the charity. Such conflicts can inhibit free and impartial discussion, result in decisions that are not in the best interests of the charity and risk the impression that the charity has not acted properly.

Declaration of interests

Potential conflicts of interest should be declared upon:
- Invitation to join council as a trustee
- The conflict of interest first arising (e.g. on appointment to the Board of a company with whom the charity has a relationship)
- The trustee becoming aware that a potential conflict of interest exists (eg when the trustee first becomes aware that a company of which he is a director has a contractual relationship with the charity).
- A declaration of interests form is available from the company secretary. all new trustees are asked to complete a declaration on appointment and all existing trustees will be asked to complete a form on adoption of this policy and to review their declared interests annually. A register of declared interests is maintained by the company secretary.

Management of conflicts of interest

The extent of a trustee's involvement in the discussions and decisions of council will depend upon the nature of their conflict of interest. In the first instance it is the trustee's duty to advise the chair of council at the start of any meeting if the trustee has any potential conflicts of interest affecting any matters on the agenda for that meeting, and the nature of such conflict.

If a trustee is likely to benefit directly or indirectly[†] from a decision of council they should refrain from involvement in discussion or decision making on that subject matter and will not be counted in the quorum. Examples would be where a trustee is also a director or significant[*] shareholder of a company with whom council is discussing a contract.

If a trustee is a carer to or is related to a user of the charity's services then they should refrain from involvement in discussion on or decision making that directly affects that patient and will not be counted in the quorum.

[†] an indirect benefit arises when the benefit falls to a person or body connected to the trustee. Examples of connected persons are members of the trustee's family, a trustee of a trust of which the trustee is a beneficiary, a firm of which the trustee is a partner or a company of which the trustee is a director. For a full list of definitions of connected persons or if a trustee has any doubt if a relationship should be treated as a conflict of interest, please consult the company secretary.

[*] significant for this purpose means holding, together with the trustee's family, more than 5% of the issued voting shares of the company.

Resources for Chapter 1 continued

The same applies if a trustee faces any other conflict of interest.

If an item under discussion might affect a trustee indirectly eg where it affects all or a number of users of the charity's services in the same way, then the trustee may participate in discussion on and decision making in relation to that benefit.

If a trustee fails to declare an interest known to the chair, the company secretary or any other trustee then they may disclose such interest on the trustee's behalf.

Ultimately, the chair will decide, if necessary after consulting fellow trustees, if a trustee has a conflict of interest and if that trustee should be permitted to participate in discussions and decisions on any given subject and if they should be counted in the quorum.

The minutes of any meeting at which a conflict of interest is declared will record:
- the nature of the interest
- an outline of the discussion
- the actions taken to manage the conflict.

Trustees with a declared conflict of interest will not be authorised as signatories to either contracts or invoices connected with such conflict.

In the case of a substantial and persistent conflict of interest which seems likely to damage the interests of the charity, the chair may ask a trustee to remove the conflict, if necessary by resigning his position as trustee.

1.2 Marie Curie Cancer Care trustees declaration of interests form

I, _____, a trustee of Marie Curie Cancer Care, have set out below my interests that might conflict with those of Marie Curie Cancer Care as required by the charity's conflicts of interest policy:

Category	*Please give details of the interest and whether it applies to yourself or, where appropriate, a member of your family or some other person with whom you have a close connection.*
Current employment and any previous employment in which you have a financial interest	
Appointments (voluntary or otherwise) eg trusteeships, directorships, professorial chairs, local authority membership etc.	
Membership of any professional bodies, special interest groups, or mutual support organisations. (It is not necessary to declare an interest if your interest in another charity is only as a subscription paying member)	
Investments in unlisted companies, partnerships and other forms of business, significant* shareholdings and beneficial interests in listed companies. *significant for this purpose means holding, together with your family, more than 5% of the issued voting shares of the company.	
Gifts or hospitality offered to you by external bodies whilst acting in your position as a trustee of Marie Curie Cancer Care and whether this was declined or accepted in the last 12 months	
Do you or your immediate family use, or care for a user of the charity's charitable services?	**Yes/No*** *Please delete whichever does not apply. If Yes please supply details.
Any contractual relationship with the charity or a subsidiary	
Any other conflicts of interest not covered by the above	

To the best of my knowledge the above information is correct and complete. I undertake to advise the company secretary of Marie Curie Cancer Care if any of the above information should change or if I become interested in any way that creates a potential conflict of interest with my position as a trustee of Marie Curie Cancer Care. I agree to review and update this declaration annually. I give my consent for this information to be used for the purposes described in the charity's conflicts of interests policy and for no other purpose.

Signed _____ (Trustee) Date _____

Resources for Chapter 1 continued

1.3 Confidentiality policy

Article from March'11 issue of *Governance*. Printed with kind permission of Robin Stephenson

Note: All model policies should be tailored to the needs of individual charities.

Employees, trustees and volunteers must not disclose to any unauthorised person any confidential information about the interests or business of the charity, its staff, trustees, beneficiaries, funders or other partners. Such disclosures may lead to disciplinary action including, in serious cases, the termination of a paid or unpaid post at the charity or the removal of a trustee. A non-exhaustive list of information which the charity considers confidential (unless such information is already legitimately in the public domain) includes:

- Any personal information about staff, trustees, beneficiaries, funders or other partners (other than details published with the consent of the person concerned) such as their name and address, personal, financial, or family circumstances.
- Information held in relation to funding applications, grant applications, joint ventures, project initiatives, strategic plans, etc. (other than those published by the charity for public consumption).
- Financial information other than information already in the public domain.
- Details of any security arrangements including IT security e.g. passwords etc.
- Individual salaries or other confidential information relating to employees.

When employees or volunteers leave the charity they must immediately return any files, documents, reference books and other papers relating directly or indirectly to the charity or its staff, beneficiaries, funders or other partners.

Employees, volunteers and trustees must be particularly alert to requests from the press or other media and should refer such requests to a senior manager or press officer (where there is one) before disclosing any information in response to such enquiries.

Restricted information within the charity

Restricted information includes confidential and sensitive information that is restricted to those members of staff, trustees, beneficiaries, funders or other partners who need the information in the course of their work. Restricted information must not be disclosed to anyone else, whether inside or outside the charity. Restricted information, whether communicated orally, electronically or in writing, should always be identified as 'Confidential' and where appropriate 'For [Named Recipient's] Eyes Only'. Such information might include:

- Proposals or plans for the future such as possible mergers.
- Special forthcoming projects, programmes, events, or initiatives before they have been announced or publicised.
- Financial and statistical information.
- Sensitive business information.
- Sensitive personal information about existing or potential beneficiaries, employees, trustees or volunteers.
- Information relating to employees or trustees including applicants for positions, leavers or joiners prior to any public announcement.

General rules in support of confidentiality

Everyone associated with the charity is encouraged NOT to:
- leave confidential information (in paper or electronic form) where it is easily visible in the office or elsewhere;
- use computer software or programmes on any electronic equipment unless they are authorised by the charity;
- give any press interviews or statements on or off the record, without first discussing with a senior member of staff;
- write personal letters on the charity's notepaper or under the charity's banner;
- discuss with staff, trustees, beneficiaries, funders or other partners the business of other staff, trustees, beneficiaries, funders or other partners, except as strictly required by their job; and
- conduct confidential conversations (including over the telephone) where you may be overheard.

NOTES

1. Employees, trustees and volunteers leaving the charity will continue to be bound by their obligations of confidentiality even after the termination of their post (whether paid or unpaid) at the charity (for whatever reason). Former employees, trustees or volunteers may not make use of non-public information gained in the course of their involvement with the charity for their own benefit or for the benefit of any other person.

2. Nothing in this policy will prevent an individual from making a 'protected disclosure' within the meaning of the Public Interest Disclosure Act 1998; (i.e. a legitimate, good faith, 'whistle-blowing' disclosure).

3. Breaches of this policy by employees or volunteers will be dealt with through the charity's disciplinary procedure. Breaches of this policy by trustees will be dealt with under the process laid down in the trustee code of conduct.

Robin Stephenson

Chapter 2
Understanding governance

2.1 | What is governance?

As a trustee you are responsible for governance so it is important to know what governance means. There are a number of definitions of governance. For example:

Good Governance: A Code for the Voluntary and Community sector, defines governance as being:
'The systems and processes concerned with the overall direction, effectiveness supervision and accountability of an organisation'.

While the Code of Governance for Members of the National Housing Federation says:
'The board's central role is to direct and control an organisation's work, that is to determine strategic direction and policies, to establish and oversee control and risk management frameworks and to ensure that the organisation achieves its aims and objectives. Management, that is the implementation of board policies, is delegated to staff.'

2.2 | What exactly is governance?

When questioned about their role, many boards will say that they
- set strategy and
- decide on policy.

In my experience most boards do neither well and anyway, **governance is much more than strategy and policy**. I will cover strategy later in this chapter. Let us concentrate for the moment on policy.

Policy

Not all policies are board policies. There will be operational policies and management policies, all of which should be delegated to your chief executive. The question is which policies are so important that they have to be board policies? A useful exercise is for a board to put time aside to consider which policies are so important that they have to be board policies, and then to plan how (and how frequently) these high-level policies should be reviewed.

Some policies are required by law to be board policies eg
- health and safety (H & S)
- safeguarding policies.

Some are required by regulation, such as
- reserves policy
- investment policies.

Some because trustees are effectively the employer, such as
- high-level outline terms and conditions of employment including disciplinary and grievance policies
- performance management
- whistle-blowing.

Other high-level board policies will relate to the work of the charity, such as
- involvement of beneficiaries and service users in decision-making.

Once these have been identified, it is worth considering how often each of these is to be reviewed. For example, by law health and safety needs to be considered annually. On the other hand, you might only want to look at your investment policy every four years. If the law is changing rapidly in a particular field, for example, employment law, you may want to review your employment policies annually. If not, you might feel that these policies should be reviewed every three years. It is easiest to draw up a table to help develop a plan to review policies. See page 27.

This table also shows whether the board or a committee of the board reviews the policy. Sometimes a policy is reviewed by a committee and later by the board. Remember, trustees do not write these policies. The task of writing policies is delegated to the executive. Trustees should concentrate on the policy itself ie what the policy is trying to achieve and should not get drawn into the minutiae.

Policy	Frequency of review (years)	Board	Finance committee	Services committee	Date of next review
Health and safety	1	✓			Nov'11
Safeguarding children	1	✓		✓	March'12
Reserves	3		✓		July'12
Anti-fraud	4		✓		Jan'13
Involvement of service users	3			✓	Nov'14
Employment terms and conditions	3	✓	✓		Nov'14

Remember: Governance is more than strategy and policy!

2.3 | Model role description for trustees

How does all this translate into what should a board actually do? There are many good model trustee role descriptions around. All say much the same thing although each might 'slice' these duties slightly differently.

I believe our key responsibilities as trustees are to hold the charity 'in trust' for current and future beneficiaries by:
- ensuring that the charity has a clear vision, mission and strategic direction and is focused on achieving these
- being responsible for the performance of the charity and for its culture
- ensuring that the charity complies with all legal and regulatory requirements
- acting as guardians of the charity's assets, both tangible and intangible, taking all due care over their security, deployment and proper application
- ensuring that the charity's governance is of the highest possible standard.

Underpinning all of these is the management of risk and of course we cannot govern our charities without appointing, supporting, developing, constructively challenging and if necessary, dismissing our chief executive.

If we stick to these five key responsibilities we will keep to our governance role and not drift into management. A much more detailed role description can be found in Resource 2.1

2.4 | The management/governance interface

Many chief executives and chairs quote the Carver model of governance, which they simplify extensively into *'governance is about identifying the "ends" and management is about deciding the "means" of achieving the "ends" as defined by the board'*, thus implying that governance and management are mutually exclusive. They are not. Andrew Hind, in his book, *The Governance and Management of Charities* (now sadly out of print and selling for large sums on e-bay!) says:

'Thus although it is fashionable to argue that trustees should only worry about the ends which the charity is seeking to achieve, while leaving management to run the organisation within the boundaries of management authority which they have received from the board, in practice trustees and senior managers have to exercise judgement jointly on the big issues as they arise. No amount of prior framework-setting can cater for every eventuality.'

Richard Chait in his book, *How to Help your Board Manage Less and Govern More*, writes:

'...we do not wish to portray the distinction between management and governance as being absolute, nor do we wish to suggest that trustees and chief executives must endure a relationship in which one never enters the other's primary domain. Governance is too complicated and too dynamic to be reduced to some inviolate division of labor. We mean to suggest only that, on the whole, boards should be more concerned with governance than management.'

In an interview for the Centre for Charity Effectiveness, Dame Mary Marsh, then chief executive of NSPCC said:

'The final tip comes from a Shell story – about developing the quality of being able to "helicopter"; this is about the capacity to have a vision and see the big picture, combined with knowing how, when and where to drill down into the detail, then knowing when to come back up again. You can't go too high up – you assume everything is OK underneath, when it might not be. You do need to get down and check'.

Besides carrying out their different but complementary roles, which may occasionally overlap, trustees and the chief executive need to recognise that they are interdependent and that they provide joint leadership to the charity.

There will always be areas which can be seen as both management and governance. If there is an open, constructive relationship based on mutual respect and understanding between the board and the chief executive, these grey areas can be discussed and agreement reached on who does what. If such a discussion generally proves difficult, it might be an idea to carry out a role analysis exercise from time to time.

2.5 | Role analysis exercise

How to carry out this role analysis exercise:
- The role analysis exercise that follows should be used as a basis for discussion in order to clarify roles.
- It is important that the chair and chief executive adapt the form adding and removing some of the subject areas and then work through the exercise together, having previously and separately thought through the issues.
- Columns should **NOT** be completed by a series of ticks. Instead descriptions need to be used. For example: *no role, carries out, full authority, proposes action, suggests options, informs, if within budget approved by the board, reports back to* ....
- A discussion with the whole board should follow.
- Roles need to be reviewed regularly because organisations develop and change. Personnel change too – the previous chair may have been a brilliant public speaker and an excellent spokesperson for the organisation; the new chair may have different skills and may prefer to leave this role to others.
- The process of discussing respective roles should in itself contribute much to a good, strong partnership between the chair and chief executive. Often, when a good relationship is established, there is little further need to refer to role descriptions. However, if an organisation is growing rapidly and roles are changing, role descriptions should be regularly reviewed and, if appropriate, changed by mutual agreement.

Chief executive's role	Subject area	Chair's role	Board's role	Delegated to .... committee
	Functioning effectively at trustee level			
	Structuring the board			
	Recruiting new trustees			
	Ensuring trustees understand their responsibilities			
	Induction, briefings, training, support of trustees			
	Board meetings, board papers, board agendas			
	Dealing with difficult or 'rogue' trustees			
	Succession planning			
	Information needs of trustees			
	Reviewing the constitution			
	Planning strategically			
	Defining the mission			
	Defining the vision			
	Leading strategic planning			
	Producing and agreeing the strategic plan			
	Producing and agreeing the corporate or business plan			
	Producing and agreeing the annual plan and targets			

Trustees   CEO   Chairs

Chief executive's role	Subject area	Chair's role	Board's role	Delegated to .... committee
	Policy			
	Deciding which policies are board policies			
	Developing a timetable to review board policies			
	Policy recommendation and development			
	Identifying and managing risk			
	Evaluation			
	Agreeing key performance indicators			
	Monitoring key performance indicators			
	Measuring the performance of the organisation			
	Monitoring the performance of the organisation			
	Appraising the chief executive			
	Reviewing the performance of the board			
	Reviewing the performance of board committees			
	Staff appraisal			
	Financial			
	Budget preparation			
	Budget approval			
	Capital purchase (major equipment, cars, buildings)			
	Building renovation/ refurbishment decision			
	Expansion decisions			
	Leasing decisions			
	Purchase of major items			
	Major repairs (more than £............)			
	Minor repairs (less than £............)			
	Emergency repairs			
	Monthly financial reporting			
	Monthly financial approvals			
	Staff salaries			
	Signing of contracts above £....			

2.5 | Role analysis exercise continued

Chief executive's role	Subject area	Chair's role	Board's role	Delegated to .... committee
	External relationships			
	Chief spokesperson			
	Spearheads lobbying			
	Spearheads fundraising			
	Media policy			
	Personnel			
	Hiring of staff			
	Dismissing staff			
	Allocating work/projects to staff			
	Staff grievances			
	Staff disciplinary procedure			
	Staff appeals (grievance, discipline, appraisal)			
	Appointing the chief executive			

Trustees CEO Chairs

2.6 | Governance in more depth

Governance today has greatly grown in sophistication. Gone are the days when well-governed charity boards concentrated solely on regulatory, compliance and financial issues. Today in well-governed charities, both the chief executive and the board realise that there are three key strands of governance:

Corporate/fiduciary governance

Most boards of trustees concentrate on financial and compliance matters ie on corporate/fiduciary aspects of governance. This is an essential and fundamental aspect of governance and one which all trustee boards, without exception, have to address.

Strategic governance

However, as Chait, Ryan and Taylor in *Governance as Leadership* point out, boards that concentrate solely on finances, compliance etc, have effectively little power or influence. Real influence and power come from developing and determining the charity's future: its vision, mission, values and strategy. Some chief executives and many trustees believe that the executive alone develops strategy, which goes to the board for approval and little else. In this situation, the chief executive is effectively disempowering the board. Thinking strategically and developing the strategy should be a joint function of trustees and executive and is, I believe, in the best interests of the charity.

Chait, Ryan and Taylor argue that trustees are well placed to *'frame problems and make sense of ambiguous situations'*. This is because, *'they see the big picture; they bring multiple perspectives and the process benefits from the interplay of ideas from people of different backgrounds'*. This process is best accomplished when executive and trustees work together to address and make sense of the complex issues that all organisations face in this rapidly changing world. Chait, Ryan and Taylor call this process '**generative governance**'. Others will argue, as I do, that this crucial process is part of the early stages of good strategic governance and not a separate strand.

Research (Chartered Institute of Management Accountants (CIMA) and International Federation of Accountants (IFAC) Enterprise Governance 2005 and others) also reinforces the importance of working strategically and has shown that the success or failure of an organisation is closely related to how effective an organisation is in a number of areas including:
- clarity of strategy
- execution of strategy
- the ability to look outward, constantly scan the environment and the ability to adapt to a rapidly changing environment and sometimes to abrupt, unexpected external changes

As a result of this research, CIMA has developed a model of governance called '**enterprise governance**'. Its two key strands are corporate governance and business governance. The latter is another name for strategic governance. CIMA has also developed a scorecard to measure business/strategic governance.

To reinforce the importance of strategic governance, one only has to go back to the fundamental role of trustees, ie *'to hold the charity in trust for future and current beneficiaries'*, which clearly requires trustees to think about, and plan for, a successful future. Strategic governance is therefore a crucial part of good governance and is the second key strand of governance.

Getting the board to think strategically and ensuring the board applies strategic thinking to much of what it does, requires thought, planning and a certain amount of engineering by the chief executive and by the chair, both of whom are key to effective governance. A good ploy is to persuade the board to regularly set an hour before board meetings (every meeting if at all possible) to consider a 'big issue'.

2.6 | Governance in more depth continued

A second step is to make sure that board papers do not concentrate on management detail but are focused on governance aspects and reflect the fact that the senior executives are thinking strategically and scanning the environment for opportunities, threats and other changes on behalf of the board. See chapter 4 for more details.

Finally a really well constructed board away-day (ideally two days with a night in between) can result in trustees and executive, metaphorically and literally, rolling their sleeves up and tackling major issues, thinking strategically and planning for the future.

This was done exceptionally well at Marie Curie Cancer Care where I was a trustee. Our chief executive, working with our new chair, arranged the first day to start with a council (ie board) meeting. After we had got board business done, the rest of the day was led by different members of the executive team and one external speaker, who framed the big issues facing the charity and brought alive our briefing papers.

On the second day, six trustees working in pairs were delegated the task of running three consecutive sessions, which took the big issues that had been framed the previous day and facilitated trustees and executives to think strategically and brainstorm the best way forward. Finally, in three mixed groups drawn from trustees and executives, and with each group led by a trustee, we were challenged with the task of coming up with the five key areas that we as trustees felt our executive should concentrate on. A hugely enjoyable, and effective two days. The organisation's thinking developed and so did the significant respect, trust and confidence that the council and the executive have for each other.

Impact governance

However there is one other strand of governance that other writers and governance gurus miss out on. All charities have to have charitable objects. In one way or another each charity is trying to improve the world or some part of the world. Its very existence becomes questionable if the charity has little effect or impact, and does little to actually achieve its objects, vision and mission. Therefore a major part of governance should concentrate on assessing the charity's performance and the impact it is having towards achieving its charitable objects; on ensuring there are appropriate high-level policies that relate directly to the achievement of charitable objects, such as policies for the safeguarding of children or vulnerable adults; on ensuring regulatory and legal compliance relating to the actual work of the charity such as residential care standards; and, on ensuring that service users, beneficiaries etc, genuinely influence what the charity does.

Therefore a major part of governance should concentrate on:
- assessing the charity's performance and the impact it is having towards achieving its charitable objects
- ensuring there are appropriate high-level policies that relate directly to the achievement of charitable objects, such as policies for the safeguarding of children or adults
- ensuring regulatory and legal compliance relating to the actual work of the charity such as residential case standards and
- ensuring that service users, beneficiaries etc, genuinely influence what a charity does.

I call this vital strand of governance 'impact governance'. Professional bodies or learned institutions may prefer to call this 'professional governance'.

So the **Dalton model of governance** (she writes pompously!) has three important strands: corporate, impact and strategic. Examples of what each strand might cover are shown below:

Corporate/fiduciary governance	Impact Governance	Strategic Governance
• Finance • Property/estate • Resources • Income generation • Audit: financial, risk, internal • Remuneration • HR: terms and conditions, • contracts • IT • Compliance: VAT, PAYE, Charity Commission ...... • Policies: investment, reserves, delegated financial authority ... - Whistle-blowing (eg fraud) - Complaints (corporate)	• Care standards • Quality of services • HR – training and education of staff and volunteers involved in service delivery • Complaints (re services) • Whistle-blowing (services) • Policies regarding service delivery: protection of vulnerable adults, children, ... - Involvement of users, beneficiaries, members - Key campaigning/lobbying themes or messages	• Environmental scans: - demographics - political changes (NHS, Social Services) - competitors - strategic alliances partnerships mergers - changes on the horizon • Planning ahead • Looking at things differently • Looking for new solutions, new ways • Tackling difficult and complex issues
UNDERPINNING ALL THREE		
Strategic thinking and planning		
Performance measurement		
Risk		

Some charities, that do not provide services, may think that impact governance doesn't apply to them. I can, for example, hear foundations and other grant-makers saying, 'It doesn't apply to us'. Not so. Foundations do not exist purely to hand out money. They exist to change lives in some way. For recipients of small grants, the reporting back and oversight regime has to be very light. On the other hand, recipients of large grants should be required to show what impact the grant is having in achieving the objectives not only of the recipient organisation but also of the funding charity.

For example the trustees of UNICEF UK will want to ensure that relatively large sums of money given to UNICEF projects run by the global organisation, have a beneficial impact on children; have proper policies to ensure that adults with abusive motives are not allowed to volunteer or work with children; that the voices of the children themselves are heard; that the project works collaboratively with others in order to make the lives of children better, etc. Impact governance applies to all charities.

2.7 | When is it appropriate for boards to get into management detail?

It is important that trustees try to stick to their 'helicopter' view of their charity. However there are times when it is right and proper for trustees to get into management detail. For example:

- if something goes wrong, the trustees might need to get into the detail in order to sort things out

or

- in the interest of good governance, the board may wish to throw a spotlight on two or three areas during the coming year. For example, you might want your auditors to take a detailed look at the tax status of those claiming to be self-employed; you might want to set up a small ad-hoc group of trustees and senior executives to ensure that the safeguarding policy and procedures are being followed or you may require a couple of trustees to take a closer look at how complaints are handled and what the charity learns from feedback and to report back.

2.8 | Finance from a governance perspective

Many trustees feel that they do not know enough about finance generally, and charity finance in particular, to fulfil their responsibility for sound financial governance. Most boards have at least one trustee who is strong financially. It is important however that all trustees play their part in financial decisions and financial monitoring. For the trustee who is not strong on finance, I list below what I believe are the minimum requirement for all trustees.

A The basics

It is important for trustees to understand fully what the different fund types are and exactly what they mean. This should be part of their induction.

All trustees need to know about:
- restricted,
- unrestricted, and
- designated funds.

'If the charity has endowments, then make sure you understand:
- permanent endowments, and
- expendable endowments.

Also you need to be introduced to SORP and its requirements.

1 The budget

You should ask about
- How the budget ties in with strategic priorities and the business plan
- For this year's budget, the assumptions on which the budget is based
- The major risks relating to the current budget and how they are being managed.
  Similarly for the new budget when it is presented for consideration and approval.

2 Measuring financial performance

Management accounts

You need to understand why management accounts are a key financial tool (i.e. measure progress against the budget) and what you should expect by way of documentation i.e.
- compare this year's monthly 'actuals' with the same set of figures for the previous year
- compare the year to date with the budget
- provide forecasts of what the end of year figure's might look like; and
- significant variations from budget, or the same period in the previous year, are explained in the introductory narrative.

Financial ratios and other key performance indicators (KPIs)

You should be aware that each board has a responsibility to decide on the financial ratios or other KPIs that they would like to monitor and the importance of tracking these statistics over time.

Examples of ratios and figures that might be tracked:
- for each type of fundraising (eg voluntary donations, legacy, shops) the most common ratio monitored is cost of raising funds to funds raised
- charities delivering residential care (eg care homes, hospices, hotels) will almost certainly want to monitor and track occupancy rates at each residential base

2.8 | Finance from a governance perspective continued

- service delivery charities may wish to measure the cost of delivering one unit of care eg one hour, one day or one week
- charities using temporary agency staff might want to monitor numbers and cost of agency staff and compare these with cost of an employee doing the same job for the same period of time.

Use of graphs to illustrate trends or to compare ratios can also be helpful.

The SOFA, balance sheet and cash flows

If you are unfamiliar with charity finance you need to be talked through the **Statement of Financial Activities (SOFA)** and explained why charity accounts are different (ie the importance of columns showing restricted and unrestricted funds). You need to know that the SOFA is essentially the income and expenditure account.

The **balance sheet** might need to be explained and how it gives a picture of the charity's assets, liabilities and reserves on the day that it was drawn up, ideally giving:
- designated funds
- restricted funds
- unrestricted funds (including fixed assets)
- unrestricted funds (excluding fixed assets)
- free reserves (ie all funds minus fixed assets, endowments and restricted and designated funds).

Cash flow projections are also valuable. They give a picture of receipts and payments in each period and anticipate cash flow for the rest of the year by looking at income over expenditure and opening and closing balances. When looking at the closing balance for each period (usually month), I like to see the figure split into restricted and unrestricted funds.

3 Insolvency

You need to be aware that

Under Charity Law trustees put themselves at risk of personal liability if they,
- in the case of unincorporated charities, commit the charity to debts which amount to more than its assets; or, in the case of charitable companies, continue to operate when they know or ought to know that they cannot avoid insolvent liquidation.

Insolvent liquidation

It is essential:
1. for trustees to ensure that restricted funds are only used for the purposes for which they were given (Remember you cannot without relevant consent – from donor or Charity Commission - 'borrow' from restricted funds to pay for activities that fall within unrestricted funds.); and

2. as soon as you think your charity might be insolvent or very near the point of insolvency, trustees must then act solely in the interest of the charity's creditors, Trustees need to speak immediately to professional advisors (e.g. auditor/independent examiner and insolvency practioner). The board must meet frequently and regularly. Careful minutes need to be kept of each meeting so that there is a record showing that the trustees were acting solely in the interests of creditors.

B Key issues for the board and every trustee

1 Relationship with auditors

Issues that all boards need to consider proactively. (Often this goes by default with trustees unaware of these documents and the part that trustees should play.)

- Will the board or a board committee (eg audit or finance) meet annually with the auditor to discuss their audit and the annual report and accounts? And will there be some time during this meeting for trustees to speak to the auditors without the executive present?
- Before the audit, will the board or a board committee consider the **audit planning letter**? If a committee, is there to be any input by the board?
- If a charitable company, each director is required to give certain undertakings to the auditor such as there is no relevant audit information of which the auditors are unaware. These declarations are made via a l**etter of representation** which is drafted by the auditors. Trustees need to consider what assurances they need in order to give similar guarantees to the auditor. The chair of trustees normally signs the letter on behalf of every director.
- Will the board or one of its committees consider the **audit findings report** which is always addressed to the trustees and often called the '**management letter**'? Management's response to the audit findings report should be considered alongside the report.

2 Internal financial controls, fraud and whistle-blowing

Issues that all boards need to consider:

- How does the board check the robustness of financial controls? (Note the new Charity Commission guidance (CC8) recommends annual review of financial controls.)
- What are the charity's anti-fraud policies and procedures and are they sufficiently robust and known throughout the charity?
- Is there a good whistle-blowing policy and procedure which are known to all staff, volunteers, service users and contractors etc?

3 Understanding risks attached to different types of income

For example:
Public service delivery contracts
Issues that all boards need to consider:

- Does the board require all public service delivery contracts to be on the basis of full-cost recovery? Will contracts covering more than one year also cover salary increases? If not full-cost recovery, how is any shortfall to be funded?
- What is the board's risk appetite regarding public service delivery contracts? Who has delegated responsibility to check contracts prior to signing, to ensure the charity does not accept risks and liabilities that the board finds unacceptable?
- Is there any risk of '**claw back**' ie the commissioning body demanding partial repayment because the charity has only delivered partially (eg only 79% of unemployed people trained by the charity found employment so local authority demands refund of 21%)?

2.8 | Finance from a governance perspective continued

4 Understanding your charity's position with regard to taxes

These should include:
- direct tax
- gift aid
- VAT
- business rates.

These are, I believe, the financial basics for all trustees whether they financially knowledgeable or not.

| Resources for Chapter 2

Resource 2.1 Model role description for trustees

Key responsibilities:

With other trustees to hold the charity 'in trust' for current and future beneficiaries by:

1. ensuring that the charity has a clear vision, mission and strategic direction and is focused on achieving these

2. being responsible for the performance of the charity and for its culture

3. ensuring that the charity complies with all legal and regulatory requirements

4. acting as guardians of the charity's assets, both tangible and intangible, taking all due care over their security, deployment and proper application

5. ensuring that the charity's governance is of the highest possible standard.

Duties and tasks to fulfil the five key responsibilities of trustees:

1. Ensuring that the charity has a clear vision, mission and strategic direction and is focused on achieving these:

To work in partnership with other trustees, the chief executive and other senior staff to ensure that
- the charity has a clear vision, mission and strategic plan that have been agreed by the board, and that there is a common understanding of these by trustees and staff
- the business, operational and other plans support the vision, mission and strategic priorities
- decision-making at board, senior management, middle and junior management reinforce the vision, mission and strategic priorities
- the chief executive's annual and longer term objectives and targets support the achievement of the vision, mission and strategic priorities
- board policies support the vision, mission and strategic priorities
- there are effective mechanisms
  - to listen to the views of current and future beneficiaries
  - to review the external environment for changes that might affect the charity
  - to reassess the need for the charity and for the services it provides, or could provide
  - to review regularly its strategic plans and priorities.

2. Being responsible, with the other trustees, for the performance of the charity and for its culture:

- to agree the method for measuring objectively the progress of the charity in relation to its vision, mission, strategic objectives/priorities, business plans and annual targets, and to receive regular reports on the performance of the charity
- to ensure that the fundamental values and guiding principles of the charity are articulated and reflected throughout the charity
- to ensure that views of beneficiaries on the performance of the charity are regularly gathered and considered by the board
- to appoint the chief executive, to set his/her terms and conditions and to ensure that the chief executive and the charity invest in the chief executive's ongoing professional development
- to receive regular reports from the chief executive on progress towards agreed strategic priorities
- to hold the chief executive to account for the management and administration of the charity
- to ensure that the chief executive receives regular, constructive feedback on his/her performance in managing the charity and in meeting his/her annual and longer-term targets and objectives

Resources for Chapter 2 continued

- to ensure that the chief executive develops a learning organisation and that all staff, both paid and unpaid, review their own performance and regularly receive feedback
- to articulate the values of the charity
- to agree and review board policies
- to ensure that there are mechanisms for beneficiaries, employees, volunteers, other individuals, groups or organisations to bring to the attention of the trustees any activity that threatens the probity of the charity.

3. Ensuring that the charity complies with all legal and regulatory requirements:

- to be aware of, and to ensure that the charity complies with, all legal, regulatory and statutory requirements
- to maintain familiarity with the rules and constitution that govern the charity, to ensure that the charity complies with its governing instruments and to review the governing instruments regularly
- if the charity has powers to delegate, to agree the levels of delegated authority, to ensure that these are recorded in writing by means of minutes, terms of reference for board committees and sub-committees, role descriptions for honorary officers, trustees and key staff, etc, and to ensure that there are clear reporting procedures which are also recorded in writing and complied with
- to ensure that the responsibilities delegated to the chief executive are clearly expressed and understood, and directions given to him/her come from the board as a whole.

4. Being guardians of all the charities assets, both tangible and intangible, taking all due care over their security, deployment and proper application:

- to ensure that the charity has satisfactory control systems and procedures for holding in trust for the beneficiaries all monies, properties and other assets and to ensure that monies are invested to the maximum benefit of the charity, within the constraints of the law and ethical and other policies laid down by the board
- to ensure that the major risks to which the charity is exposed are reviewed annually and that systems have been established to mitigate or minimise these risks
- to ensure that the income and property of the charity is applied for the purposes set out in the governing document and for no other purpose, and with complete fairness between persons who are properly qualified to benefit
- to act reasonably, prudently and collectively in all matters relating to the charity and always to act in the interests of the charity
- to be accountable for the solvency and continuing effectiveness of the charity and the preservation of its endowments
- to exercise effective overall control of the charity's financial affairs and to ensure that the way in which the charity is administered is not open to abuse by unscrupulous associates, employees or volunteers; and that the systems of control are rigorous and constantly maintained through regular evaluation and improvement in the light of experience
- to ensure that intangible assets such as organisational knowledge and expertise, intellectual property, the charity's good name and reputation, etc, are properly valued, utilised and safeguarded
- if the charity owns land, to know on a continuing basis what condition it is in, if its boundaries are being encroached upon, what can be done with it and how it is or should be used. in particular, to ensure that any property which is a permanent endowment is preserved and invested in such a way as to produce a good income while at the same time safeguarding the real value of the capital
- to ensure that all income due to the charity is received and that all tax benefits are obtained and all rating relief due is claimed.

5. **Ensuring that the charity's governance is of the highest possible standard:**

- to ensure that the charity has a governance structure that is appropriate to a charity of its size/complexity, stage of development, and its charitable objects, and that enables the trustees to fulfil their responsibilities
- to reflect annually on the board's performance and your own performance as a trustee
- to ensure that the trustee board has the skills required to govern the charity well, and has access to relevant external professional advice and expertise
- to ensure that there is a systematic, open and fair procedure for the recruitment or co-option of trustees
- to ensure that there are succession plans for the chair and the chief executive
- to participate in individual and collective development and training of trustees
- to abide by the code of conduct for trustees
- to ensure that major decisions and board policies are made by the trustees acting collectively.

Chapter 3
Delegating authority

3.1 | Introduction

Under charity law, trustees are the
'persons having the general control and management of the administration of the charity'.

Therefore
- trustees are ultimately responsible for the affairs of the charity
- trustee responsibility is both collective and individual
- delegation to others does not absolve a trustee of responsibility.

In addition
- delegated authority must be in writing
- individuals and committees with delegated authority need to report back and be held to account
- delegated authority should be reviewed regularly.

3.2 | Delegation

Delegation to the chief executive

The management of the charity is delegated to the chief executive. There are two key areas of work for a chief executive:

- to provide leadership to the charity and to be responsible for the management and administration of the charity within the strategic, policy and accountability frameworks laid down by the board of trustees
- together with the chair to enable the board of trustees to fulfil its duties and responsibilities for the proper governance of the charity and to ensure that the board receives timely advice and appropriate information on all relevant matters.

A more detailed model job description can be found at Resources 3.1. See also Chapter 6 on the role of the chief executive in good governance.

How boards delegate

Boards tend to delegate to the chief executive in a number of different ways. These include clarity and agreement on:

1. the chief executive's job description

2. the strategic framework

- the values, vision and mission of the organisation;
- the strategic priorities of the organisation
- the business/corporate plan
- the organisation's annual objectives and plan
- the chief executive's annual objectives

3. the policy framework

- board policies within which the organisation must be managed and arrangements for their review

4. levels of delegated authority

- clearly recorded levels of financial delegation to chief executive, financial director etc
- clear guidelines on who and within what limits decisions can be made between meetings of board

5. the accountability framework

- how performance of the organisation will be measured;
- how chief executive's performance will be measured; and
- independent checks and assurances.

Delegation to the chair

A chair of trustees has no special duties (other than those of a trustee and chairing trustees meetings and the annual general meeting) and no special authority other than those delegated to the chair by the board of trustees. Charities that only allow their chair to chair meetings usually have poor governance. The chair needs to play a leadership role to the board and is usually delegated the line-management of the chief executive on behalf of the board.

The key delegated duties of a chair of trustees are usually:
- to provide leadership to the board and to ensure that trustees fulfil their duties and responsibilities for the proper governance of the charity
- to support, and where appropriate, to challenge the chief executive and to ensure that the board as a whole works in partnership with executive staff.

A more detailed role description can be found in Resource 3.2.
See also Chapter 5 on the role of the chair in good governance.

Delegation to the treasurer

A treasurer has no special duties (other than those of a trustee and chairing meetings of the finance committee) and no special authority other than those delegated by the board of trustees.

The key delegated duties of the treasurer are usually:
- on behalf of the board of trustees to oversee all financial aspects of the charity so as to ensure its short and long-term viability
- to assist the chair of trustees, other honorary officers and the chief executive in ensuring that the board of trustees fulfils its duties and responsibilities for the proper financial governance of the charity.

A more detailed role description can be found in Resource 3.3.

3.3 | Accountability framework

Routine holding to account

It is important that trustees ensure that those to whom they delegate are doing a good job.

However to really make people accountable, including the trustees themselves, it is crucial to create a culture where everyone wants to learn, develop and become more effective.

To do this it is essential to have a good performance management policy and procedures and to invest resources in the professional development of everyone involved, paid staff as well as volunteers. In order to learn, there has also to be a culture of welcoming feedback from others: colleagues, service users, volunteers, etc. While in some rare cases complaints can lead to disciplinary action, in the main feedback should be used to learn and improve.

Performance of individuals

Part of the charity's performance management policies will include the ongoing and formal performance appraisal sessions for all staff. Clearly the chief executive's performance needs to be appraised (see chapter 9) but so should the performance of other key people in delivering strong effective governance, for example, the chair of trustees (see Chapter 5), other honorary officers and chairs of board committees.

Performance of board committees

Most board committees report back to the board by circulating their minutes, or an abbreviated version of their minutes, to the board. Ideally these reports should carry a cover sheet, which not only draws to trustees' attention key issues about which trustees need to be aware but also highlights decisions that trustees are being asked to make, albeit with recommendations from the committee. The cover sheet should also highlight decisions made by the committee under delegated authority.

In addition, each committee should be asked to do take time out once a year (or every two years if annually isn't really feasible) to:
- review its own performance against its terms of reference
- ask members of the committee
- whether they feel the committee is effective and adding value to governance
- how the committee could become more effective
- whether they are happy with their chair, the quality of the papers, quality of discussions and decision-making, etc.

Audit committees should also be encouraged to get feedback from the external auditor on the performance of the audit committee.

In addition all committees should be required annually to report back on:
- what they have achieved in the last 12 months
- what they hope to achieve in the next 12 months
- what they plan to do differently in order to increase their effectiveness
- what changes, if any, are needed to their terms of reference.

At regular intervals (usually every four to five years) a governance review should be carried out which should include looking at the committee structure of the board.

Performance of the charity

To measure the effectiveness of an organisation and its impact is an extremely difficult task and one which is always 'work in progress'. The task of identifying and/or developing a tool for measuring organisational performance is one which is usually delegated to the executive. There are several performance measurement tools available which range from PQASSO for smaller charities to the balanced scorecard for large, more complex organisations. Most charities develop their own ways of measuring performance against their strategic and business plans. Smaller charities are likely to include a report on the performance of the charity within the chief executive's report to the board. Most charities should have a separate agenda item at each board meeting to receive an honest appraisal on the performance and progress of the charity, ie both good news and bad.

'Spotlights' or independent checks and balances

Once a year, the board should consider which areas of the organisation's work it needs to examine in more detail. Sometimes, the board might want external experts to come in and prepare an independent report (eg health and safety or checking that correct taxes especially PAYE are being paid, or that financial controls are sound) or they might want a small group of trustees to carry out the checks (eg making sure that safeguarding policies and procedures are being followed) or they may ask the executive to take a closer look at a particular area of work (eg making sure sensitive data is secure). It helps to have 'spotlights' carried out in a planned and systematic way.

Evaluating effectiveness should lead to reviewing the powers and authority that have been delegated by the board, ie reviewing role descriptions of key people such as the chair or the chief executive and terms of reference of committees as well as levels of financial delegation, etc.

3.4 | Delegation to board committees

Deciding upon which board committees are needed should be part of a wider governance review.

Governance reviews

Generally governance reviews should be carried out approximately every five years. Ideally such reviews should take place when things are relatively quiet and on an even keel. It also helps enormously if work has already been done on the strategic direction of the charity and there is clarity about what the charity would like to achieve in the next five years or so.

It might be an idea to set up a small ad-hoc committee, if you do not already have a governance or nominations committee, to steer the governance review. Ideally the steering group will consist of a couple of trustees (including the chair of trustees), the chief executive and the company secretary (if you are a company).

Reviewing governing documents

If you have a good idea of what the board would like the charity to achieve in the next few years, now is a good time to review your governing documents. This is particular useful as the governing document can be:
- brought into line with Companies Act 2006 and Charities Act 2006
- ensure that all future plans fall within your charitable objects and that you have the necessary powers to do everything you plan to do.

It is also a good idea to make sure that your governing document is written in plain English and not in a way that can only be understood by lawyers.

Further, this is an opportunity to introduce good governance practice ie introduce limited terms of office for trustees and honorary officers. See also chapter 7.

Try to keep powers as extensive as possible and do not go into too much detail. For example, do not name board committees; instead just make sure you have the power to set up and delegate to board committees. You may also wish to make sure that you can, if the board so wishes, have non-trustees as committee members. This will give the board the flexibility to bring in expertise without necessarily asking people to serve as trustees as well.

For the redrafting or rewriting of governing documents, it is important that you use a firm of lawyers that specialise in charities rather than general solicitors who may have a small number of charity clients. Most firms will be willing to give you a fixed price for the work as long as you are clear about the changes you want.

Educating trustees before you start

Before the review process begins it is a good time to remind trustees of their role, duties and responsibilities, their commitment to the charity and what is expected of them as well as a reminder of circumstances that might make trustees personally liable. Remind them what governance is and look at various models of governance. This can be done by sending trustees on appropriate external courses or you may prefer to commission a governance specialist to facilitate a session with the full board and the senior executive team (who also need to understand the fundamentals of governance).

Review of Board committees

Once you know what the charity would like to achieve in the coming years, you will be able to identify the skills and experience you need on the board. For example, if you have decided (subject to having the necessary powers) to involve the charity in campaigning, you might want one or more trustees with campaigning experience. Similarly if you are thinking of going into public service delivery or starting a major building project, you may want to have trustees with experience of public service contracts or property matters respectively.

See section 3.2 for information on delegation to board committees.
See also chapter 7 on recruitment of trustees.

Reviewing governance committee structures

Not all charities have the power in their governing documents to set up and delegate to committees so check your current governing documents first. If need be, you can ensure that you get this power when you review your governing documents.

I always suggest that when you review your governance structure (ie committee structure), you start with a blank sheet, that is, you consider what sort of committee structure is needed to fulfil the board's responsibilities for the proper governance of the charity and for the charity to achieve its strategic objectives. Consider too which committees need to be 'permanent' and which could be ad-hoc committees. Boards, in my experience, do not use time-limited, ad-hoc committees enough.

Do you need any advisory and/or task groups? Try not to make the committee structure too large and complex. When deciding on the committee structure bear in mind the workload each committee will generate for your staff. If you aren't careful, your chief executive and senior team will find themselves spending most of their time servicing committees.

The most common committees are:
- finance
- audit
- governance.

Model terms of reference for all three are included in Resources 3.4, 3.5 and 3.6.

Some very large charities do not have a finance committee and rely instead on a very good treasurer, an effective finance director and good financial controls and processes. These charities are often dominated by trustees from the for-profit sector who are financially strong and who have good business acumen. The finance director therefore reports directly to the board and ad-hoc committees scrutinise the budget, etc.

Generally larger charities and more complex charities have a separate audit committee. If you plan to have an audit committee, you would be advised to consider whether it should be chaired by a suitably qualified outsider who is totally independent of the charity. Check that you have the power to appoint non-trustees to committees and that not all board committees have to be chaired by a trustee. If you do not have the appropriate powers make sure you get these powers when your governing document is reviewed.

If you decide that a separate audit committee is not required, then make sure that the audit function is given to another committee, such as the finance committee. Make sure too that the audit function covers both financial and non-financial matters and looks at all risks. If another committee has responsibility for the audit function, it is a good idea for this committee to arrange to sit purely as the audit committee at least twice a year.

If governance needs improving, then a governance committee can lead the development of better governance. However consider whether this needs to be a 'permanent' committee or whether it could be an ad-hoc group with a specific time-limited remit.

Charities delivering services often also have a services committee.

3.5 | Delegation to board committees continued

Some boards like to have a fundraising or development committee and others like to have a human resources committee. If you decide to have a fundraising or development committee it is important to remind yourself that the trustees' role is to govern and not to fundraise (unless you are a US non-profit organisation, which expects all trustees to bring money in). If you are too small to have specialist Human Resources (HR) expertise on the staff, it might be an idea to buy in these services. If you are lucky enough to have an HR department then the chances are that you are unlikely to need an HR committee although you may want to have an HR specialist or an employment law specialist as a trustee.

Once you have decided on the committee structure then you need to make sure that you have:
- terms of reference for all committees
- clear reporting lines
- mechanisms for committees' effectiveness to be assessed
- regular reviews of terms of reference
- another review of the governance structure after about five years, or earlier if needed.

Consideration should also be given as to the best way to review the effectiveness of board. This should include reviewing the quality of board papers and whether the right issues are being considered by the board and its committees. See chapter 4 on the right issues.

Trustees CEO Chairs

| Resources for Chapter 3

Resource 3.1 Chief executive: A model job description

Responsible to: the board of trustees as a whole, but usually line-managed by the chair of trustees on behalf of the board.

Key responsibilities:

1. to provide leadership to the charity and to be responsible for the management and administration of the charity within the strategic, policy and accountability frameworks laid down by the board of trustees

2. together with the chair to enable the board of trustees to fulfil its duties and responsibilities for the proper governance of the charity and to ensure that the board receives timely advice and appropriate information on all relevant matters.

Duties and tasks to fulfil the key responsibilities:

1. To provide leadership to the charity and to be responsible for the management and administration of the charity within the strategic and accountability frameworks laid down by the board of trustees.

1.1 Leadership

- to lead, inspire and motivate staff and volunteers
- to assist the board in agreeing the values, ethos, vision and mission of the charity
- to lead the review and development of a medium to long-term strategy for the charity within its objects, vision, and mission, and to obtain the approval of the board
- to develop the work of the charity in order to achieve the agreed strategic plan and its objects, vision and mission and thus to ensure that the charity is focused on achieving the strategic priorities
- to ensure that the charity's values, ethos and policies are relevant, fair and consistently implemented
- to develop an organisation that is constantly seeking ways to learn and to improve its performance
- to develop and maintain an environment that attracts and retains the best staff and volunteers.

1.2 Management

- to be accountable to the board for the proper and effective management of the charity
- to run the charity efficiently and effectively by ensuring that the charity has an appropriate management structure and management systems in order to fulfil its strategic objectives and to carry out its work
- to ensure that all management policies and decisions support the agreed vision, mission, values, philosophy and strategic priorities of the charity
- to ensure that business, operational and annual plans to underpin the strategic plan are developed, agreed and implemented
- to identify appropriate methods for monitoring the performance of the charity and to report back to the trustees on the performance of the charity against its strategy, its business, operational and annual plans, and against the annual budget as approved by the board
- to ensure that the recruitment, management, training and development of staff reflect good employment practice and are directed towards achieving the charity's objectives
- to ensure that the charity is aware of best practice and that it constantly works to achieve this within the constraints laid down by the trustees and resources available.

1.3 Finance and risk

- to be responsible overall for the financial health of the charity including developing, overseeing and monitoring an effective programme of income generation

Resources for Chapter 3 continued

- to ensure that the major risks to which the charity is exposed are reviewed regularly by the board and the executive team, and systems have been established to mitigate these risks; and to ensure a risk analysis is automatically carried out when taking on new work or proposing new work to the board
- to ensure that there are effective mechanisms to ensure the robustness of external and internal controls (financial and non-financial).

1.4 External and internal relations

- to foster good communications throughout the charity and externally
- to develop, as appropriate, the charity's public profile and foster good relationships with government, statutory, voluntary and private bodies and other external stakeholders
- to set up mechanisms for listening to the views of current and future beneficiaries on the performance of the charity as well as on areas for future development
- to scan the external environment for changes that may affect the charity, to advise the trustees proactively and to take necessary action.

1.5 Legal and regulatory compliance

- to ensure that the charity fulfils all its legal, statutory and regulatory responsibilities.

2. Together with the chair to enable the board of trustees to fulfil its duties and responsibilities for the proper governance of the charity and to ensure that the board receives timely advice and appropriate information on all relevant matters.

2.1 Strategy and planning

- in partnership with the chair, to ensure that the trustees set the values, ethos, vision, mission, strategic objectives and strategic priorities for the charity.

2.2 Ensuring high-quality governance

- draw the board's attention to matters that it should consider and decide
- ensure that the board receives all necessary advice, guidance and information on matters relating to current performance, the short- and long-term future of the charity, regulatory and legal compliance and other appropriate issues; making sure that such advice, guidance and information are timely, honest, balanced and relevant
- to ensure that the staff understand and support the governance role of the board and that there is a positive and constructive working relationship between the board and the executive
- to ensure with the chair that the board of trustees reviews regularly the charity's, governing instruments, the charity's governance structure and to assist with the board's assessment of its own performance
- in partnership with the chair to ensure that the board's delegated authority is recorded in writing, understood fully by staff and volunteers and that all agreed reporting procedures are followed
- to work closely with the board to ensure that the board has on it the skills it requires to govern the charity well, and that the board has access to relevant external professional advice and expertise
- to assist the chair in ensuring that there is a systematic, open and fair procedure for the recruitment or co-option of trustees, future chairs of the board and future chief executives
- to work with the chair to ensure that all members of the board receive appropriate induction, advice, information and training (both individual and collective) thus getting the best thinking and involvement of each member of the board.

2.3 Board meetings

- to ensure that the board is given the information it needs to perform its duties
- in partnership with the chair, to develop an annual programme of board and committee meetings and board away-days
- in partnership with the chair to ensure that the right and appropriate items reach board agendas and that high-quality papers support each item on the agenda
- to assist the chair in ensuring that the board focuses on its governance role by making sure that the board agenda and papers do not draw the board away from governance and into unnecessary detail and management issues
- to report regularly to the board of trustees on the performance of the charity, progress towards the strategic priorities and the achievement of board policies
- to submit high-level policy proposals for the approval of the board or assist the board in the development of these policies and to be responsible for the efficient and effective achievement of these policies
- to implement board decisions.

2.4 Relationships with the chair of trustees

- To have regular one-to-one meetings with the chair at which the chair and chief executive can talk openly, discuss progress and problems, agree expectations of each other, plan the board's annual programme together and prepare together for meetings [The chief executive and chair should ensure that there are no 'surprises' between chair and chief executive at board meetings or elsewhere]
- In close consultation with the chair to agree respective roles in representing the charity and acting as spokesperson at public functions, public meetings and to the press/media

Resources for Chapter 3 continued

Resource 3.2 Chair of trustees: A model role description

Key responsibilities:

1. to provide leadership to the board and to ensure that trustees fulfil their duties and responsibilities for the proper governance of the charity

2. to support, and where appropriate, to challenge the chief executive and to ensure that the board as a whole works in partnership with executive staff.

Duties and tasks to fulfil the key responsibilities:

1. To provide leadership to the board and to ensure that trustees fulfil their duties and responsibilities for the proper governance of the charity.

1.1 To guard the long-term future of the charity by ensuring that:

- the board sets the mission, vision, strategy and high-level policies for the charity within the powers and restrictions in its charitable objects and governing instruments
- the board takes steps to monitor the performance of the charity and to ensure that the charity satisfies all regulatory and legal compliance requirements
- major risks to which the charity is exposed are reviewed regularly and systems are established to mitigate these risks without the charity becoming totally risk-averse
- the charity has a satisfactory system for holding in trust for the beneficiaries monies, properties and other assets and ensure that monies are invested to the maximum benefit of the charity, within the constraints of the law and ethical and other policies laid down by the board
- the charity's financial dealings are systematically accounted for, audited and publicly available
- internal controls and systems (both financial and non-financial) are audited and reviewed regularly
- the board and the charity are fair and open to all sections of the community in all the charity's activities
- the board and the charity hear the voices and views of key stakeholders, especially beneficiaries.

1.2 To ensure the highest possible standards of governance by ensuring that:

- the charity has a governance structure that is appropriate to a charity of its size/complexity, stage of development, and its charitable objects and that these structures and the governing instruments are reviewed regularly
- the board delegates sufficient authority to its committees, the chair, the chief executive and others to enable the business of the charity to be carried on effectively between meetings of the board
- the board's delegated authority is recorded in writing by means of terms of reference for board committees, role descriptions for honorary officers and for key staff, etc; and, the board monitors use of these delegated powers
- the board has on it the skills it requires to govern the charity well and these skills are utilised, and that the board has access to relevant external professional advice and expertise
- there is a systematic, open and fair procedure for the recruitment and co-option of trustees, future chairs of the board and future chief executives
- all members of the board receive appropriate induction, advice, information and training (both individual and collective)
- trustees act reasonably, always act in the interests of the charity and comply with the charity's code of conduct for trustees
- the board of trustees regularly reviews its performance.

1.3 To ensure the proper and efficient conduct of board meetings by:

- chairing trustee meetings effectively, seeking consensus, balancing the need for full debate on key questions with the expeditious despatch of business so as to reach clear and agreed decisions as swiftly as possible
- encouraging all trustees to participate and to feel free to challenge constructively both the chair and the chief executive
- taking an active role in ensuring that board agendas are meaningful and reflect the key responsibilities of trustees
- ensuring that the chief executive and his/her staff provide the board with relevant, timely and accurate information in order to allow the board to discharge its responsibilities. This should include alerting the board to major risks, informing the board of current and future key issues, including significant trends, and informing the board about external changes which may impact on the charity
- ensuring that board decisions are made in the best, long-term interests of the charity and that the board takes collective ownership of these decisions
- ensuring that decisions taken at meetings of the board are implemented
- ensuring that that there is an annual programme of board and committee meetings, carefully structured agendas and high-quality briefing papers providing timely information and concentrating on governance.

2. To support, and where appropriate, to challenge the chief executive and to ensure that the board as a whole works in partnership with executive staff

2.1 To support the chief executive by:

- ensuring there are clear and open processes for the recruitment (and if necessary dismissal) of the chief executive, and for setting and reviewing the remuneration package of the chief executive
- ensuring that the board focuses on its governance role and does not slip incrementally, or otherwise, into the management role
- arranging regular, but not over-frequent, meetings with the chief executive and by developing a very professional relationship with the chief executive within which each can speak openly about concerns, worries and challenges
- providing leadership to the chief executive to ensure that the charity is run in accordance with the decisions of the board and the charity's governing documents and that there is clarity about the charity's objectives at all levels
- supervising the chief executive on behalf of the board (unless other arrangements are made), always remembering that the chief executive is responsible to the board as a whole and not to any one individual trustee or sub-group of trustees
- ensuring the chief executive's performance is reviewed regularly
- ensuring the chief executive has the opportunity for professional development and has appropriate external professional support
- in partnership with the chief executive, to agree respective roles in representing the charity and acting as spokesperson.

2.2 To make sure that the board understands and fulfils its responsibility to hold the chief executive and the executive team to account by ensuring that:

- when necessary, the chair and the trustees challenge the chief executive constructively and only in the best interests of the charity and as 'critical friends'
- the chief executive is clear about the key performance indicators by which he/she will be held accountable

Resources for Chapter 3 continued

- the chief executive understands his/her crucial responsibility to provide relevant, honest, timely, high-quality information and advice to the board of trustees
- there are appropriate mechanisms, both internal and external, to verify that the board receives a balanced and honest picture of how the charity is doing.

2.3 To ensure the board works in partnership with management by:

- ensuring through the chief executive, that the staff understand the role of the board and that the chief executive provides an effective link between the board and staff
- ensuring that staff are aware of the board's appreciation of their successes and hard work
- ensuring that, through the chief executive, a performance evaluation process is in place for everyone in the organisation and that the charity invests in the development of staff
- ensuring that whenever practicable, trustees visit various parts of the charity, attend a few events organised by the charity and have informal opportunities to meet the senior management team, staff and beneficiaries.

Resource 3.3 Treasurer: A model role description

Key responsibilities:

1. **on behalf of the board of trustees to oversee all financial aspects of the charity so as to ensure its short- and long-term viability**

2. **to assist the chair of trustees, other honorary officers and the chief executive in ensuring that the board of trustees fulfils its duties and responsibilities for the proper financial governance of the charity.**

Duties and tasks to fulfil the key responsibilities:

1. On behalf of the board of trustees to oversee all financial aspects of the charity so as to ensure its short- and long-term viability.

In partnership with the chief executive, finance director and members of the finance committee
- to ensure that the charity operates within the financial guidelines set out in current legislation, by the charity commission, in the charity's constitution and by the board
- to ensure that the charity has adequate financial and internal audit controls and that these are monitored and reviewed regularly
- to identify and bring to the attention of the board, any financial risks facing the charity that the chief executive or finance director have not already reported to the board
- to ensure that the charity's financial resources are sufficient to meet the charity's current and future needs, and to advise the board on the board's reserves policy, and to ensure that this policy is reviewed and monitored regularly
- to scrutinise the proposed annual budget, and advise and guide the board accordingly
- to scrutinise management accounts, performance against budget, trading performance etc, and to advise the board accordingly
- to scrutinise and evaluate regularly the charity's cash flow position, and to inform the board of any concerns
- to ensure that funding received for specific purposes is separately accounted for and spent for the purposes for which it was given.
- to ensure that all income due to the charity is received and that all tax benefits are obtained and all rating relief due is claimed.
- to review longer term forecasts of capital resources and of income and expenditure, and to review and monitor financial trends within the charity and the sector within which the charity operates
- to meet the external auditor and the internal auditor once a year, independently from the finance director and other senior staff
- to formally present the accounts to the annual general meeting drawing to members' attention all relevant matters, and to respond to questions from the floor
- to chair or be a member of appropriate board committees such as the finance, audit, investment and remuneration committees.

Resources for Chapter 3 continued

2. **To assist the chair of trustees, other honorary officers and the chief executive in ensuring that the board of trustees fulfils its duties and responsibilities for the proper financial governance of the charity.**

- to ensure that the charity has satisfactory control systems and procedures for holding in trust for the beneficiaries all monies, properties and other assets and ensure that monies are invested to the maximum benefit of the charity, within the constraints of the law and ethical and other policies laid down by the board
- to ensure that the income and property of the charity is applied for the purposes set out in the governing document and for no other purpose, and with complete fairness between persons who are properly qualified to benefit
- to keep the board informed of its financial duties and responsibilities
- to advise the board on the financial implications and operational risks arising from board decisions – especially the board's strategic and policy decisions
- to advise the board on the financial strategy proposed by the senior management team and to review and monitor the financial strategy on behalf of the board
- in consultation with the chair of trustees to advise the chief executive and the finance director on the level, quantity and frequency of financial information and reporting required by the board to allow the board to fulfil its legal and statutory responsibilities
- to work with the chief executive, finance director and accountant to ensure that financial information is both accurate and presented in such a way that facilitates good financial governance
- to ensure that intangible assets such as organisational knowledge and expertise, intellectual property, the charity's good name and reputation etc. are properly valued, utilised and safeguarded
- if the charity owns land, to know on a continuing basis what condition it is in, if its boundaries are being encroached upon, what can be done with it and how it is or should be used. in particular, to ensure that any property which is a permanent endowment is preserved and invested in such a way as to produce a good income while at the same time safeguarding the real value of the capital.

Resource 3.4 Terms of reference for a governance committee

Approved by the board of trustees on ....20...

1. Composition, attendees, quorum and reporting

- The governance committee will consist of not less than ... trustees appointed by the board, and the chief executive. The chair of trustees is normally a member of the governance committee.

(There are difference of views as to whether the chief executive should be on the governance committee or not. I advise that he/she should. Others disagree. Whether the chair of trustees should be the chair of the governance committee is very much a matter for the individual charity. With a significant growth in the duties and responsibilities of chairs of professionally managed charities, it may be wise to allocate the chairing of this committee to another trustee although the chair of trustees is likely to be an active member of this committee. However, the chair should not be involved in selecting his/her successor.
It is important to have people with a range of backgrounds on the governance committee. Committee members also need to be good judges of character.)

- The board will appoint the chair of the governance committee.

(The chair of the governance committee needs to be both fair and impartial, needs to be a skilled board member and knowledgeable about the charity. If external advertising or external agents [eg head-hunters/search agents] are not being used, the chair and members of the committee will need to have access to extensive networks.)

- Members of the governance committee may serve for not more than ... years.

- The governance committee will report back regularly and at least annually to the board of trustees.

2. Overall responsibility

Take delegated responsibility on behalf of the board of trustees for ensuring effective and improving governance

Main duties

- to consider and make recommendations to the board on all matters relating to governance
- to consider and advise the board on the composition and balance of the board
- to be responsible for nominating and determining the process for selecting candidates to be recommended for appointment to the board and committees
- to develop and recommend to the board policies and procedures for:
- the induction of new trustees
- reviewing the effectiveness of the board
- the appraisal of trustees
- the training and development of trustees
- to ensure that board members are inducted, trained/developed and appraised.

Financial limitations

The committee has no delegated financial powers.

Resources for Chapter 3 continued

Resource 3.5 Terms of reference for a finance committee

Approved by the board of trustees on ....20...

1. Composition, attendees, quorum and reporting

- The finance committee will consist of not less than .....trustees appointed by the board of whom one will be appointed chair.
- The chair of the finance committee will be appointed by the board. (The treasurer is usually the chair of the finance committee)
- Any trustee not being a member of the finance committee may attend a meeting of the finance committee with the prior agreement of the chair of the finance committee/chair of trustees.
- The chief executive, the finance director and such other members of staff as the chair may require shall be in attendance at meetings.
- Until otherwise determined by the board of trustees, a quorum shall consist of ... members of the committee.

2. Overall responsibility

Take delegated responsibility on behalf of the board of trustees for overseeing all financial aspects of the charity so as to ensure short and long term viability and report back to the board accordingly.

3. Main duties

3.1 Financial

- to ensure that the charity operates within the financial guidelines set out in current legislation, by the Charity Commission, the charity's constitution and by the board of trustees
- on behalf of the board of trustees to ensure that the charity's financial obligations are met
- to regularly review and advise the board of trustees on the appropriate regulatory framework within which the charity must function, including ensuring adequate financial controls
- to advise the board of trustees on the financial implications and operational risks arising from board decisions – especially the board's strategic and policy decisions
- to review longer-term forecasts of capital resources and of income and expenditure, and to review and monitor financial trends within the charity and the sector within which it operates
- to formulate for the board to approve and agree, and regularly to review and monitor, a financial strategy and a reserves policy that will help to achieve the charity's objectives, as set out in the board's current strategic plan and business plan
- to advise on, scrutinise and evaluate a draft annual budget for the approval of the board, ensuring that it is compatible with, and supports, the charity's objects and the strategic, business and annual plans
- to work with the chief executive and other senior executive staff (for example finance director, accountant) to ensure that financial information is both accurate and presented in such a way that it facilitates good governance and management
- to consider regularly the charity's management accounts and monitor performance against the approved budget
- to scrutinise and evaluate regularly the charity's current and forecast cash flow and to inform the board of any concerns
- to approve, within the limits laid down by the board, emergency unbudgeted expenditure
- to approve, within the criteria specified by the board, expenditure of a significant nature on new initiatives

- to formulate (where a separate investments committee does not exist), for board approval and regularly to review an appropriate investment policy; to ensure that it is adhered to and to monitor investment performance against policy and report back to the board accordingly
- to establish (where a separate remuneration committee does not exist), and regularly review the charity's remuneration policy and, as part of the budgeting process, advise the board of trustees on remuneration

3.2 Audit [If this is not covered by a separate audit committee]

- to determine the frequency of tendering for external auditing services
- to consider the appointment of the external auditor and assess independence of the external auditor,
- to recommend the audit fee to the board and pre-approve any fees in respect of non audit services provided by the external auditor and to ensure that the provision of non audit services does not impair the external auditors' independence or objectivity
- to discuss with the external auditor, before the audit commences, the nature and scope of the audit and to review the auditors' quality control procedures and steps taken by the auditor to respond to changes in regulatory and other requirements;
- to oversee the process for selecting the external auditor and make appropriate recommendations through the board to members at the annual general meeting
- to scrutinise and advise the board on the contents of the draft audit report and to review the external auditor's management letter and management's draft response, and to formulate for board use any written representations that may be needed by the auditors in connection with the charity's statutory accounts or any other financial statements
- to discuss with the external auditors any problems or reservations arising from the draft external audit report and draft management letter, reporting relevant issues back to the board, and advising the board accordingly
- to review the performance of the charity's auditors and advise the board on any changes that ought to be made to their terms of engagement.

3.3 Whistle-blowing

- to review the charity's procedures for handling allegations from whistle-blowers and to encourage a culture within the charity whereby each individual feels that he or she has a part to play in guarding the probity of the charity, and is able to take any concerns or worries to an appropriate member of the management team or in exceptional circumstances directly to the chair of the audit committee
- to review the appropriateness of the charity's whistle-blowing policy and follow-up actions taken by management
- to review the charity's procedures for detecting fraud.

3.4 Risk

- to ensure there are robust systems and policies for identifying, managing and reporting risk
- to ensure that senior management and the board are aware of, and taking appropriate action with regard to major risks.

3.5 Other

- to ensure that contingency and disaster recovery plans are in place and are regularly tested

4. General

- to provide minutes of all meetings for review at meetings of the board of trusteesto review annually the finance committee's terms of reference and its own effectiveness and recommend any changes to the board.

Resources for Chapter 3 continued

Resource 3.6 The audit committee

In developing these model terms of reference I have tried to include the widest scope of duties for each of the key committees. I have also taken into consideration the recommendations of the Smith Report, Audit Committees Combined Code Guidance.

When discussing the relationship between the audit committee and the board, the Smith Report emphasises: *'the most important features of this relationship cannot be put into a code of practice: a frank, open working relationship and a high level of mutual respect are essential, particularly between the audit committee chair and the board chair, the chief executive and the finance director. The audit committee must be prepared to take a robust stand, and all parties must be prepared to make information freely available to the audit committee, to listen to their views and to talk through the issues openly.*

In particular, the management is under an obligation to ensure the audit committee is kept properly informed, and should take the initiative in supplying information rather than waiting to be asked. The board should make it clear to all directors and staff that they must cooperate with the audit committee and provide it with any information it requires.'

The Smith Report goes on to say:
'Many of the core functions of audit committees set out in this guidance are expressed in terms of 'oversight', 'assessment' and 'review' of a particular function. It is not the duty of audit committees to carry out functions that properly belong to others, such as the company's management in the preparation of the financial statements or the auditors in the planning or conducting of audits. To do so could undermine the responsibility of management and auditors. Audit committees should, for example, satisfy themselves that there is a proper system and allocation of responsibilities for the day-to-day monitoring of financial controls but they should not seek to do the monitoring themselves.

However, the high-level oversight function may lead to detailed work. The audit committee must intervene if there are signs that something may be seriously amiss. For example, if the audit committee is uneasy about the explanations of management and auditors about a particular financial reporting policy decision, there may be no alternative but to grapple with the detail and perhaps to seek independent advice.

Under this guidance, audit committees have wide-ranging, time-consuming and sometimes intensive work to do.'

Terms of reference for an audit committee

Approved by the board of trustees on ....200...

1. Composition, attendees, quorum and reporting

- The audit committee will consist of not less than .....trustees appointed by the board on the recommendation of the governance committee and others with appropriate skills and expertise of whom at least ....are external and independent of the charity.
- At least one member of the audit committee will have significant, recent and relevant financial experience.
- The chair of the audit committee will be appointed by the board.
- The chair of trustees will not be a member of the audit committee.
- The chief executive, the finance director, director of operations/services, internal auditor and such other members of staff as the chair of the audit committee may require shall be in attendance at any or all meetings.
- The external auditor will be asked to attend at least one meeting of the audit committee each year. There will be at least one meeting, or part of one, in which the external auditors attend without management present.

- Until otherwise determined by the board of trustees, a quorum shall consist of .... members of the committee.
- Appointments to the audit committee will be for a period of up to three years extendable by no more than two additional three-year periods.
- There will be at least three audit committee meetings each year, held to coincide with key dates within the financial reporting and audit cycle.
- The audit committee will report back regularly and at least every ....months to the board of trustees.
- The board will review the audit committee's effectiveness annually

2. Authority

The audit committee is authorised by the board to:
- investigate any activity within its terms of reference
- seek any information that it requires from any employee or trustee of the charity, and all employees and trustees are directed to cooperate with any request made by the committee
- obtain outside legal or independent professional advice and such advisors may attend meetings as necessary.

3. Overall responsibility

It is the responsibility of the audit committee:
- to monitor the integrity of the financial statements of the charity, reviewing significant financial reporting issues and judgements contained in them
- to review the charity's internal financial control system
- to monitor and review the effectiveness of the charity's internal audit function
- to ensure effective policies and procedures for managing risk and to assess the effectiveness of these
- to make recommendations to the board in all matters in relation to the external auditor.

4. Main duties

4.1 Internal controls and risk management

4.1.1 Internal audit

Where there is no internal audit function, the role of the audit committee is to consider annually the need for such a function and to report to the board either why such a function is or is not needed.

It is the responsibility of the audit committee:
- to review the internal audit programme and ensure that the internal audit function is robust, adequately resourced and has appropriate standing within the charity
- to ensure that there is a programme of regular audits in all key areas, for example: legal, risk, health and safety, investment, insurance and financial (including statutory annual audits, VAT, PAYE), to contribute to these reviews and to consider management's responses
- to review management's and the internal auditor's reports on the effectiveness of systems for internal financial control, financial reporting and risk management
- to receive reports from the internal auditor on any significant findings and consider management's response and to receive assurances that any audit committee approved recommendations of the internal audit are implemented within the agreed timetable by management
- to review the internal auditor's annual report

Resources for Chapter 3 continued

- to ensure the effective coordination of the internal and external audits
- to approve the appointment or dismissal of the head of internal audit

4.1.2 Whistle-blowing

- to review the charity's procedures for handling allegations from whistle-blowers and to encourage a culture within the charity whereby each individual feels that he or she has a part to play in guarding the probity of the charity, and is able to take any concerns or worries to an appropriate member of the management team or in exceptional circumstances directly to the chair of the audit committee
- to review the appropriateness of the charity's whistle-blowing policy and follow-up actions taken by management
- to review the charity's procedures for detecting fraud.

4.1.3 Risk

- to ensure there are robust systems and policies for identifying, managing and reporting risk
- to ensure that senior management and the board are aware of, and taking appropriate action with regard to major risks.

4.1.4 Other

- to ensure that contingency and disaster recovery plans are in place and are regularly tested.

4.2 Financial statements and reporting

- to review and challenge where necessary the accuracy of information provided in regular financial reports to the board, the annual report and the annual accounts
- to review, and challenge where necessary, the actions and judgements of management, in relation to the interim and annual financial statements before submission to the board, paying particular attention to:
  - critical accounting policies and practices, and any changes in them
  - decisions requiring a major element of judgement
  - the extent to which the financial statements are affected by any unusual transactions in the year and how they are disclosed
  - the clarity of disclosures
  - significant adjustments resulting from the audit
  - unadjusted mis-statements in the financial statements
  - significant adjustments resulting from the audit
  - the going concern assumption
  - compliance with accounting standards
  - reviewing the charity's statement on internal control systems prior to endorsement by the board and to review the policies and process for identifying and assessing business and other risks and the management of those risks by the charity.

4.3 External auditors

- to determine the frequency of tendering for external auditing services
- to consider the appointment of the external auditor and assess independence of the external auditor
- to recommend the audit fee to the board and pre-approve any fees in respect of non audit services provided by the external auditor and to ensure that the provision of non audit services does not impair the external auditors' independence or objectivity

- to discuss with the external auditor, before the audit commences, the nature and scope of the audit and to review the auditors' quality control procedures and steps taken by the auditor to respond to changes in regulatory and other requirements
- to oversee the process for selecting the external auditor and make appropriate recommendations through the board to members at the AGM
- to scrutinise and advise the board on the contents of the draft audit report and to review the external auditor's management letter and management's draft response, and to formulate for board use any written representations that may be needed by the auditors in connection with the charity's statutory accounts or any other financial statements
- to discuss with the external auditors any problems or reservations arising from the draft external audit report and draft management letter, reporting relevant issues back to the board, and advising the board accordingly
- to review the performance of the charity's auditors and advise the board on any changes that ought to be made to their terms of engagement
- to monitor and review the external auditor's independence, objectivity and effectiveness, taking into consideration relevant UK professional and regulatory requirements
- to develop and implement policy on the engagement of the external auditor to supply non-audit services, taking into account relevant ethical guidance regarding the provision of non-audit services by the external audit firm.

4.4 General

- to consider other topics as directed by the board
- to oversee any investigations of activities within the audit committee's terms of reference
- where the monitoring and review activities of the audit committee reveal cause for concern, or scope for improvement, to make recommendations to the board on action needed to address the issue or to make improvements
- to review annually its terms of reference and its own effectiveness and recommend any changes to the board
- to ensure that all new members of the audit committee receive induction and all members of the audit committee, including the chair, receive continuing training which covers, among other things, the role of internal and external auditing and risk management.

Chapter 4
Discussing the right issues and being well informed

Trustees **CEO** Chairs

4.1 | Introduction

Because trustees can be personally liable in certain circumstances, some trustees get scared and feel they need to know everything about a charity. If a trustee knows everything about a charity, the charity is doing very, very little. The key question is what and how much you need to know in order to govern effectively.

Remember, if I were a chief executive up to no-good, I would flood my trustees with information and management detail. So concentrate on quality not quantity and ensure that the board of trustees is discussing the right issues for effective governance.

Guard against being disempowered

Ultimate responsibility for the charity lies collectively with the full board of trustees as does ultimate authority over the charity. Trustees should ensure that no individual or groups of individuals ever undermine the board's ultimate authority or stewardship role. Boards are often disempowered unwittingly.

Here are a few ways to disempower a board of trustees (or an idiot's guide to disempowering a board!).

- Ensure that the board meets fairly infrequently. Make sure most major decisions are urgent and cannot wait until the next trustees' meeting. This way all or most major decisions can be made by the chair or the chair and chief executive together or by a small select inner cabinet.
- Ensure board agendas are full of issues that have nothing to do with governance (ie avoid anything to do with strategy, guarding of the charities assets, compliance issues, performance of the charity and developing good governance) and get the board to concentrate on issues which will distract them from governance and keep them busy. Better still get them to spend most of the meeting discussing and disagreeing over 'matters arising from the previous meeting'.
- Put all major proposals under 'Any other business' (AOB). By the time they reach AOB, trustees will agree to anything in their eagerness to get home.
- Flood the trustees with information. Make papers exceedingly long and full of unintelligible acronyms and technical terms. Trustees will never read the papers and if you are challenged, tell them you included the decision in a paper to the board which they approved.
- Fill board papers with management detail and get trustees focused on operational matters. In addition ensure that the chief executive's report is full of lots of interesting but unimportant information such as who is pregnant and who received an award for long-service. Avoid telling them about the big issues, opportunities, challenges and risks facing the charity or about the external environment and how the charity can develop.
- Tell the trustees that their role is solely to do with approving strategy and agreeing board policies (which are written by senior staff). Tell them everything else is management. Don't tell them about their ultimate responsibility for the performance of the charity and the charity's compliance with law and regulation or that ultimate authority lies collectively with the board as a whole and not with anyone else.
- Get the board to delegate everything to numerous board committees on which carefully chosen (by you) staff and non-trustees serve. You will then find it much easier to get committees to make the decisions you want.

4.1 | Introduction continued

To avoid being disempowered trustees need to ensure that they:
- understand the importance of the trustee role
- understand what their duties, responsibilities and personal liabilities are
- understand what governance is really all about
- make sure the board has the skills, expertise, experience and commitment to provide effective governance
- make sure that all delegate authority of the board is in writing and regularly reviewed
- introduce a matters arising chart and either scrap AOB or make sure that nothing can be brought under AOB unless the chair of trustees is informed at least 24 hours in advance
- make sure that board agendas help trustees fulfil their governance role and trustees' duties and responsibilities
- make sure trustees receive high-quality board papers that are succinct and to the point, concentrate on governance issues and arrive with trustees in good time
- are clear about how the performance of the charity, the chief executive, the chair and board committees are to be measured
- take time out to reflect on the effectiveness of governance and how it can be improved.

4.2 | Board papers

The quality of governance depends very much on the quality of information received by the trustees. Trustees are very dependent on the chief executive to provide high-quality, timely and relevant papers. The chief executive should take this responsibility very seriously and give it the time it deserves.

It is quite a skill to ensure that the papers focus the board on governance issues. In my experience, when chief executives complain that their trustees like to concentrate on management detail rather than governance, it is not uncommon to find that board papers presented to trustees are all about management issues and management detail. If the chief executive gives trustees management detail, trustees will inevitably be drawn into management. So it is the chief executive's responsibility to ensure that board and committee papers focus on governance issues.

Ground rules for board papers

Simple ground rules for board papers will also help. The chair and chief executive should try to get the trustees to identify and agree on these. Here is a list of possible ground rules. As always these should be adapted to the needs of the charity and the board.

- All papers will arrive five to seven days before the meeting in order to give trustees at least one weekend to read the papers.
- All papers will arrive at the same time and appropriately bound together with pages numbered throughout.
- Papers tabled at the meeting will not be accepted except in very exceptional circumstances.
- All papers will be taken as read at the meeting.
- All papers will be succinct and to the point.
- All longer papers (and there will be few of these) will carry a one or, at the very most, two page, analytical summary.
- Assessment and management of risk should be an essential part of all major proposals (including the budget) that are put to the board.
- All papers will carry a cover sheet explaining very succinctly the reason for the paper coming to the board and will draw out the key governance issues. The cover sheet should indicate clearly the name of its author and the name of the member of the senior management team who is responsible. (See example)
- The first time they are used all acronyms will be written in full (followed by the acronym in brackets) and all technical terms will be explained briefly (not more than two or three lines) in a footnote or as an appendix to the paper.

Cover sheets

One way of ensuring that trustees concentrate on governance is to have a cover sheet for each board or committee paper. Cover sheets should highlight key governance issues in each paper. Correctly used cover sheets, well thought out agendas and high-quality papers will help to ensure that the business of the board is carried out much more effectively. See Resources 4.1 for an example cover sheet.

4.2 | Board papers continued

Presenting a business case for a decision

The executive cannot expect decision-makers such as trustees to simply back a hunch – they will need a business case to support a proposal put to them. The key elements of a good business case for a major proposal to the board are:

- articulate clearly what is being proposed
- explain briefly why this work is necessary/advisable? (for example to solve a problem or to extend the work of the charity – give reason)
- briefly report on any 'market research' you have completed with beneficiaries (or others) to hear their views on what is needed
- explain which options are being considered, their advantages, disadvantages and associate risks
- explain what professional advice was sought and give an accurate summary of the advice received
- explain why the option you propose is the best and how it will help further the charity's strategic objectives
- explain how risk will be managed including details of any contingency plans
- financial implications – include assumptions made and summary financial forecasts (include more detailed financial forecasts in an appendix) and draw attention to the timing and responsibility for critical decisions regarding whether or not to go ahead. Explain clearly how financial risks will be managed
- confirm that your proposals fall within the charity's charitable objects and that the governing documents give trustees all the necessary powers
- explain what success will look like and how it will be measured
- give a clear timetable for implementation.

4.3 | Information and the chief executive

The trustees depend on the chief executive to provide them with the information they need to govern well. A good chief executive needs to work with the chair to ensure that the information is timely, balanced, honest and succinct. Most boards receive most of their information via their chief executive.

It is important for the chief executive, to develop a relationship with trustees based on openness, honesty, respect and trust. A relationship which sees the chief executive and trustees totally committed to achieving the organisation's objects and sees each other as partners in leading and achieving the organisation's mission.

I carried out research into what chairs and chief executives would like to see in a chief executive's report, Vic Cocker, former chair of WaterAid, summed up the views of several chairs when he wrote:

'It is important that there is a culture of 'bad news up front' – rather than leaving it to emerge later'. He added: *'Trustees should pay particular attention to the tone of the report. Also whether the chief executive is in good heart and whether the team is functioning well.'*

Individual information styles

What kind of personality is the chief executive? Is he/she an optimist or a pessimist? Is the chief executive sufficiently confident of his/her own ability to give trustees the good news and the bad news?

Broadly speaking chief executives fall into three main categories:
- Those who will only give trustees the good news, who underplay any problems and put a very positive spin on everything. Chairs and trustees can be lulled in to a false sense of security and it is often only when the chief executive leaves that the board discovers huge problems which were kept well hidden from the trustees. The chair has a duty to ensure, however difficult the task may be, that this does not happen and that there are both internal and external checks and assurances that will give the board an honest, balanced picture of how the organisation is performing and what challenges are on the horizon.
- Those who are very mindful that trustees carry ultimate responsibility for the organisation and that trustees can, in certain circumstances, be personally liable. As a result when they report to trustees they concentrate on problems, risks and bad news and always present the worst-case scenario. For example, budgets will be very pessimistic so trustees are fully aware of what the worst financial position might be. Quite often, chief executives in this group will forget to give the board the good news and to tell trustees about the many achievements of the organisation. Board meetings can therefore be constantly worrying and depressing. However, as a trustee, I prefer to have a chief executive from this group rather than the chief executive who always tells me everything in the garden is rosy. If you are a chief executive that falls in this category, make sure you include highlights and successes in each report to the board and ensure there are objective tools for measuring the performance of the organisation.
- Those who always give a very balanced and honest view of the current situation and also on what lies ahead. However brilliant an organisation is, there will always be some things that are not working out as well as they should and there will always be risks and challenges for a chief executive. A highly professional chief executive who is also confident of his/her own ability to do the job well, and who sees leadership of the organisation as a partnership with the board, will ensure that he/she gives trustees a very balanced view of what is happening and what the problems are as well as keeping the trustees informed about what might be on the horizon. This is the category in which chief executives should aim to be.

4.3 | Information and the chief executive continued

The chief executive's report

Most but not all organisations have a separate chief executive's report to the board. Information required from a chief executive may be covered in the different board papers. Some or all of these papers may be written by the chief executive or by other members of the senior management or leadership team. A chief executive's report to the board is recommended as it is a mechanism for communicating directly with the board and gives the chief executive the opportunity to raise with the trustees various issues that may not otherwise be brought to their attention.

If there is a chief executive's report, what should it cover ideally? When posed with this question as part of my research for this publication, Robin Stephenson, former director of corporate affairs at The Health Foundation summed up the difficulties of answering the question. He writes:

'The contents of a chief executive's report to the board of trustees will vary depending upon a number of factors, in particular:
  • *the nature of the organisation's activities*
  • *the size of the organisation*
  • *the stage of the organisation's development*
  • *the size of the executive team*
  • *the frequency of board meetings*
  • *other regular reports to the board*
  • *other methodologies adopted to keep trustees informed'*

But even though it can be difficult arriving at the perfect content for a report, trustees, chairs and chief executives alike are in agreement about style and format. They felt that the report should be:
  • short (ideally not more than four to five pages),
  • broad in thrust but exact in language
  • informed and balanced in presentation
  • timely in relation to developing events
  • focussed on necessary policy decisions
  • forward looking
  • honest and open.

What to leave out: Interesting but unimportant information

A chief executive's report that is full only of 'chatty' or 'housekeeping' items disempowers the board and sidetracks trustees away from the important governance issues into interesting but trivial information and into management. This tactic is sometimes used as a ploy by a tiny number of chief executives to keep trustees away from the major decisions and in ignorance of what is really happening in the organisation.

To deal with interesting chat, suggest that a regular newsletter is circulated between meetings to trustees (often called a 'board newsletter') giving trustees all the interesting but relatively unimportant 'bits and pieces' about the work of the organisation and its people.

It is part of a chief executive's professional duty to provide the board with the information trustees need to govern well. Their role description should clearly indicate the responsibility to ensure that the board receives timely advice and appropriate information on all relevant matters.

If the chief executive is not giving the trustees the level and quality of timely information and advice that they need, the chair needs to discuss these needs openly with the chief executive. It may be that as a new chief executive he/she is only imitating their former chief executive.

If this is the case it is up to the board through the chair to articulate what information they need from the chief executive. Remember it is what the board collectively wants and needs that is important and not just what the chair feels is needed. If the chief executive is not sure the chair is reflecting the collective view of the board, the chief executive should try including *board information and advice needs* as an item on the next agenda or on the programme for the next board away-day.

At the end of the day, if the chief executive repeatedly fails to keep trustees appropriately informed then the board should take disciplinary action.

Framework for a chief executive report

It can be difficult to identify what a chief executive report should contain ideally. Based on my research with chairs and chief executives, the following is a framework that most chairs taking part in the survey wanted and which can be tailored to the charity's and trustees' needs. (Note: not every item below needs to be covered in every chief executive's report or in every pack of board meeting papers.) Remember the report needs to be succinct, to the point and ideally not more than five sides of A4.

Yesterday and today
- a synopsis of how the organisation is doing (what is going well and what is not)
- highlights of current successes and achievements including good PR, awards, plaudits and peer recognition
- shift in the positioning of strategy implementation which has been made necessary by changes in resources, constraints and performance
- the current (not more than five) top risks and how they are being managed
- early warning of contentious issues, reputational issues, and legal and contractual risks including threatened litigation and progress of actual litigation
- feedback from stakeholders especially beneficiaries;
- the chief executive's current worries ('What keeps the chief executive awake at night') together with hopes and concerns
- any personal angles or advice on the issues on the board's agenda
- progress of any major campaigns being run by the organisation and the organisation's responses to major consultation on issues that are likely to affect the organisation.

Tomorrow
- issues on the horizon that might impact on the organisation either positively or negatively or which may develop into major risks
- regular environmental scans and reports on changes, opportunities, challenges etc.
- proactive consultation of trustees on emerging issues
- analysis of trends and what this might imply for the organisation's future (for example: drop in income, increasing costs, drop in the number of volunteers, greater demands for some services, fewer beneficiaries)
- any actual or potential ethical dilemmas
- strategic or tactical, medium or long-term, needs of the organisation including positioning of the organisation, possible partnerships.

Major management issues
- key staffing changes, changes in the management structures, key management issues and significant management decisions of which the trustees need to be aware.

4.4 | Minutes of board meeting

Minutes of board meetings are a permanent record of when the meeting occurred, the main points of the discussions, decisions that were taken and actions that were required. They are legal documents. If anything significant goes wrong, the courts, regulators and the police might want to examine minutes of meetings. It is therefore important to ensure appropriate and accurate minutes are kept. Minutes may become particularly important to provide evidence that the board acted prudently (see sections on personal liabilities and on duty of prudence in Chapter 1 section 1.3, 1.4 and 1.5.)

Normally, minutes will include the following:
- name of the charity
- date, time and place of the meeting
- trustees present, and executive and professional advisers in attendance
- names of trustees who sent apologies
- declaration (or not) of conflicts of interest and actions taken
- brief account of key points of discussions and debates (see Chapter 1 section 1.5)
- decisions made (including the names of any dissenters who want their names recorded in the minutes as dissenters)
- reports and documents introduced, accepted or noted
- future action required
- time meeting ends
- once the minutes have been formally approved as an accurate record at the next meeting, the signature of the chair

Many sets of minutes are unnecessarily long and detailed. Minutes are not meant to be a verbatim account, nor a transcript, of the meeting. They are an accurate record of the decisions made, actions required and the action taken. If a major decision is required and if there is a general discussion on a subject not requiring an immediate decision, only relevant key points of the discussion/debate should be included in the minutes. For good governance, it is vital that trustees, individually and collectively, use independent judgment and feel able to express opinions and concerns honestly and freely. In order to avoid the risk of personal liability, it is advised that names or direct quotations should not be recorded in relation to any discussion or debate.

Conflicts of interests that have been declared or raised, and decision made by the board regarding these conflicts, must be recorded in the minutes. If no conflicts of interest are declared then a note to this effect must also go in the minutes.

Minutes should be written in plain English so that anyone reading the minutes is able to understand what decisions were made and the reasons why. Minutes that solely provide a record of the decisions made and actions required are not sufficient. Enough information should be included for minutes to be a useful resource at a later stage.

The minute taker may wish to record electronically (routinely or only for long, complex meetings) the whole meeting. This must not happen without the knowledge and approval of the board. The board will need to have a written policy on how long the electronic recording is to be kept (eg the recordings have to be destroyed immediately after minutes have been written; or immediately after minutes have been formally approved as accurate; or x months after the meeting; or are kept forever).

Minutes are a legal record and can be used by regulators or by the courts if there are questions of legal liability. It is vitally important that they are accurate and provide an audit trail for all major decisions.

Minutes should be circulated to the board as soon as possible to trustees and certainly before the next board meeting. Trustees who spot minor mistakes or require minor corrections should ideally contact the chair copying in the minute-taker.

Minutes of meetings together with written copies of professional advice taken by the trustees should be kept in a safe but accessible place.

Matters arising

Some boards spend most of their time discussing 'matters arising' A time saver is to have a rolling 'matters arising' or 'action required' chart showing the status or progress of actions required from the previous meeting and actions from earlier meetings that have not been completed. Items remain on the chart until they are completed and the board has been informed. The chart is also a useful mechanism for the chair to check that action required by the board or a board committee is carried out.

Sample matters arising / actions required chart (incomplete)

Minute number	Item	Action required	By whom	By when	Progress
6.3	Marketing strategy	Identify potential competitors	Dir. of Marketing	March '11	Included in this meetings board papers
11	Trading company	Business plan required	MD of trading company	Nov '11	On schedule

4.5 | Improving agendas

Mention of the word 'agendas' causes most people to switch off and think about something else. Yet agendas dictate what a board will address. Therefore getting the agenda right is a vital task: one which is shared by the chair, the chief executive and the company secretary. Although the chief executive and/or the company secretary will almost certainly write the first draft of the agenda, all chairs of trustees should see it as their responsibility to ensure that the right issues are discussed by the board.

However most chairs will need their chief executive's and company secretary's guidance to ensure this happens. The worst boards are happy for the chief executive or the company secretary to dig out the previous agenda for the corresponding meeting the year before and just change the date. This is a certain sign of a feeble board and weak governance.

It is vital that board agendas ensure that trustees fulfil their duties and responsibilities as trustees and company directors, ie, do board agendas cover the five areas of responsibility as given in the trustees' role description (see Resource 2.1); or cover the three key strands of governance – corporate/fiduciary, impact, strategic (see chapter 2, section 2.7 for further information)?

In order to ensure that the board addresses the right issues at the right time so as to support all that the charity is trying to achieve, it is strongly recommended that there is clarity at all levels of what is to be achieved in the coming year.

The following should be major contributors to developing agendas:

Clear annual work plan for the board and its committees

Each year, having agreed vision, mission, aims and strategic priorities the board should agree:
- the key objectives for the coming year for the charity
- the key objectives for the coming year for the chief executive
- a work plan for the coming year for the board and a programme of issues that the board wishes/needs to address during the year
- work plans for the coming year and programmes of issues that each board committee wishes/needs to address during the year.

From these the chief executive or company secretary should develop a programme/timetable showing clearly which objectives/issues are to be tackled at each meeting of the board and its committees.

High-level board policies

Trustees delegate authority in a number of different ways. One such way is through high-level board policies. It is therefore important to clarify which policies are board policies (eg health and safety, safeguarding children and vulnerable adults. employment), how often each is to be reviewed and whether the board or one of the board's committees will review the policy. Once a chart is drawn up showing all this information, it is relatively easy to draw up a programme/timetable for review of board policies indicating clearly whether the board or one of its committees will carry out each review. These are then added to the relevant agendas at the relevant times. See chapter 3 on delegated authority for further information

Annual programme of planning, monitoring and reviewing

Every board and every board committee should have an annual programme of planning, monitoring and reviewing (eg budget, financial performance against budget, strategic objectives and performance against these).

Annual programme of spotlights

It is important for the board to consider which two or three areas of the charity's work, the trustees would, during the course of the year, like to spotlight. For example, trustees may decide that they want to

- bring in independent experts to test whether sensitive data (about beneficiaries, staff, donors etc) is adequately protected
- review whether the trustees' safeguarding policies and procedures are being consistently applied
- check that the charity is meeting all tax liabilities (especially with regard to self-employed staff) and obtaining all tax rebates
- review whether or not service users and beneficiaries are still very much at the heart of the organisation.

It helps to identify and plan these in advance.

Unexpected issues

There should also be room on the agenda for the trustees to consider unpredictable opportunities or challenges.

Risk

Although risk will be covered formally by the board at least once a year as a separate agenda item (as required under SORP 2005), consideration of risk and risk management should be embedded throughout the charity. It should therefore underpin all papers to the board including the budget. The board should consider high-level risks, both current and future, and how these are changing. The board should also oversee the management of these risks by the executive, and should not be drawn into risk management detail.

Fulfilling duties and responsibilities of trustees

In addition agendas should ensure that trustees fulfil their responsibility to hold the charity 'in trust' for current and future beneficiaries by:

- ensuring that the charity has a clear vision, mission and strategic direction and is focused on achieving these
- being responsible for the performance of the charity and for its fundamental values, ethos and philosophy
- ensuring that the charity complies with all legal and regulatory requirements
- acting as guardians of the charity's assets, both tangible and intangible, taking all due care over their security, deployment and proper application
- ensuring that the charity's governance is of the highest possible standard.

Similarly each board agenda should be checked to ensure that the three strands of governance are covered: corporate, strategic and impact. See page 35 for details.

4.6 | Standard items on agendas

Agendas usually start with:
- apologies for absence
- minutes of previous meeting for approval
- matters arising
- declaration of any conflicts of interest with matters on the agenda.

Followed by:
- chief executive's report
- report on performance of the charity against its strategic, business/corporate, annual plans (for smaller charity's, this might be included in the chief executive's report)
- financial matters.

Then come various items identified through a number of different mechanisms
- strategic matters
- items from the board work plan for the year
- board policies for review/approval
- report on any board 'spotlights'
- delegated authority reports eg board committees
- compliance issues
- other important matters requiring board time.

and finish with
- short review of the meeting (see section 4.12 below)
- any other business
- dates of meetings for next 12 months.

In order to ensure that trustees have adequate time to discuss key issues and make decisions without making meetings too long, the following may be useful:
- Indicate which are the key discussion items on the agenda for example by printing them in bold. There should be at most two or three major items for consideration.
- Items on the agenda which will only be discussed at the meeting if at least one trustee indicates to the chair at least 24/48 hours before the meeting that he/she wishes the item to be discussed, will be clearly shown eg by an *.
- Any matter to be brought up under 'Any other business' should be notified to the chair at least 24/48 hours before the meeting ie a '*' item.
- Reports from committees are often a '*' item. If this is the case, it is advisable that each committee prepares an annual report for the board which is discussed. It should cover major issues the committee has dealt with in the last year; what it proposes to deal with in the coming year and any matters of significance and risk that need to be brought to the board's attention.

If you are the chair, at the end of each meeting you should check how people think the meeting was run. A general question 'How did you find today's meeting?' is not recommended. Most trustees, eager to leave, are most likely to say 'fine' even if they feel unhappy with the meeting. It is important that the chair guides the short discussion with **one or two** pertinent questions such as:

- Did the right agenda items come to the board?
- Did the board papers arrive in good time and serve their purpose to inform and enable the trustees to make enlightened decisions? How can the papers be improved?
- Did we concentrate on making policy decisions and discussing issues that are truly the board's responsibility or did we drift into discussing management issues or matters of detail?
- Did the chief executive have an opportunity to openly discuss current and likely future major issues with us?
- How did we work as a team on the issues before us?
- Did we remember to recognise and celebrate success?
- Was the meeting too long or too short?
- Was there sufficient time to discuss issues?
- Did we spend too long discussing issues?
- How can we make the next meeting more effective?

Annual review of agendas

The chair or the governance committee or the audit committee should examine the board agendas in the past year in order to ensure that trustees are fulfilling their duties and responsibilities for the charity. This review will indicate gaps as well as how the agenda design process can be improved.

4.7 | Resources for chapter 4

Resource 4.1 Sample cover sheet for board of trustees

Board of trustees meeting		Date of meeting	
Title of paper:			
Prepared by:	Date written:	Status: [eg For info, decision]	Agenda item:

Analytical Summary: Drawing out key governance issues:

Financial summary [If relevant]

Risks

Recommendation:

Resources for Chapter 4

Resource 4.2 Sample annual work plan for board and board committees

	January meeting	April meeting
Board of trustees	• Remuneration, fees and budget for next year • Health and safety policy and annual review • Review emergency plan	• Consider overall performance of the charity during previous year against the agreed key performance indicators • Annual analysis of complaints, lessons learnt and action taken
Finance committee	• Finalise budget for board approval • Update on health and safety matters • Marketing plans including trends • Scrutiny of trading company's effectiveness	• Annual report and accounts for previous year • Consider public benefit and the current scheme to provide financial assistance to those who cannot afford the fees • Sit as audit committee to review auditor's management letter and review auditor's performance
Services committee	• Scrutinise and review performance against key service performance indicators for previous year. • Agree programme for review of relevant policies relating to services • Staff/beneficiary ratios and trends	• Annual analysis of complaints, lessons learnt and action taken • Accessibility audit and compliance with Disability Discrimination Act
Governance committee	• Review effectiveness of board committees against terms of reference and plans for the year • Succession planning • Skills, experience audit of the board • Review recruitment, induction and ongoing training of trustees	

Chapter 5
The role of the chair in good governance

Introduction

> Note: This chapter is addressed to chairs but should also be read by other trustees and by chief executives in order to understand the role of the chair in good governance. The whole of this publication, not just this chapter, is relevant to chairs.

The role of the chair is key to good governance. Although trustees' authority comes from collective decision making, the chair plays a critical role in providing leadership to the board in order to ensure both good governance and the fulfilment of the trustees' responsibilities.

Expectations of chairs of trustees can be high and many writers on governance fan the belief that chairs of trustees need to be paragons of virtue and be able to walk on water. It is important to have high expectations of yourself and of others but it is equally important to remember that neither chairs, nor trustees, nor chief executives are, or can be, perfect. We are all human with our own weaknesses and strengths. Together with the chief executive, you can, through your own actions, develop an organisation that constantly seeks to learn and to improve performance. So ask for feedback and learn from it.

Richard Gutch, former chair of the Association of Chief Executives of Voluntary Organisations (ACEVO), writes:

'Chairing a board well requires a particular, soft, skill, which to some extent can only be developed through practice. Giving everyone a chance to contribute (but not too much), knowing when to bring a discussion to a conclusion (but not too early) and taking people with you for the greater good of the organisation, without them feeling manipulated (even though they may have been) are some of the hallmarks of a good chair. As Elizabeth Vallance, chair of ICAN, put it: "If a trustee comes up to me after a meeting and says 'what I really wanted to say was x', then I've failed". Or as Prof. Martin Bobrow, chair of the Muscular Dystrophy Campaign, rather more bluntly said: "The role of the chair is to negotiate common sense between people who temporarily lose their common sense".'
Governance July 2010

Chairing is a much underestimated skill. Few of us are born with chairing skills. Instead we learn and develop the expertise needed to do a really sound job. A successful chair does not just chair board meetings skilfully. The role is a much wider one. The trustees will expect you as chair to ensure that they fulfil their responsibilities. They will expect you to support, supervise and act as a 'critical' friend to the chief executive. They will expect you to ensure that the chief executive provides the board with the information that trustees need for the proper discharge of their duties. They will expect you to lead the way to setting up mechanisms, structures and systems to ensure that governance is strong. They will expect you to support the chief executive in making management strong too.

A successful chair needs to be clear about what the role entails:
- to understand what is required of trustees and what governance is all about
- to be able to deal with difficult and often sensitive issues that every charity, however good it is, has to face
- to help the board achieve clarity in terms of what is expected of the chief executive and of the charity and how success will be measured
- to make sure all the trustees adhere, to the Nolan Committee's seven principles for those in public life: selflessness; integrity; objectivity; accountability; openness; honesty and leadership.

5.2 | Understanding your role as chair

General advice to all chairs of trustees

Whether you are an existing chair or whether you have been recently selected/elected to the position, much of the advice below should be relevant.

1. Whether or not you are new to the charity, spend time getting to know each trustee – ideally by arranging one-to-one meetings with each trustee. Try to find out how each trustee would like to see governance improved; sound them out about your ideas to strengthen governance; explore how the board can better use their skills and expertise. Repeat this process every couple of years. (If you wanted, this could be part of the process of evaluating the effectiveness of the board, of each individual trustee and of you.)

2. Even if you are an experienced chair or have been a trustee of the same charity for many years, make sure that an induction programme is planned in advance when you are first appointed as chair. Think also about how you might develop a support network of chairs of trustees with whom you can share ideas, problems, etc.

3. You will need to provide leadership to the board. Be very clear about the role and responsibilities of trustees. As chair you will need to ensure that collectively, the board fulfils these responsibilities. Understand the fundamental differences between governance and management but also be aware that there are grey areas which can be seen as both management and governance. To clarify grey areas, encourage open discussion with key staff.

4. Do not surround yourself with clones of yourself or people who will always agree with you. Make sure that trustees have on the board, the skills, experience and expertise to ensure that the charity is well governed.

5. Persuade your fellow trustees that it is important that the board takes time out regularly to review its own performance. Under your leadership this can be viewed as a learning and development process. Make sure your own performance is reviewed regularly too.

6. Understand and know your governing instruments, or make sure that the appropriate member of staff knows and can advise the board on the powers that the board has, and can check that the charity's work falls within its charitable objects. Make sure that governing instruments are regularly reviewed and updated so that they keep pace with the developments in the charity and give the charity the scope to carry through future plans.

7. Board agendas should be constructed around the role and responsibilities of the board. As chair you should play a key role in drawing up agendas. The quality of decision-making depends very heavily on the quality of information received by the board. Although the papers are likely to be written by others, it is a crucial role of the chair to ensure that trustees receive timely, high-quality information that concentrates on governance issues. It is also the chair's role to ensure that board decisions are implemented and that actions required are carried out.

8. Get to know your chief executive better and develop a strong professional working relationship with the chief executive. Ask the chief executive how the governance can be improved and strengthened and discuss any ideas you may have. Arrange to meet the chief executive regularly but not too frequently and don't set up an office in the building. Try to develop a very honest and open relationship with the chief executive based on mutual understanding and respect. However, remember the board must hold the chief executive to account for the management of the charity and for fulfilling the strategic priorities. The board under your leadership should be supportive and, whenever appropriate, constructively challenging.

9. Line-managing the chief executive on behalf of the board is almost certainly going to be one of your duties. Find out what arrangements are in place for the chief executive's appraisal and, between formal appraisals make sure you have regular (ideally at least quarterly) one-to-one review or supervision meetings with the chief executive to discuss the chief executive's performance against mutually agreed objectives and other relevant issues. See chapter 3 section 3.3 on delegation to the chief executive and chapter 9 on appriasing the chief executive.

Finally
10. Being a chair is a serious business but try to make it an enjoyable experience.

5.3 | Understanding the role and responsibilities of a chair of trustees

A first step for all chairs of trustees must be to understand the extent, limitations and demands of the role. Clarity of the chair of trustees' role not only helps the chair but also the remaining trustees and the chief executive. There are a number of model role descriptions available. Most have much in common, saying the same thing but in a slightly different way and emphasising different aspects of the role. However the role of the chair of trustees has evolved, as indeed governance has over the last decade, so it is important to use a role description which has kept up-to-date with these changes and which reflects the greater emphasis on strategy, risk, accountability and performance. All model documents need to be modified to the needs of your charity. See Resource 5.1 for a model role description for a chair of trustees.

Demands

- You must be committed to the work of the charity and have sufficient time to carry out your duties well
- You have to be in sympathy with the aims, ethos and values of the charity
- You must adhere to the Nolan Committee's seven principles for those in public life: selflessness; integrity; objectivity; accountability; openness; honesty and leadership
- You must provide leadership to the board. (This does not mean making all the decisions and expecting the board to rubber-stamp your decisions.)
- You must accept the democratically made decisions of the board even though you may not agree with them. If you cannot live with a decision then you need to consider whether you can continue as chair
- If things go very wrong and, for whatever reason, you no longer have a chief executive capable of sorting out the major problems that threaten the charity, then you and/or possibly some of the key trustees might, in extreme circumstances, have to step into the breach and run the charity
- You must ensure that the board of trustees fulfils its responsibilities. To do this you must understand what governance and the role of the board are.

Understanding governance

Understanding governance particularly in the field of charity law is essential. Therefore you need to make sure you read and absorb contents of chapters 1 and 2. Make sure all trustees and the chief executive read and absorb these chapters as well.

Understanding the role of the board

A deep understanding of the trustee role helps chairs of trustees to ensure that the board fulfils its responsibility and enables trustees of charities to govern well. Yet, very few trustees, even the most experienced, fully understand the extent of their role. The model role description below will, I hope, help to clarify what the role of the board is. When adopting model documents it is important to tailor the document to reflect your charity, its needs and its stage of development.

Model role description for trustees

The key responsibilities:

With other trustees to hold the charity 'in trust' for current and future beneficiaries by:
- ensuring that the charity has a clear vision, mission and strategic direction and is focused on achieving these
- being responsible for the performance of the charity and for its culture
- ensuring that the charity complies with all legal and regulatory requirements
- acting as guardians of the charity's assets, both tangible and intangible, taking all due care over their security, deployment and proper application
- ensuring that the charity's governance is of the highest possible standard.

In order to do all this trustees need:
- to appoint, support and professionally develop and if necessary, remove the chief executive
- to manage risk actively.

See Resource 2.1 for a more detailed role description for trustees.

Personal liability of charity trustees

As a chair of trustees it is important to understand when trustees may be personally liable. Even if your charity is registered as a limited liability company or a royal society and you have trustee indemnity insurance, trustees can in certain circumstances be personally liable. Your liability is increased if the charity is not incorporated. Ann-Marie Piper of Farrer & Co explains:

Personal liability of trustees

If ever there was a subject to stir nodding heads during trustee training, this is it. However, for most charity trustees, the risks are often overstated.

In terms of trustee liability there is a big distinction between charities that are incorporated and those that are not.

1 Incorporated charities

Most modern charities are set up as companies and the very good reason for this is that their trustees get the protection of limited liability. Very basically, this means that the liabilities incurred in the normal running of the charity are those of the charity and not the trustees. Should the funds of the charity be insufficient to meet the liabilities, then generally the charity will need to be put into insolvent liquidation but the trustees personal assets will not be in jeopardy.

Limited liability is, however, not absolute. It can be lost, and trustees can be personally liable, if:
- *the charity trades whilst it is insolvent*– the normal company insolvency rules apply equally to charities*
- *if the charity fails to comply with any of a long list of statutory obligations, such as payment of PAYE and national insurance contributions*
- *if the trustees commit a breach of trust which results in a loss to the charity (see below).*

2 Unincorporated charities

Unincorporated charities include charitable trusts and unincorporated associations (often called clubs or societies) and, perhaps less well known, charities set up by will and Charity Commission scheme.

Such charities suffer from two handicaps:
- *they lack a 'legal personality' and*
- *they do not have the benefit of limited liability status.*

5.3 | Understanding the role and responsibilities of a chair of trustees continued

Because they lack a legal personality (ie a separate legal existence) contracts must be entered into in the names of their trustees, rather than in the name of the charity. If something goes wrong this means that it is the trustees who are in the frontline – they can be sued by the charity's creditors (for an amount which exceeds the value of the charity's assets). The trustees have a right to recover the any amount disbursed on the charity's behalf but this is of little use if there are insufficient funds in the charity.

In addition, the trustees of such charities can also be liable for failing to comply with statutory obligations and for breaches of trust which result in a loss to the charity.

3 Breaches of trust

A breach of trust occurs when a charity trustee fails in his or her duties. They can arise from actions the trustees take or fail to take. Examples include making grants for purposes not covered by the charity's constitution and failing adequately to supervise the staff of the charity.

It is important to understand that personal liability is in prospect only if the breach also results in a loss to the charity.

Trustees liable for a breach of trust are those in office at the time of the breach. Subsequent trustees can also be liable if they know (or should have known) of the breach and fail to rectify matters.

The law recognises that with the best will in the world and, even after following all the rights steps, sometimes things will go wrong and it contains a mechanism to allow 'innocent' trustees to be excused from liability.

Trustee indemnity insurance – the answer to a trustee's prayer?

Trustee indemnity insurance is generally of limited value – if the trustees act reasonably (even if they get things wrong) they will generally be excused liability for their breaches of trust. If they don't, the policy is unlikely to pay out.

Most charity lawyers agree that the cost of the premiums would be better spent on converting an unincorporated charity to give the trustees the protection of limited liability.

* Very basically a body is insolvent if it cannot meet either of the following tests: (1) the balance sheet test – the value of its assets exceeds that of its liabilities or (2) the going concern test – it can meet its debts as they fall due.

This article first appeared in the July 2005 issue of **Governance: essential information for effective trustees**

See sections 1.4 and 1.6 and articles at the end of this chapter by Lindsay Driscoll Resource 5.4 'When liability begins and ends', and on Resource 5.5 'Breach of trust'.

5.4 | Your relationship with the chief executive

As chair of trustees, you will almost certainly have, on behalf of the board, to line manage the chief executive. This includes not only providing support but also acting as a 'critical friend'. You will need to ensure there is clarity about what the board expects the charity to achieve and each year you will need to agree, in consultation with the board, the chief executive's annual goals/objectives. You will need to ensure that the chief executive's performance is regularly reviewed and that he/she receives professional development and support. If you have no line management experience, you may wish to suggest to the board that line management of the chief executive is carried out by another trustee.

As a trustee, but also in your role supervising the chief executive, both you and the chief executive will need to be able to develop a real understanding of each others' roles and see the relationship as a partnership within which each of you has a different, complementary and crucial role. You will need to meet regularly but not over frequently. You will need to make yourself available between meetings to give advice or to be kept abreast of important developments or sometimes just to listen.

Model role description for a chief executive

The chief executive is responsible to the board of trustees as a whole but usually line-managed by the chair of trustees on behalf of the board.

Key responsibilities:
- to provide leadership to the charity and to be responsible for the management and administration of the charity within the strategic, policy and accountability frameworks laid down by the board of trustees.
- together with the chair to enable the board of trustees to fulfil its duties and responsibilities for the proper governance of the charity and to ensure that the board receives timely advice and appropriate information on all relevant matters.

See Resource 3.1 for a mole detailed version of a chief executive's job description.

5.4 | Your relationship with the chief executive continued

Balancing support with constructive challenge

A decade or two ago, a commonly held view was that a board of trustees' only role was to appoint a chief executive, leave the running of the charity to the chief executive and support him/her through thick and thin.

How times have changed. We live in an age of greater scrutiny and much greater accountability. If disaster strikes, trustees will have to bear the brunt of any consequences of mismanagement. While chief executives may lose their jobs, they do not suffer the same level of consequences as trustees, who carry full legal responsibility for the charity.

The boards that do best in strategically maximising the impact and effectiveness of their charity are those who combine a high degree of support for the chief executive with a high level of constructive challenge. Naturally, this does not mean that chief executives need to be constantly challenged but only when appropriate and always constructively. Although many chief executives would rather not be challenged, the best will welcome it as long as it is done helpfully. Constructive challenges lift most of us to a higher level of performance. Strong governance needs to be teamed with strong management. To make either weak would be a disservice to the charity.

The different stances a board takes with regard to support and challenge is shown in the diagram below which is taken from DfES **Governing the School of the Future** (ISBN 1 84478 296 4) and which was based on page 9 of **Research Matters** No 20, Summer 2003, NSIN, Institute of Education, University of London.

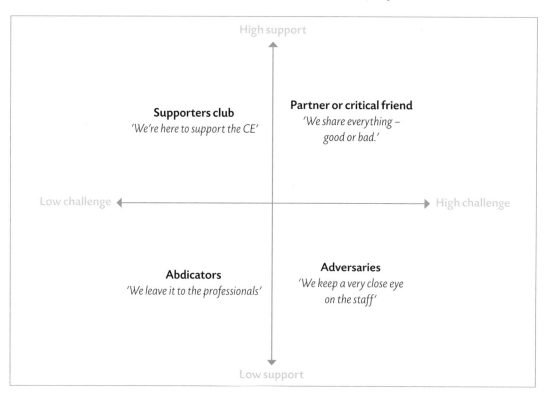

As chair, you may wish to ask trustees to think about which quadrant they collectively fall into and which quadrant they feel as individuals describes their mode of working.

Recognising the five modes of board behaviour: The Julia Unwin model

Julia Unwin identified five modes in which high performing boards operate.

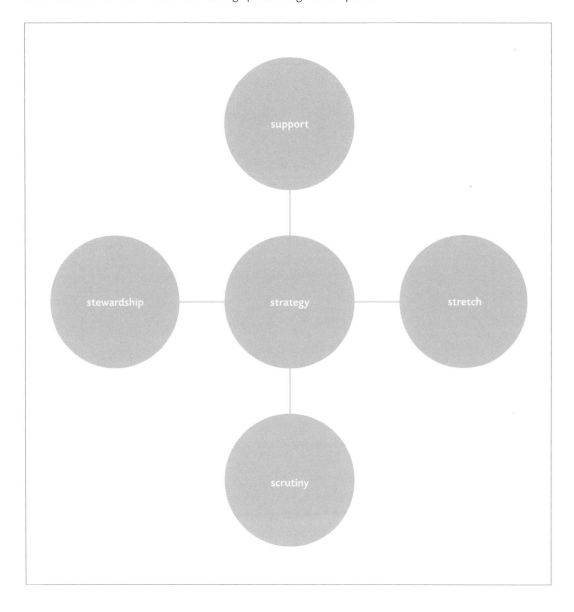

5.4 | Your relationship with the chief executive continued

While very good boards use all of these modes, excellent boards know which they are using and when. In Julia's own words, the five modes are:

1. Support

There are times when the function of the board is to support. not just to encourage the executive, but also to enable the executive team to work by ensuring that the infrastructure of the organisation works – that staff are employed, that systems work, and also that they are encouraged and enabled to do their work.

Boards in support mode say:
- *Have you got what you need to do that?*
- *We really ought to celebrate that.*
- *We really can't allow you to be treated like that.*

2. Stretch

There are times when the board needs to stretch the organisation. It needs to challenge and improve what is put to it.

Boards that are stretching say:
- *Can't we do any better than that? Can we create a strategic alliance for this?*
- *Have you thought of doing it differently? Couldn't we develop a social enterprise to do this?*
- *Surely we can improve by more than 5%?*

3. Scrutiny

Oversight and scrutiny go hand in hand. Boards in scrutiny mode examine the propositions put to them, challenging them and holding them to account.

Scrutinising boards say:
- *But this really doesn't make sense. We can't change our services in this way.*
- *Have you thought of the implications of doing this?*
- *I don't think you have made the case that ....*

4. Stewardship

In stewardship mode boards safeguard the assets of the organisation. They protect the money, the good name, the long term survival of the organisation.

Boards which are carrying out their stewardship role say:
- *But will the money be here in five years' time?*
- *Are we giving away our intellectual property too cheaply?*
- *Is risk to our reputation too great if we do this?*

5. Strategy

Boards also make strategy. They listen to what others have to say, consult the experts and their stakeholders, and in the end they make the big decisions that affect the future direction of the organisation.

Boards in strategy mode say:
- *The external environment means that we have to re-think...*
- *This is a golden opportunity to open our doors to people from...*
- *We can come out of this a stronger organisation.*

In my experience of working with successful boards, the use of the 5 S register, and an awareness of which mode is appropriate when, enables boards to really govern with confidence. The risks boards face are when they need to be making strategy, and in fact they are offering support, or when they are so busy husbanding the resources of the organisation, that they don't offer that vital sense of stretch.'

First published in **Governance**, March, 2006

The chief executive and the chair may wish to discuss in advance which mode might apply to each item or part of each item on the agenda. For example, the chief executive might feel that it would be helpful that on, say item 8 on the agenda, the board 'stretched' the executive in order to achieve even more. Or, the chair may warn that the proposal in, say item 5 was likely to come under hard 'scrutiny' by the board. The chief executive may remind the chair that it would be appropriate to congratulate the executive on their achievements under, say, item 6. This will influence how the chair introduces each item and facilitates the discussion.

You will also need to agree with the chief executive how he/she will report back to the board and how you will ensure, on behalf of the trustees, that the board receives the information and guidance it needs to govern well. See chapter 3 delegated authority section 3.2.

5.4 | Your relationship with the chief executive continued

The chief executive role in providing information to the board

You are advised to read chapter 4 which focuses on exploring the information needs for good governance and designing agendas that ensure the board fulfils its duties and responsibilities.

Both you and the trustees are very dependent on your chief executive for receiving the information you need to govern well, to make good decisions and to fulfil your responsibilities. A good chief executive will work with you to ensure that the information trustees need is provided and that it is timely, balanced, honest and succinct.

To ensure that your chief executive is open with trustees about the issues and challenges facing the charity, it is important to develop a relationship of mutual respect in which trustees and chief executive are totally committed to achieving the charity's objects and see each other as partners in achieving the charity's mission.

If your chief executive is not giving the trustees the level and quality of timely information and advice that you need, discuss these needs openly with him/her. It might be that as a new chief executive, they are only imitating what their former chief executive did or what another chief executive does. First, be clear about what the trustees need from the chief executive to govern well. Make sure that the chief executive's role description (see Resource 3.1 for a model role description for chief executives) clearly states the chief executive's responsibility *'to ensure that the board receives timely advice and appropriate information on all relevant matters'*.

If having done this, the chief executive's report and the other papers to the board give little of what is needed by trustees to govern well and to make informed decisions, why not to put *'information and advice needs of the board'* as an item on the next agenda or on the programme for the next board away-day? Remember it is what the board collectively wants and needs that is important and not just what you, as chair, feel is needed. Always keep in mind that you are acting on behalf of the board.

At the end of the day, if every tactic fails then the board must insist on getting what it wants and needs, and when it needs it, and should take disciplinary action if the chief executive refuses or is unable to comply.

As the chair, you need to make sure the information for which the board asks will enable trustees to govern well and does not stray into management.

Planning the work of the board

Every board needs to be clear about its planning and reporting cycles. For example, with financial planning and reporting, the board needs to know in which month it will set the budget and when it will receive the end of year accounts for approval. In addition, at every board meeting there should be a report to the board showing financial performance against the budget and with forecasts for the end of the financial year. Prior to the approving of the budget, remuneration levels will need to be considered and, if services are provided by the charity, what fees should be charged for each service. Both will need to fit in with the budgeting process. If there is a finance committee, this committee will need to meet a couple of weeks prior to the board meeting in order to scrutinise more carefully the various plans, recommendations and reports.

Examples of planning, monitoring and reviewing cycles:

1 Planning cycles:
- strategic planning (strategic review followed by strategic planning leading to corporate or business plans, clear annual objectives for the organisation, the chief executive and the board)
- financial planning (annual and longer term)

2 Monitoring cycles:
- the performance of the organisation against its strategic objectives and its corporate and annual plans
- financial performance against its long-term business plan and annual budget
- the performance of the chief executive in delivering the strategic plans and against the chief executive's annual objectives

3 Reviewing cycles:
- regular reviews of all board policies (see Chapter 2 section 2.3).
- review of changes in the legal and regulatory frameworks within which the charity has to operate
- governance review, including a review of the governing instruments and the structure of board committees and sub-committees
- environmental scans (including demographic, political, public opinion…)

Governance work or action plan

Another helpful tool is to have a governance action or work plan for the year, which shows not only all the key requirements of the various planning and reporting cycles but also adds in various other objectives that the board would like to achieve during the course of the year. An example of a charity's governance plan for a 12 month period is given on the next page.

5.5 | Planning the work of the board continued

Example of a board governance plan

	Jan	March	May	July	September	December
Financial (in addition to usual financial performance reports)	Budget	Review financial targets	Scrutinise draft annual report and accounts and recommend for approval	Review financial Key Performance Indicators to see if they are still the right ones	Review finance committee's performance and terms of reference	Review remuneration policy and general levels of remuneration. Review of CE's remuneration
Audit			Annual report from audit committee to board			Half yearly audit report including annual risk audit
Annual one-off reports	Analysis of complaints for previous 12 months with action taken and lessons to learnt		Independent audit report on health and safety with management's action plan			
Review of board policies	Crisis management/ major incident policy and plan	Complaints policy	Child and vulnerable adults protection policy	Heath and safety policy	Data protection policy	Reserves policy
Other reviews	Set chief executive's objectives for the new financial year	Strategic planning process for next 5 years begins with strategic review		Performance review of the chief executive	Performance of the board	Agree board's and board committees' objectives and work plan for the new financial year

Each committee of the board should have a similar annual plan

5.6 | Delegated authority

Clarity on delegated authority is vital and should be recorded in writing. In your leadership role, you will need to make sure that the board delegates clearly and in writing; that those to whom the board delegates are held to account and that all delegated authority is regularly reviewed. Read Chapter 3 for further details on delegated authority.

Remember boards delegate in a number of different ways. For example:
- agreement on values, ethos, vision and mission
- clear strategic plan, business plan and annual plans
- clear list of board policies and arrangements for their review
- role descriptions for the chair, the treasurer (if you have one) and the chief executive
- terms of reference for all board committees
- clearly recorded levels of financial delegation (eg budget, signatories for cheques and electronic bank transfers, upper limits for orders, payment of invoices without approval of the chair of trustees/chair of the financial committee)
- clarity on who can make decisions, and within what limits, between meetings of board.

5.7 | Building the right team to govern well

Stagnant boards usually lead to stagnant charities. It is important to refresh the board on a regular basis to ensure that some trustees are always looking at the charity with 'fresh eyes'. See chapter 7 for information on the recruitment, induction and ongoing development of trustees.

In order to ensure that governance is effective in your charity, you will need to take a leadership role in getting trustees to review how potential trustees are identified, inducted and how all trustees continue to learn and develop. As trustees, we take huge care when identifying, appointing and developing our chief executive. We need a proper process for identifying, appointing and developing trustees because effective governance is vital to the long-term health of the charity.

Retention of trustees

Governing a charity well is not an easy task. Chait, Holland and Taylor in *Improving Performance of Governing Boards* came to the stark conclusion that, *'effective governance by a board of trustees is a relatively rare and unnatural act'*. They argue that this is because, *'the tides of trusteeship carry boards in the wrong direction: from strategy towards operations, from long-term challenges towards immediate concerns, from collective action toward individual initiatives'*. Regrettably, they conclude, that most boards just drift with the tides and as a result trustees are little more than high-powered, well-intentioned people engaged in low-level activities. Combine this with the legal responsibilities of trustees and it is no wonder that charities sometimes have difficultly recruiting and retaining trustees that bring added-value to the governance of charities.

In order to identify factors that attract, motivate and retain good trustees, it may help you as chair to look at why trustees leave.

Reasons for leaving

Reasons commonly given by trustees for leaving a charity prior to completing their term of office include:

- **Trivia**
  Issues that come before the board are a mishmash of trivial matters disconnected from each other and from the business strategy. This can be the result of an under-performing chair of trustees, or a chief executive who wants to keep trustees away from the important issues, or a charity that has not articulated or is not focused on its vision, mission, strategic direction or business strategy.

- **Decision making**
  Decision making is slow and inconclusive. Decisions are either not made, or trustees and staff do not really know what was decided, or decisions made at one meeting are reconsidered and changed a few meetings later. This can be the result of poor chairing, or a lack of leadership, control and follow through by the chair.

- **Disengaged**
  Decisions are made by sub-committees or individuals (for example the chair and/or the chief executive) and the board is asked to 'rubberstamp'. Board meetings can be tightly scripted with decisions predetermined and with trustees having little scope to influence the outcome. Trustees in this situation should articulate their views, should suggest a governance review and rethink how the board delegates its authority.

- **Lack of support**
  Trustees feel out of their depth or excluded and there is no support or training which will allow them to develop into valuable trustees. They often leave claiming they do not have time to give to the charity.

- **Information**
  Trustees drown under a deluge of information full of uninterpreted data and facts or meaningless waffle.

Trustees CEO Chairs

- **At war**

  The board is dysfunctional with large egos and much jostling for power, which the chair cannot or does not wish to address. Trustees who are not involved in the power play start absenting themselves from unpleasant board meetings and eventually claim 'lack of time' when they leave. Instead they need to get together to remove those trustees who are more concerned by their position and authority than they are about achieving the objects and mission of the charity. If necessary they should seek the advice and help of the Charity Commission on the grounds that the assets of the charity may be in danger because of the lack of leadership and accountability by the trustees.

- **Founder syndrome**

  The board is dominated by the founder. This occurs when the organisation functions purely according to the personality and wishes of a prominent trustee or the chief executive who is usually, but not always, the founder of the charity. Many founders cannot make the transition from a highly entrepreneurial, reactive, individualistic style to a more pro-active, consensus-managed, forward-planning leadership style. The charity tends to struggle from one crisis to another until eventually the founder is forced out.

- **Stagnant membership**

  Most of the trustees have been there for decades and have no desire to listen to a different point of view especially from a new trustee who 'doesn't know how things are done'. The new trustee soon leaves. This can often only be put right when the chair changes and the new chair carries out a governance review bringing in terms of office, etc., and perhaps moves long-serving trustees to position that given them status but little authority such as honorary life members or vice-presidents.

- **Breakdown in trustee/staff relationship**

  The trustees and staff are locked into a vicious cycle of mutual mistrust and misunderstanding. This is enormously damaging to the charity and often very difficult to put right. Appointing strong external help, such as a professional governance adviser to the board, can help to resolve problems, as the outsider can act as a mediator between trustees and managers, persuade both sides to introduce better practice, and get trustees and senior management to focus on achieving the charity's objects and mission rather than putting all their energies into fighting each other. At times, the situation only changes when there is a change at the top, when either the chair or chief executive leaves, or they both do.

- **Stormy waters**

  The charity hits a rough patch, for example financial difficulties, and some trustees want to jump ship. If the charity is well governed and trustees feel confident that they have acted reasonably, this situation is less likely to arise. When a charity is poorly governed and poorly managed, trustees may be tempted to hand in their resignation when times get tough but they ought to remember that resigning does not protect them from the consequences of their actions, or lack of actions, when they were trustees.

5.7 | Building the right team to govern well continued

Attracting, motivating and retaining effective trustees

In order to attract, motivate and retain good trustees, the board under your leadership needs to make sure that:

- the charity has a clear vision, mission, strategic objectives and business plan, and that there is a common understanding of these by trustees and staff, and that the trustees are focused on working in partnership with management to achieve these
- there is an open and clear process for identifying skills needed on the board, and for identifying and selecting new trustees. Potential trustees should be given sufficient information about the charity, their role and commitment in order that they can make an informed decision as to whether or not they wish to allow their name to go forward for selection/election to the board. Ideally this process should be master-minded by a nominations or governance committee
- the charity invests time, money and other resources in the development of better governance
- new trustees are provided with initial and ongoing support, training and development, and that there are regular board away-days
- the board reflects regularly on its performance and leads by example in the development of the charity as a learning organisation
- the board reviews regularly its governing documents and the governance structure
- the board records in writing delegated authority and reporting procedures as well as having clear terms of reference for board committees and role descriptions for honorary officers and trustees, and reviews these regularly
- the board develops planning and reporting cycles, ensures through the chair that agenda items are pertinent and that trustees receive timely, accurate and succinct information and advice to allow them to govern well
- the chair ensures that each trustee plays an active part in the governance of the charity and brings added value
- the board and staff recognise that although trustees may not formally benefit from the charity, most trustees gain something from their involvement in the charity and that it is important that they do so
- there is an excellent working partnership between the board and management based on mutual respect, trust, honesty and openness
- the trustees enjoy being trustees and can have fun!

Problems with trustees

Dealing with poor attendance by a trustee

From time to time, most boards of trustees have problems with fairly regular non-attendance by one or more trustees. Keeping a register of trustee attendance at board meetings and publishing the register annually usually helps to improve the attendance rate. However, what should boards do if a particular trustee rarely attends?

The chair of trustees is responsible for dealing with poor trustee attendance. You need to check whether the governing documents or, if the charity has one, the code of conduct for trustees say anything about poor attendance. If it does, tackling the issue becomes easier. Either way, first find out why the trustee is not attending trustee meetings.

There can be a number of reasons including:
- the trustee is so busy that attending trustee meetings never becomes a priority.
- there is something in the trustee's personal or professional life which might mean that temporarily he/she cannot give the charity the time he/she would like to give
- the trustee is unwell but does not want to make this public
- the trustee received little or no induction and support when first appointed and has difficulty getting to grips with the issues brought to the board
- trustee meetings achieve little so the trustee does not see much point in attending
- trustee meetings are so acrimonious or dysfunctional that she/he does not want to be part of them.

What next? This very much depends on the reason for the trustee's continued absences. Taking each of the reasons given above, in the same order, possible courses of action can be:
- If trustee meetings never or rarely become a priority for an over-busy trustee, you as chair need to tell him/her tactfully but firmly that it is time to step down as a trustee.
- If the trustee's personal or professional life is affecting their attendance temporarily, why not suggest, with the approval of the board, that the trustee takes a 6 or 12 month sabbatical from being a trustee? If the situation is much more permanent, the trustee will need to resign.
- If the trustee is unwell then the nature of the medical problem will indicate whether the trustee needs a short sabbatical until he/she is strong enough to return to full trustee duties or whether he/she needs to resign as it is unlikely that he/she will want, or be able, to take on the full range of trustee duties again.
- If inadequate or no induction is making the trustee ineffective, assure the trustee that the fault lies with the charity. Discuss what might be done to assist. Reassure the trustee that his/her experience, skills etc are very much needed. Arrange a belated induction programme and organise a more experienced trustee to be his/her mentor. Personally provide support for the trustee and facilitate his/her participation in discussions at trustee meetings.
- If the board is not functioning effectively, carry out a full governance review (ideally facilitated by an objective outsider). Major surgery will be needed which might include finding a new chair of trustees and replacing some or all trustees! The achievement of the charitable objects and the interests of the charity's beneficiaries are paramount. The interests of trustees or staff are secondary.

5.8 | Problems with trustees continued

If clauses relating to non attendance are not in the code of conduct for trustees or in the governing instruments, consideration should be given to adding appropriate clauses, for example in the code of conduct:

'Trustees are expected to attend most if not all trustees' meetings and to participate fully in discussions and the decision-making processes. Trustees who without good cause do not attend any trustees meetings within a six-month period will be in breach of this code of conduct and will be removed from the trustee board.'

or in **the governing instruments** [1]:

'A trustee will cease to be a trustee if he or she is absent without permission from the trustees from all their meetings held within a period of six consecutive months and the trustees resolve that his or her office be vacated.'

Different types of problematic trustees

- **Quiet as a mouse**

  The 'quiet as a mouse' trustee is usually meticulous at attending board meetings but says very little if anything during the meeting. Later they might approach the chair or chief executive to rather hesitantly make an excellent point which the board would have benefited from during the meeting.

  A one-to-one meeting with you is the best way forward. You will need to build the trustee's self-confidence. Suggest perhaps an experienced but sensitive trustee as a mentor. Suggest attending a course on the role, responsibilities and liabilities of trustees. Perhaps get them involved in a working group or board committee that draws on their experience and expertise, and at which they might be less nervous about speaking. If you try everything but there is no improvement then the time is right to gently but firmly let the trustee know that the board needs trustees to take active part in board and committee meetings.

- **Section trustee with a personal agenda**

  Often the personal agenda is not discovered until the trustee has been in post for a few meetings. All board discussions are then are taken in a direction which reinforces the trustee's personal agenda.

  One US not-for-profit organisation has dealt with this issue by having 1-3-2 year terms of office instead of the more common two sets of three years. In other words the trustee with a personal agenda is not offered a second term of office after the first year. Other solutions are having a good induction scheme which covers: conflicts of interests, codes of conduct, the collective authority that lies with the board, the importance of democratically made decisions, objectivity etc. In a quiet word early on, you can point out that the offending trustee is coming across to you and to other trustees as having a personal agenda. Explain why this is unacceptable and how important it is to keep to the matter being discussed and taking a dispassionate and objective view on all issues. Remind the trustee of Lord Higgs' advice to non-executive directors. Support the trustee in changing their behaviour. If all attempts fail and the trustee's personal agenda continues to prevent him/her in fulfilling their duty to be objective, then take the necessary steps to remove the trustee either informally or formally – the latter is sadly more likely.

- **The dominant trustee**

  This trustee feels she or he has all the answers. They are probably the first to speak on any issues and sound as though they are the expert on every topic. They tend to speak rather loudly and forcefully. It is strongly implied that anyone who disagrees must be a fool! The remaining trustees tend not to speak up.

[1] Model governing instruments may be obtained from the Charity Commissions website www.charity-commission.gov.uk

As chair you need to actively ask other trustees for their views perhaps trying to get some of them to speak before the dominant trustee. When summing up the discussion, make sure you include views of other trustees. It is also advisable to have a quiet word with the dominant trustee. He or she may not be aware of their behaviour and when informed will, with your help and support, try to amend their rather over-powering response. He or she might take offence and decide to resign and benefit another charity with their expertise. More likely, they stay and after a slight improvement, revert to their dominating behaviour. In which case you will need to be firm in meetings and make clear that the views of all trustees carry weight. You may also want to introduce individual trustee appraisal, based on trustees and executive giving their views (Chatham House Rules) on each trustee. This can then be used to get the message home to the dominant trustee.

- **The bullying trustee**
  The bullying trustee is a nasty version of the dominant trustee. If the charity doesn't already have an anti-bullying policy (which includes bullying of and by trustees), grievance procedures for staff and trustees and code of conduct for trustees with a process for dealing with breaches, then you must make sure these are introduced and known to trustees and staff alike.

  You will need to deal with a bullying trustee very firmly. He or she will need to be informed that such behaviour is wholly unacceptable ad must cease immediately. Keep careful records of incidents, complaints, actions taken etc. You will need to decide whether the individual is capable of change or not. If the former, provide support and help. Take firm action if bullying behaviour does not cease. If the latter you will have the very difficult task of persuading the board of the decisive action that will need to be taken to remove the trustee and informing the offending trustee that he or she must step down or be removed as a trustee. Seek legal advice and follow agreed procedures.

- **The trustee who discloses confidential information**
  This is a tricky one. I know of one charity where the chair was convinced that he knew where the source of the leak was but had actually identified the wrong person mainly because he didn't like that particular trustee and was eager to find an excuse to get rid of her. So the first step is to be able to prove where the leak came from. This can be extremely difficult to do. In one case, a charity hired private detectives to get the necessary evidence!

  You should make sure that the board has a clear confidentiality policy (see Chapter 1 resource 1.3) and procedures which are known to all trustees and to the executive. Make sure that all papers that are confidential are marked 'strictly confidential' on each page. If necessary uniquely number all copies and collect them in at the end of the meeting. Remind trustees of which matters are confidential and must not be repeated elsewhere. Remind trustees that the board and executive should be able to talk openly at all board (and board committee) meetings in the confidence that their comments will not be repeated outside the board room. Take and follow legal advice if the breach is serious.

5.9 | Powers to remove trustees

The governing documents of every charity should be reviewed regularly. Trustees need to be constantly aware of the objects of the charity (as working outside the objects can mean that trustees are personally liable) and of the powers given to trustees in the governing documents. It is also important to have the power to remove a trustee. If your charity is a registered company, trustees automatically have this power, but in practical terms it helps to have the power clearly articulated in the articles of association. This power of removal should be supported by a code of conduct and role descriptions for trustees, and a proper and fair procedure for the removal of a trustee. Quite often personal intervention by you as the chair of trustees can resolve the situation without the need for formal processes.

Where the removal of a trustee is necessary for serious reasons, such as a trustee who is constantly disruptive, who discloses confidential information, who has been dishonest, or who is unable to accept a democratic board decision etc, it is important for you as chair to ensure that the proper procedures for removing a trustee are followed and that advice is obtained from the charity's legal advisers.

Quite often a trustee needs to be removed not for a misdemeanour but because the trustee rarely attends board meetings or contributes little or nothing to the governance of the charity.

The process for removing a trustee should be the same:
- be clear about what the core problem is and gather evidence
- give the offending trustee the opportunity to change their behaviour
- put the case for removal to the board, having taken legal advice
- always give the trustee the right to defend him/herself
- always have an appeal system.

Prevent problems arising by having appropriate training for trustees; appropriate policies (eg anti-bullying, confidentiality), a code of conduct, limited terms of office, board and individual trustee appraisal etc.

5.10 | Conclusion

This chapter covers a great deal, which I hope will be particularly useful to you as a chair of trustee. Inevitably there will be aspects of this complex role which have not been covered. However, I hope the chapter and this publication goes some way in helping you as chair to lead the trustee board to effectively govern a modern, professionally managed charity.

One of the key lessons I have learnt over the years is the importance of celebrating and recognising success, not just of the staff and the charity but of the trustees as well – and don't forget yours as chair. Be generous in your praise of other peoples' work. Not only will they greatly appreciate your words but it will also help to make being a 'critical friend' easier.

Finally, because very few people will actually thank you for all that you do for your charity, I would like to say that without you and hundreds of thousands of other chairs like you, communities, society, the country and the world would be a lesser place. So 'thank you' for all that you do in the interests of your charity.

Resources for Chapter 5

Resource 5.1 Model role description for a chair of trustees

Duties and tasks to fulfil the key responsibilities:

11. To provide leadership to the board and to ensure that trustees fulfil their duties and responsibilities for the proper governance of the charity.

11.1 To guard the long-term future of the charity by ensuring that:

- the board sets the mission, vision, strategy and high-level policies for the charity within the powers and restrictions in its charitable objects and governing instruments
- the board takes steps to monitor the performance of the charity and to ensure that the charity satisfies all regulatory and legal compliance requirements
- major risks to which the charity is exposed are reviewed regularly and systems are established to mitigate these risks without the charity becoming totally risk averse
- the charity has a satisfactory system for holding in trust for the beneficiaries moneys, properties and other assets and ensure that moneys are invested to the maximum benefit of the charity, within the constraints of the law and ethical and other policies laid down by the board
- the charity's financial dealings are systematically accounted for, audited and publicly available
- internal controls and systems (both financial and non-financial) are audited and reviewed regularly
- the board and the charity are fair and open to all sections of the community in all the charity's activities
- the board and the charity hear the voices and views of key stakeholders, especially beneficiaries.

11.2 To ensure the highest possible standards of governance by ensuring that;

- the charity has a governance structure that is appropriate to a charity of its size/complexity, stage of development, and its charitable objects and that these structures and the governing instruments are reviewed regularly
- the board delegates sufficient authority to its committees, the chair, the chief executive and others to enable the business of the charity to be carried on effectively between meetings of the board
- the board's delegated authority is recorded in writing by means of terms of reference for board committees, role descriptions for honorary officers and for key staff, etc; and, the board monitors use of these delegated powers
- the board has on it the skills it requires to govern the charity well and these skills are utilised, and that the board has access to relevant external professional advice and expertise
- there is a systematic, open and fair procedure for the recruitment and co-option of trustees, future chairs of the board and future chief executives
- all members of the board receive appropriate induction, advice, information and training (both individual and collective)
- trustees act reasonably, always act in the interests of the charity and comply with the charity's code of conduct for trustees
- the board of trustees regularly reviews its performance.

11.3 To ensure the proper and efficient conduct of board meetings by:

- chairing trustee meetings effectively, seeking consensus, balancing the need for full debate on key questions with the expeditious despatch of business so as to reach clear and agreed decisions as swiftly as possible
- encouraging all trustees to participate and to feel free to challenge constructively both the chair and the chief executive
- taking an active role in ensuring that board agendas are meaningful and reflect the key responsibilities of trustees
- ensuring that the chief executive and his/her staff provide the board with relevant, timely and accurate information in order to allow the board to discharge its responsibilities. This should include alerting the board to major risks, informing the board of current and future key issues, including significant trends, and informing the board about external changes which may impact on the charity
- ensuring that board decisions are made in the best, long-term interests of the charity and that the board takes collective ownership of these decisions
- ensuring that decisions taken at meetings of the board are implemented
- ensuring that that there is an annual programme of board and committee meetings, carefully structured agendas and high quality briefing papers providing timely information and concentrating on governance.

12. To support, and where appropriate, to challenge the chief executive and to ensure that the board as a whole works in partnership with executive staff

12.1 To support the chief executive by:

- ensuring there are clear and open processes for the recruitment (and if necessary dismissal) of the chief executive, and for setting and reviewing the remuneration package of the chief executive
- ensuring that the board focuses on its governance role and does not slip incrementally, or otherwise, into the management role
- arranging regular, but not over frequent, meetings with the chief executive and by developing a very professional relationship with the chief executive within which each can speak openly about concerns, worries and challenges
- providing leadership to the chief executive to ensure that the charity is run in accordance with the decisions of the board and the charity's governing documents and that there is clarity about the charity's objectives at all levels
- supervising the chief executive on behalf of the board (unless other arrangements are made), always remembering that the chief executive is responsible to the board as a whole and not to any one individual trustee or sub-group of trustees
- ensuring the chief executive's performance is reviewed regularly
- ensuring the chief executive has the opportunity for professional development and has appropriate external professional support
- in partnership with the chief executive, to agree respective roles in representing the charity and acting as spokesperson.

Resources for Chapter 5 continued

12.2 To make sure that the board understands and fulfils its responsibility to hold the chief executive and the executive team to account by ensuring that:

- when necessary, the chair and the trustees challenge the chief executive constructively and only in the best interests of the charity and as "critical friends"
- the chief executive is clear about the key performance indicators by which he/she will be held accountable
- the chief executive understands his/her crucial responsibility to provide relevant, honest, timely, high-quality information and advice to the board of trustees
- there are appropriate mechanisms, both internal and external, to verify that the board receives a balanced and honest picture of how the charity is doing.

12.3 To ensure the board works in partnership with management by:

- ensuring through the chief executive, that the staff understand the role of the board and that the chief executive provides an effective link between the board and staff
- ensuring that staff are aware of the board's appreciation of their successes and hard work
- ensuring that, through the chief executive, a performance evaluation process is in place for everyone in the organisation and that the charity invests in the development of staff
- ensuring that whenever practicable, trustees visit various parts of the charity, attend a few events organised by the charity and have informal opportunities to meet the senior management team, staff and beneficiaries.

Trustees CEO Chairs

Resource 5.2 A simple model code of conduct for trustees

Printed with kind permission of Charity Trustees Network

It is the responsibility of trustees to:

- **Act within the governing document and the law** – being aware of the contents of the charity's governing document and the law as it applies to [charity name].
- **Act in the best interest of [charity name] as a whole** – considering what is best for the charity and its beneficiaries and avoiding bringing [charity name] into disrepute.
- **Manage conflicts of interests effectively** – registering, declaring and resolving conflicts of interests. Not gaining materially or financially unless specifically authorised to do so.
- **Respect confidentiality** – understanding what confidentiality means in practice for [charity name], its board and the individuals involved with it.
- **Have a sound and up-to-date knowledge of [charity name] and its environment** - understanding how [charity name] works and the environment within which it operates.
- **Attend meetings and other appointments or give apologies** - considering other ways of engaging with the board if unable to attend a meeting.
- **Prepare fully for meetings and all work for [charity name]** – reading papers, querying anything you don't understand and thinking through issues in good time before meetings.
- **Actively engage in discussion, debate and voting in meetings** - contributing positively, listening carefully, challenging sensitively and avoiding conflict.
- **Act jointly and accept a majority decision** – making decisions collectively, standing by them and not acting individually unless specifically authorised to.
- **Work considerately and respectfully with all** – respecting diversity, different roles and boundaries, and avoiding giving offence.

Trustees are expected to honour the content and spirit of this Code.

Signed _____

Name _____

Date _____

Resources for Chapter 5 continued

Resource 5.3 A longer model code of conduct for trustees

Printed with kind permission of Charity Trustees Network

I will respect and uphold the values of [organisation name]
[list values of organisation]

GENERAL

- I will act within the governing document of [organisation name] and the law, and abide by the policies and procedures of the organisation. This includes having a knowledge of the contents of the [governing document] and relevant policies and procedures.
- I will support the objects and mission of [organisation name], championing it, using any skills or knowledge I have to further that mission and seeking expert advice where appropriate.
- I will be an active trustee, making my skills, experience and knowledge available to [organisation name] and seeking to do what additional work I can outside trustee meetings, including sitting on sub-committees.
- I will respect organisational, board and individual confidentiality, while never using confidentiality as an excuse not to disclose matters that should be transparent and open.
- I will develop and maintain a sound and up-to-date knowledge of [organisation name] and its environment. This will include an understanding of how [organisation name] operates, the social, political and economic environment in which it operates and the nature and extent of its work.
- I will use [organisation name]'s resources responsibly, and when claiming expenses will do so in line with [organisation name] procedures.
- I will seek to be accountable for my actions as a trustee of [organisation name], and will submit myself to whatever scrutiny is appropriate.
- I accept my responsibility to ensure that [organisation name] is well run and will raise issues and questions in an appropriate and sensitive way to ensure that this is the case.

MANAGING INTERESTS

- I will not gain materially or financially from my involvement with [organisation name] unless specifically authorised to do so.
- I will act in the best interests of [organisation name] as a whole, and not as a representative of any group – considering what is best for [organisation name] and its present and future beneficiaries and avoiding bringing [organisation name] into disrepute.
- Unless authorised, I will not put myself in a position where my personal interests conflict with my duty to act in the interests of the organisation. Where there is a conflict of interest I will ensure that this is managed effectively in line with [organisation name] policy.
- I understand that a failure to declare a conflict of interest may be considered to be a breach of this code.

MEETINGS

- I will attend all appropriate meetings and other appointments at [organisation name] or give apologies. If I cannot regularly attend meetings I will consider whether there are other ways I can engage with [organisation name].
- I will prepare fully for all meetings and work for the organisation. This will include reading papers, querying anything I do not understand, thinking through issues before meetings and completing any tasks assigned to me in the agreed time.
- I will actively engage in discussion, debate and voting in meetings; contributing in a considered and constructive way, listening carefully, challenging sensitively and avoiding conflict.

- I will participate in collective decision making, accept a majority decision of the board and will not act individually unless specifically authorised to do so.

GOVERNANCE

- I will actively contribute towards improving the governance of the trustee board, participating in induction and training and sharing ideas for improvement with the board.
- I will help to identify good candidates for trusteeship at [organisation name] and, with my fellow trustees, will appoint new trustees in accordance with agreed selection criteria.

RELATIONS WITH OTHERS

- I will endeavour to work considerately and respectfully with all those I come into contact with at [organisation name]. I will respect diversity, different roles and boundaries, and avoid giving offence.
- I recognise that the roles of trustees, volunteers and staff of [organisation name] are different, and I will seek to understand and respect the difference between these roles.
- Where I also volunteer with the organisation I will maintain the separation of my role as a trustee and as a volunteer.
- I will seek to support and encourage all those I come into contact with at [organisation name]. In particular I recognise my responsibility to support the chair and the senior staff member.
- I will not make public comments about the organisation unless authorised to do so. Any public comments I make about [organisation name] will be considered and in line with organisational policy, whether I make them as an individual or as a trustee.

LEAVING THE BOARD

- I understand that substantial breach of any part of this code may result in procedures being put in motion that may result in my being asked to resign from the trustee board.
- Should this happen I will be given the opportunity to be heard. In the event that I am asked to resign from the board I will accept the majority decision of the board in this matter and resign at the earliest opportunity.
- If I wish to cease being a trustee of [organisation name] at any time, I will inform the chair in advance in writing, stating my reasons for leaving.

Signed _____

Name _____

Date _____

[2] Holding trustees are individuals who are appointed to hold the legal title of charity property.
[3] See article on 'breach of trust' in May 2008 issue of **Governance**

Resources for Chapter 5 continued

Resource 5.4 When does the liability of trustees begin and end?

Article from July'08 issue of **Governance**. Printed with kind permission of Lindsay Driscoll

When does the liability of trustees begin and end?

When a charity gets into financial or other difficulties, sometimes the first reaction of trustees is to resign in order to escape liability.

Resignation will often not achieve that result, but the circumstances in which trustees will remain liable and for how long will depend on a range of factors including the legal structure, the type of liability and the extent of any indemnities. Although this is a simple question it covers some complex issu es and situations. *This article can only be a very simplified summary and detailed legal advice will always be required.*

Incorporated charities
The position is probably most straightforward in the case of trustees of a charitable company. In this case as the debts are those of the company itself, there is unlikely to be any contractual liability following resignation although there could be some cases where liability for negligence could continue as well as liability for wrongful trading.

Unincorporated charities
The position is more complicated in the case of unincorporated charities. Here trustees will generally continue to be personally liable under a contract they entered into when a trustee but will generally have the benefit of an implied indemnity from charity assets.

Employment and unincorporated charities
A situation which can arise in an unincorporated charity is the question of who is liable where there is a breach of contract of employment, is it the trustees at the time the contract was created or those where the breach occurred. As the new trustees continue to pay the employee and adopt the contract it will usually be novated automatically, that is a new contract is created on the same terms between different parties, so that it will normally be the trustees at the time of the breach who would be liable.

Leases and unincorporated charities
Another situation where problems can occur is when trustees have entered into a lease or other long term liabilities. They often retire long before the lease has ended but if there is a breach of covenant it would generally be the original signatories rather than the current trustees who would be liable. For this reason it is essential that trustees entering into a lease or who give a personal guarantee should take proper advice. The same is true of holding trustees[2] in a charitable unincorporated association.

Breach of trust[3]
Whatever the legal structure, potential liability for a breach of trust committed whilst a trustee will continue after the trustee has left the board. A trustee who resigns in order to facilitate a breach of trust could be liable along with those who actually commit the breach. An example of this is where a trustee resigns to take up employment with the charity without proper procedures and authority.

Liabilty for decisions made before you are appointed
Will a new trustee be liable for a breach of trust committed before the trustee took office? Generally not but if trustees become aware of a breach committed before their appointment they are under an obligation to take steps to rectify the situation if possible. If they fail to do so they could also be liable.

[4] a wrongful act, not including a breach of contract or trust, that results in injury to another's person, property, reputation, or the like, and for which the injured party is entitled to compensation

Liabilty after you have left

How long does the potential liability exist after the retirement of the trustee? This will be governed by the rules on the limitation of actions. This means that a claim against the trustee whether for breach of contract or tort[4] will normally be barred by statute six years after it has occurred although sometimes the time limit starts later, for example where the claimant is a minor. In the case of breach of trust there are some situations where a claim may be brought at a later date and if there is fraud or a fundamental breach of trust, it can be brought at any time.

Lindsay Driscoll
Trustee, Dance United
Charity lawyer

lindsayjdriscoll@btopenworld.com

Resources for Chapter 5 continued

Resource 5.5 Breach of trust

Article from May'08 issue of **Governance**. Printed with kind permission of Lindsay Driscoll

Breach of trust

Most trustees know that being 'in breach of trust' raises the possibility of being personally liable. What exactly is 'breach of trust' and in what circumstances does this lead to personal liability?

The fundamental duty of all charity trustees is to further the purposes of the charity and administer it in accordance with the charity's governing document and the requirements of charity law. Failure to do so will result in a breach of trust.

A breach of trust may take many forms; perhaps the most common one is where trustees suffer from mission drift and carry out activities outside the objects clause for example where a charity set up to assist the homeless in England extends its activities to Wales or a charity to help children with cancer assists adults. Another example would be where a charity campaigned on issues unrelated to its purposes.

Trustees may also fail in their duty to further the charity's purpose and thus be in breach of trust where they are not meeting the public benefit requirement. Full discussion of this is set out in the Charity Commission's guidance on public benefit which was published in accordance with the Charities Act 2006 earlier this year.

A breach of trust will occur where the trustees carry out actions or make payments where they have no power to do so. A common example of this is where trustees receive benefits which are not authorised either by their governing document, by the Charities Act 2006 or by the Charity Commission. Other examples are where trustees spend permanent endowment where this is not authorised under the new provisions of the Charities Act 2006 or where they sell or charge land where there is no express or implied power to do so.

The other main situation where trustees are in breach of trust is where they fail in their duties to protect the charity's assets and resources and observe their duty of care and duty of prudence. Examples of this are where the trustees fail to ensure that there are adequate internal financial controls or fail to take proper investment advice or fail to insure charity property with resulting loss to the charity.

What are the consequences where a trustee commits a breach of trust? This will very much depend on such factors as whether the trustees acted in good faith, the severity of the breach and the amount of loss to the charity.

In extreme cases, the Charity Commission may take regulatory action against the trustees concerned, which could include giving directions to the trustees or appointing new trustees. The Commission can also take court proceedings against the trustees personally for the recovery of funds lost to the charity as a result of a breach of trust. However, this very rarely occurs where the trustees have acted in good faith and under the Charities Act 2006 the Commission, as well as the court, can now relieve the trustees of any liability to pay provided they have acted honestly and reasonably and ought fairly to be excused.

How can charity trustees protect themselves from the consequences of a breach of trust? The first step must always be for trustees to be fully aware of their legal responsibilities and the provisions of their governing document and to take proper professional advice whenever necessary. The governing document may limit the liability of trustees for breach of trust, in some circumstances, through an indemnity or exemption clause.

The trustees may also consider whether trustee liability insurance is appropriate. This will generally cover breach of trust claims, however it cannot extend to liability arising out of conduct which the trustee knew or reasonably should have known was not in the interests of the charity. Under the Charities Act 2006 charities may now buy indemnity insurance for their trustees without an explicit power to do so.

Lindsay Driscoll
Trustee, Dance United
Charity Lawyer and until recently Legal Charity Commissioner

lindsayjdriscoll@btopenworld.com

Resources for Chapter 5 continued

Resource 5.6 Model procedures for trustee whistle-blowing

Article from May'08 issue of **Governance**. Printed with kind permission of Robin Stephenson

Model procedures for trustee whistle-blowing

Whilst more often considered from the perspective of an employee, what do you do if you believe you've uncovered some significant wrongdoing, perhaps involving other trustees or senior members of staff; where do you go, who do you raise it with, what is the appropriate procedure for dealing with it?

It might be of considerable assistance, and reassurance, to trustees if the charities they represented had a procedure to cater for such situations. One solution is to put in place a whistle-blowing policy for trustees. This can be done quite easily by adapting those drawn up for employees.

Set out below is a sample policy with procedures that charities might like to adopt or adapt for this purpose. The model has been drafted with a larger charitable organisation in mind but there is no reason why smaller charities cannot embrace the principles and put a simplified policy in place, tailored to their own circumstances and resources. Having at least some guidelines and procedure in place is better than having none at all.

Whistle-blowing policy (trustees)

1 Assurance

The board of trustees and chief executive are committed to maintaining the highest standards of honesty, openness and accountability and recognise that all trustees have an important role to play in achieving this goal.

On rare occasions a trustee may become aware or suspect that someone inside or connected with the charity is doing something improper or even illegal, but they may feel apprehensive about voicing their concerns. This may be because they feel that speaking up would be disloyal to their colleagues or to the organisation itself. Or it may be because they do not think that their concerns will be taken seriously or because they are afraid that they will ostracised for raising them. However, the charity expects any trustee with knowledge, or reasonable suspicion, of wrongdoing to raise their concern.

The charity takes all misconduct and malpractice very seriously, whether committed by trustees, staff, volunteers, advisers, suppliers or contractors; this document sets out a procedure by which trustees can report any concerns they may have.

2 What sort of activities should be reported using this procedure?

The sort of misconduct or malpractice that the charity would expect trustees to report would, of course, include criminal offences including fraud and corruption, but also:

- unfair practices in relation to the work of the charity
- financial impropriety
- failure to comply with legal obligations
- unfair treatment or discrimination, or bullying
- actions which endanger the health or safety of beneficiaries, staff, volunteers, trustees or the public
- actions which cause damage to the environment
- actions which could damage the reputation of the charity; or
- actions which are intended to conceal any of the above.

It is impossible to give an exhaustive list of the activities that constitute misconduct or malpractice and it will not always be clear that a particular action falls within one of the above categories. Trustees must use their own judgement. However, the charity encourages trustees to raise concerns rather than keep silent. If you raise a concern in good faith then, even if it is not confirmed by an investigation, your concern will be valued and appreciated and you will not be subjected to any detriment by reason of your actions. In contrast, anyone making false reports, maliciously or for personal gain, will be dealt with appropriately.

3 How to raise a concern?
You can raise a concern orally or in writing. The charity would normally expect you to raise your concern internally to the chair of trustees or the treasurer or other designated officer.

Which of these individuals is the most appropriate will depend on the seriousness of the matter and who you think is involved. If, under the circumstances, you do not feel comfortable about raising your concern with any of these persons, then you can report instead to any other trustee e.g. the vice chair or even the president.

Trustees should state at the time if they want to raise the matter in confidence so that appropriate arrangements can be made.

4 Do I need proof of wrongdoing?
The charity does not expect trustees to have absolute proof of any misconduct or malpractice that they report. However, you must have some sound reasons for your concern.

5 Will the charity protect my identity?
The charity will do everything it reasonably can to keep your identity confidential, if you so wish. However, there may be circumstances (for example, if your report becomes the subject of an internal disciplinary inquiry or a criminal investigation) where you may be needed as a witness. Should this be the case the charity will discuss the matter with you at the earliest opportunity.

6 How will the matter be investigated?
Once you have raised your concern with the charity you will receive an acknowledgement of receipt normally within five working days.

The charity will then need to make preliminary enquiries to decide whether a full investigation is necessary. If such an investigation is necessary then, depending on the nature of the misconduct, your concerns will be either:
- investigated internally (by management or trustees appointed for that purpose), or
- referred to the appropriate external person (for example the external auditors, the Charity Commission or the police) for investigation.
- Subject to any legal constraints, the charity will inform you of the outcome of the preliminary enquiries, full investigation and any further action that has been taken.

7 What can I do if I am unhappy with the way the charity has dealt with my concern?
If a trustee is unhappy with the outcome of an investigation, the charity would prefer that they pursue their concern through the internal grievance procedures in the first instance.

If they are still not happy they may wish to raise their concern with an external organisation, such as the Charity Commission or the police.

Resources for Chapter 5 continued

8 Independent Advice

If you feel you need independent advice at any stage, you may like to contact the independent charity Public Concern at Work. Public Concern at Work is an independent charity that promotes good practice, compliance with the law and accountability in the workplace. It is entirely self funding and relies on modest subscriptions from employing organisations for its existence.

Public Concern at Work is recognised as a leader in its field and its work has been endorsed by Government, the Committee on Standards in Public Life, the TUC, the CBI and the Institute of Directors. Among the services it provides to organisations in the public, private and voluntary sectors are:

- a helpline staffed by qualified lawyers providing advice, free of charge, primarily for employees but also open to trustees;
- a consultancy service assisting clients in developing and implementing effective whistle-blowing policies; and
- policy packs for employers.

Public Concern at Work can be contacted at Suite 301, Baldwins Gardens. London EC1N 7RJ. www.pcaw.co.uk 020 7404 6609 helpline@pcaw.co.uk

9 External Contacts

It is hoped that this policy gives trustees all the reassurance they need to raise any concerns internally. However, the charity recognises that there may be circumstances (for example, where the wrongdoing is extremely serious) where it may be appropriate for you to report your concerns to an outside body, such as the charity's external auditors, the Charity Commission or the police. Public Concern at Work will be able to advise you on such an option and the circumstances in which it may be appropriate for you to contact an outside body.

10 Conclusion

While the charity cannot predict the outcome of an investigation prompted by any concerns raised by trustees, it will handle the matter fairly and properly. By using this procedure, trustees will help the charity to achieve this.

External Auditors
[insert details]

Robin Stephenson
Trustee, The Public Service Broadcasting Trust
Consultant, governance and legal affairs

advice@robinstephenson.co.uk

Resource 5.7 Model procedures for trustee grievances

Article from March'08 issue of **Governance**. Printed with kind permission of Robin Stephenson

Model procedures for trustee grievances

Whilst more often considered from the perspective of an employee, what do you do if you are a trustee with a grievance, especially if it concerns your treatment by a fellow trustee or perhaps by the chair or chief executive?

It might be of considerable assistance, and reassurance, to trustees if the charities they represented had procedures to cater for such situations. One solution is to put in place a grievance procedure for trustees. This can be done quite easily by adapting those drawn up for employees.

Set out below is a sample policy that charities might like to adopt or adapt for this purpose. The model has been drafted with a larger charitable organisation in mind but there is no reason why smaller charities cannot embrace the principles and put a simplified policy in place, tailored to their own circumstances and resources. Having at least some guidelines and procedure in place is better than having none at all.

Trustee grievance procedure

This procedure is intended to facilitate the resolution of grievances that a trustee may have concerning their treatment by another trustee, a member of staff or the board of trustees. It is expected that in most cases trustees will be able to resolve such grievances through informal process but where that is not possible or appropriate trustees are encouraged to use the formal grievance procedure.

1 Introduction
The charity places responsibility upon all trustees to develop constructive working relationships underpinned by the charity's values so that:
- the individual needs and expectations of trustees are respected
- any individual trustee's problems are dealt with promptly, fairly and frankly; and
- confidentiality is respected.

There may be occasions when a trustee has a grievance about the way they have been treated. In such cases the charity's policy is to encourage free communication between trustees and the chair to ensure that questions and problems can be aired and, where possible, resolved quickly and to the satisfaction of all concerned. While many issues can and will be resolved informally, the formal grievance procedure is available to provide an open and fair way of addressing concerns with a view to resolving them as quickly and effectively as possible.

So, where a trustee has a grievance relating to their treatment they are encouraged to raise it first informally with the chair. If they remain dissatisfied following such initial informal discussions, or the grievance concerns their treatment by the chair, the following procedure should be followed:

2 Formal grievance
1 The trustee should set out the grievance in writing to the chair*. (If the grievance relates to the chair, the trustee may raise the matter with the vice chair or such other trustee designated to hear grievances in such circumstances.) The trustee should set out clearly details of the nature and extent of the grievance.

The chair* will send the trustee a written acknowledgement of receipt of the grievance and invite the trustee to submit any further information required and to attend a formal meeting to discuss the grievance. This meeting will take place within seven working days of the date of that acknowledgement provided:
a) the trustee has provided the chair* with all requested information relating to the grievance; and
b) the chair* has had a reasonable opportunity to consider that information.

Resources for Chapter 5 continued

The trustee can choose to be accompanied to the meeting by a fellow trustee. Should the trustee wish to be accompanied, they should inform the chair* accordingly in advance of the meeting concerned.

2 At the meeting, the trustee will have the opportunity to explain his grievance and may call witnesses. The chair* may require any other person that the grievance concerns to attend the meeting and give evidence. All parties will be given the opportunity to question any other parties present through the chair*. If witnesses are called, they may only remain in the meeting whilst they give evidence and answer questions. The chair* will consider the oral and written submissions made, asking clarification and questions of the aggrieved trustee, any other party and witnesses as necessary. At the end of the meeting, the trustee will be given the opportunity to sum up their grievance.

3 The meeting will be adjourned while the chair* considers the matter and reaches a decision. The chair* will then either reconvene the meeting and give his decision orally to the trustee confirming it in writing within seven working days, or he will notify his decision in writing to the trustee within seven working days of the meeting. The trustee will then have the right of appeal.

3 Appeal

If the trustee is dissatisfied with the outcome of the meeting they may appeal in writing to the board of trustees within ten working days of receipt of written notification of the decision. The trustee must state the full grounds of their appeal and provide all necessary supporting documentation. A further meeting will be held to consider the appeal, which will be heard by a panel of at least three trustees excluding any who heard the initial grievance or who are the subject of the grievance. A decision will be given in writing to the trustee within ten working days of the appeal being heard. That decision will be final.

4 Supporting advice

The board of trustees is responsible for ensuring that decisions are consistently applied in accordance with this grievance procedure.

The Secretary** is responsible for advising the chair and trustees on the application of procedure and principles in relation to all grievance matters and for helping maintain this consistency. The Secretary** must be consulted at all stages under the formal procedure and is also there to advise during any informal process.

[* or his designated alternate]
[** or other designated officer or adviser]

Robin Stephenson
Trustee, The Public Service Broadcasting Trust
Consultant, governance and legal affairs

01273 813087
advice@robinstephenson.co.uk

Chapter 6

The role of the chief executive in good governance

6.1 | Introduction

Note: This chapter is addressed to chief executives but should also be read by other trustees and by chairs in order to understand the role of the chef executive in good governance. The whole of this publication, not just this chapter, is relevant to chief executives.

Research shows that failing charities usually have weak, ineffective governance. Good governance on its own does not guarantee the success of an organisation as strong governance cannot make up fully for weak management. So your first priority as chief executive is to ensure excellence of management and that the organisation is focused on achieving its strategic aims and priorities. Your second priority is to help the board to ensure the charity is well governed.

Your role as chief executive is key to good governance. Boards of trustees are dependent on you:
- to provide them with timely, accurate information
- to report back accurately on the performance of the charity
- to keep them informed of compliance with, and changes to, the legal and regulatory frameworks
- to scan the environment in which the charity works
- to alert them to current opportunities and threats and those that may be on the horizon
- to help frame strategic thinking and priorities
- to guide them, when necessary, to good governance practice.

Although as a chief executive you will work very closely with your chair of trustees, you need to remember that trustees have collective authority and responsibility. The chair plays a critical role in providing leadership to the board, in order to ensure both good governance and the fulfilment of the trustees' responsibilities, but do not make the mistake of not building a strong relationship with each and every one of your trustees. If in doubt, it is the views of the trustees acting collectively that count and not any contrary views of any individual trustee, even the chair.

Remember too that we are all human and make mistakes. Boards of trustees make mistakes too. Build up a relationship with your board and the chair which is based on mutual trust and respect. Get to know them well but keep to a professional relationship – do not muddy the waters by becoming over-friendly with one or more trustees! At the end of the day they are your bosses and you are answerable and accountable to them collectively.

Together, and in different ways, you and the board will provide leadership to the charity. Good, strong governance balanced by good, strong management is a winning formula that creates opportunities and enhances the success of the organisation. Achieving this has to be the aim of every chief executive, every chair and every trustee board of a professionally managed organisation.

It is tempting, when so much needs to be done, to ignore governance matters and the board and to get on with the work of driving the charity forward and achieving its vision. However, chief executives who do this, do so at their peril. They often suddenly find that misunderstandings have arisen that haven't been addressed or that the board's thinking has developed in a completely different way and is totally at odds with your and your senior management team's vision for the future. When this happens, it is usually too late to try to develop a good professional working relationship with your trustees. The outcome is often that the chief executive moves on.

6.1 | Introduction continued

How much of a chief executive's precious time should be spent on governance? I recall one chief executive telling me that governance matters took up 50% of his time. I very much hope that he is the exception and not the rule. Most chief executives who work at developing this crucial relationship with the chair and the board of trustees, appear to spend 15–25 % of their time on governance or related matters. Give this time willingly and not grudgingly. You are a very important person as you are key to both strong management and strong governance. Give both your attention.

If you have complaints about your board of trustees or your chair, don't be tempted to confide in your senior colleagues within your charity. Nor should you try to turn them against the trustees. Behave very professionally at all times. Get support and advice from other chief executives whose views you respect and who have the confidence to tell you what you might not want to hear. I'm a great believer in mentors – have more than one as you will need mentors in different aspects of your professional life.

Do not get down-hearted and feel that your relationship with your trustees is most likely to end in problems – most chief executives have a good relationship with their boards and really successful chief executives always do.

In *Lost in Translation: a complete guide to chair/chief executive parnerships* published by NCVO, Tesse Akpeki sums this up by writing:

A chief executive's guide to making the most of your board
- cultivate a positive attitude toward the board
- put aside time out of your busy schedule for working with the board
- bring human skills to your dealings with the board: sensitivity, tact and a willingness to listen
- take initiatives to the board in the first stages of the development process: let them have input before firm plans are put in place
- help the board feel satisfaction and a sense of ownership about the organisation's work
- develop your own knowledge of board leadership and governance practice
- let staff and senior managers know you think the board's role is vital
- attend to communication (quality and systems): both are essential to keeping relations healthy
- pay close attention to your relationship with the chair
- view your own performance review as an opportunity to strengthen your working relationship with the board.

6.2| The chief executive's role in good governance

As with all significant roles, there are two aspects to the chief executive's role in good governance:
- the harder, more technical aspects and processes
- the softer issues such as relationships and communications.

This chapter starts with the former and then leads onto the softer issues, which in many ways can cause the chief executive greater headaches.

The more technical aspects and processes

Many of these are covered elsewhere in this publication. It is particularly important to read and absorb chapters 1, 2, 3 and 4. You are also advised to read the chapters addressed to your chair of trustees (chapter 5) and to use the remaining chapters as a resource.

The chief executive's role

The chief executive's role has two key areas of responsibility:
- **to provide leadership to the charity and to be responsible for the management and administration of the charity within the strategic, policy and accountability frameworks laid down by the board of trustees**
- **together with the chair to enable the board of trustees to fulfil its duties and responsibilities for the proper governance of the charity and to ensure that the board receives timely advice and appropriate information on all relevant matters.**

It is on the second of these that this chapter concentrates. It can be expanded as follows:

Strategy and planning:

- in partnership with the chair, to ensure that the trustees set the values, ethos, vision, mission, strategic objectives and strategic priorities for the charity.

Ensuring high quality governance:

- to draw the board's attention to matters that it should consider and decide
- to ensure that the board receives all necessary advice, guidance and information on matters relating to
- current performance
- the short- and long-term future of the charity
- results of environmental scans
- external factors that could impact on the charity
- analysis of trends within the charity
- regulatory and legal compliance and other appropriate issues
 making sure that such advice, guidance and information are timely, honest, balanced and relevant
- to ensure that the staff understand and support the governance role of the board and that there is a positive and constructive working relationship between the board and the executive
- to ensure with the chair that the board of trustees regularly reviews the charity's governing instruments and governance structure and to assist with the board's assessment of its own performance
- in partnership with the chair to ensure that the board's delegated authority is recorded in writing, understood fully by staff and volunteers and that all agreed reporting procedures are followed
- to work closely with the board to ensure that the board has on it the skills it requires to govern the charity well, and that the board has access to relevant external professional advice and expertise

6.2 | The chief executive's role in good governance continued

- to assist the chair in ensuring that there is a systematic, open and fair procedure for the recruitment or co-option of trustees, future chairs of the board and future chief executives
- to work with the chair to ensure that all members of the board receive appropriate induction, advice, information and training (both individual and collective) thus getting the best thinking and involvement from each member of the board.

Board meetings

- to ensure that the board is given the information it needs to fulfil its duties and responsibilities
- in partnership with the chair, to develop an annual programme of board and committee meetings, board away days and board training
- in partnership with the chair to ensure that the right and appropriate items reach board agendas and that high-quality papers support each item on the agenda
- to assist the chair in ensuring that the board focuses on its governance role by making sure that the board agenda and papers do not draw the board away from governance and into unnecessary detail and management issues
- to report regularly to the board of trustees on the performance of the charity, progress towards the strategic priorities and the achievement of board policies
- to submit high-level policy proposals for the approval of the board or assist the board in the development of these policies and to be responsible for the efficient and effective achievement of these policies
- to implement board decisions.

Relationships with the chair of trustees

- to have regular one-to-one meetings with the chair at which you and the chair can talk openly, discuss progress and problems, agree expectations of each other, plan the board's annual programme together and prepare together for meetings (the chief executive and chair should ensure that there are no 'surprises' between chair and chief executive at board meetings or elsewhere.) and
- in close consultation with the chair to agree respective roles in representing the charity and acting as spokesperson at public functions, public meetings and to the press/media.

6.3 | The chief executive's role in understanding governance

The first point that all chief executives must understand is that trustees are collectively responsible for governance and for the charity. The chair is responsible for providing leadership to the board and ensuring that governance is effective and that trustees fulfil their responsibilities. This is why it is important for both you and the chair, more than any other trustee, to understand what governance really means.

Make sure you fully understand the fundamentals of good governance (see chapter 1) and what governance is (see chapter 2). Ideally make sure your senior leadership team also understands these two chapters and realise why it is essential that senior managers give governance time.

Your role as chief executive should be to ensure that your trustees fulfil the full remit of their responsibilities; and that board structures, agendas, board papers, away days, trustee training, etc support them in addressing all three strands of governance (corporate, strategic and impact). See chapter 2 'Understanding governance'.

6.4 | Making sure trustees are discussing the right issues and being well informed

Detailed advice on this topic can be found in Chapter 4.

Improving meeting agendas and board information

Mention of the word 'agendas' causes most people to switch off and think about something else. Yet agendas dictate what a trustee board will address. Therefore getting the agenda right is a vital task: one which is shared by the chair and by you, the chief executive. Although you, or possibly the company secretary, will almost certainly write the first draft of the agenda, chairs should see it as their ultimate responsibility to ensure that the right issues are discussed by the board. However most boards will need their chief executive's guidance to ensure this happens.

The quality of governance depends very much on the quality of information received by the trustees. Trustees are very dependent on you, to provide high-quality, timely and relevant papers. Take this responsibility very seriously and give it the time it deserves or delegate some of it to other members of your senior management team as long as you are confident that members of the senior management team understand the importance of board papers and committee papers.

It is quite a skill to ensure that the papers focus the board on governance issues. In my experience, when chief executives complain that their trustees concentrate on management issues rather than governance, it is not uncommon to find that their board papers focus mainly on management issues and management detail and are therefore the main cause of the problem.

It is very tempting when there are so many pressures on your time to send trustees a paper which was written for management. Every chief executive has done so at some stage of their career. However resist the temptation! It will only draw trustees into management detail instead of concentrating on governance. Remember: If you distribute to your board papers full of management details they will discuss management details! There is a real skill in writing good papers for the board. It takes time and effort.

It is important for you to develop a relationship with your trustees based on openness, honesty, respect and trust. A relationship which sees you and your trustees totally committed to achieving the organisation's objects and sees each other as partners in leading and achieving the organisation's mission.

In particular read section 2 in Chapter 4 on how to disempower a board. Make sure you neither consciously nor subconsciously do anything to disempower your board.

Insufficient or unhelpful information

It is part of your professional duty to provide the board with the information they need to govern well. Your job description should clearly indicate your responsibility to ensure that the board receives timely advice and appropriate information on all relevant matters.

If you are not giving the trustees the level and quality of timely information and advice that they need, the chair needs to discuss these needs openly with you. It may be that as a new chief executive you are only imitating a former chief executive with whom you have worked.

If this is the case you should expect the board through the chair to articulate what information they need from you. Remember it is what the board collectively wants and needs that is important and not just what the chair feels is needed. If you are not sure the chair is reflecting the collective view of the board, try including board information and advice needs as an item on the next agenda or on the programme for the next board away-day.

Remember, if you repeatedly fail to keep them appropriately informed then the board should take disciplinary action. Sometimes, you as chief executive, might need to guide your board on what they need to discuss and what information they need to govern well.

Your chief executive's report

It can be difficult to identify what a chief executive's report should contain ideally. Based on my research with chairs and chief executives, a framework has been identified which reflects the views of chairs and chief executives, which you can tailor to your own charity's and trustees' needs. (Note: not every item in the framework needs to be covered in every chief executive's report or in every pack of board meeting papers.) Remember your report to the board needs to be succinct, to the point and ideally not more than five sides of A4.

For more information read chapter 4 'Discussing the right issues and being well informed'.

6.5 | Trustee recruitment: your part in building a strong refreshed board

Detailed advice on recruiting trustees can be found in Chapter 7.

The role of the chief executive in the recruitment of trustees is not to dictate or, in any way, to put pressure on the trustees to select or not select any potential trustee. Trustees will almost certainly seek your advice at various stages of the process. Your role is also to facilitate the recruitment process and to brief potential trustees from the chief executive's perspective. The chair and/or the nominations committee will want to do the same from their perspective.

Many boards when starting the process of finding new trustees will ask their chief executive and other contacts if they know of any suitable candidates. The trustees will almost certainly ask your views on the suitability of potential trustees; nevertheless, it is important to remember that the decision to appoint, or not, rests collectively with the board and not with you as the chief executive.

A tiny minority of boards prohibit the chief executive being involved in the identification of new trustees. I believe this is a mistake for two reasons: first, because a chief executive is likely to have a much wider network of people who have the potential to be good trustees; and secondly, because the chief executive's objective assessment of potential trustees can aid the process of finding the most suitable and effective trustees.

A few leave the task of finding new trustees entirely to the chief executive. This is highly inappropriate so resist the temptation to find every, or most, trustees and, in particular, resist the temptation to fill the board with people who will readily endorse everything you propose and never challenge you. You should play a part in the identification, recruitment, and induction of trustees but equally, you need to recognise that the board should take responsibility for its renewal.

If you find your charity is still not convinced that the board needs good recruitment processes to identify future trustees, you need to persuade your chair to take the lead towards establishing a more open, professional recruitment procedure. To start this process, remind trustees of the requirement, under the Statement of Recommended Practice (SORP) 2005, to report on the method your charity uses for the recruitment, induction and training of trustees. The fact that recruitment is now a factor in reporting should convey the importance of proper recruitment procedures to your board.

Providing information to potential trustees and clarifying expectations

Your board will need your help in making sure that sufficient information is provided to potential trustees including the commitments that are expected of all trustees. See chapter 7.2 for information requirements for potential trustees.

Inducting new trustees

Without induction, trustees can take a year or more to understand the organisation sufficiently in order to contribute anything of real value to its governance. The chair, with your help, can ensure that new trustees can contribute sooner by establishing and implementing a trustee induction process.

In particular, it would help if you had informal sessions with new trustees on the following:
- the vision, mission and strategic plans of the organisation
- the organisation's big issues and how they are being addressed.
- major risks facing the charity and how they are being managed.

Ideally the finance director should cover sessions on:
- charity financial regulations and how to read the financial information provided to trustees

and the chair should explain:
- the governance structure and how it helps the trustees to fulfil their duties and responsibilities;
- the board's policies and the mechanisms used to review these regularly; and
- how the board reflects on its performance, how it assesses the performance of its chief executive and how it measures the performance of the organisation.

Trustees should be encouraged to go on externally run courses (as run by **Governance** www.civilsociety.co.uk/trusteetraining) on the expectation, duties and responsibilities of trustees, the difference between governance and management, etc. This will also be an opportunity to meet trustees from other charities and to share experiences.

In addition, you will probably want to arrange for new trustees to visit the charity and have the opportunity to:
- meet and get to know you and members of the senior management team
- walk around the main office and talk to staff and volunteers
- visit one or more of the service delivery centres or projects.

Creating a trustee handbook

To improve board performance and support new trustees, the board is likely to look to you or the company secretary, to provide a trustee handbook/manual. This can either be delivered online, in a traditional loose-leaf folder version or on a CD. See resource 7.7

See Chapter 7 for detailed information on recruiting trustees.

6.6 | Performance appraisal

This is covered in great detail in Chapter 9 'Appraising the chief executive'.

All of us, and chief executives are no exception, need candid and constructive feedback on our performance. This is not only to provide reassurance that we are doing well, but also to help us to learn and to develop professionally. During my many years working with chief executives, they have expressed, frequently and sometimes privately, the need for honest, objective feedback as to whether or not they are doing a good job. Chief executives often get mixed messages from their trustees.

The chief executive, who is so crucial to the success of an organisation, probably needs performance feedback more than anyone else in the organisation. This is because the more senior you are, the less likely that staff or volunteers will tell you honestly if they feel that you can do things better. In addition, the extraordinary demands of the role mean that you have less time to reflect on your own performance and how it can be improved unless time is regularly put aside for your appraisal.

Other impediments to you getting honest informal feedback on your performance include:
- you may work very long hours, so no one feels they should fault you in any way
- the need for you to provide leadership and to act as a role model to staff, volunteers, etc. can sometimes make it more difficult for you to receive less than fulsome praise.

Reviewing your performance should be a rewarding exercise for all those concerned and for the charity. Planning and preparation, openness and honesty and a genuine desire to learn and to be constructive will ensure the success of the ongoing review of your performance. Do not forget to take time out to celebrate your achievements and those of the board and of the charity.

6.7 | Softer issues: working effectively with the chair and the trustees

The days when the board felt that its only duty was to appoint the chief executive and support him/her through thick and thin are long past. Today everyone, and especially trustees, who carry ultimate responsibility, is held accountable by regulators, the public, the media and the courts. The board therefore has to hold the chief executive to account.

You will therefore be line-managed. This will almost certainly be done by the chair, on behalf of the board. This should include not only providing you with support and ensuring you receive appropriate professional development but the chair should also act as a 'critical friend' to you. If the chair has no line-management experience, the board may decide that your line management is carried out by another trustee.

Each year you will need to agree with your board your annual goals/objectives. Also try to persuade your board and board committees to be clear about what they should aim to achieve each year in order to help the charity and you achieve the annual objectives set by the board.

Your relationships with the chair

Both you and the chair will need to be able to see the relationship as a partnership within which each of you has a different, complementary and crucial role. You will need to meet regularly but not over frequently. Keep the chair proactively involved about key developments, contentious issues, developments in the environment that may result in tactical, strategic or other changes. The chair will need to make him/herself available between meetings to give advice or to be kept abreast of important developments or sometimes just to listen to you.

The chair will need to ensure that your performance is regularly reviewed and that you receive professional development and support. Discuss the process of reviewing your performance with the chair and then take proposals to the board. It is always better to take the initiative with this rather than leave it to the board to suggest methods of appraisal. For ideas, see chapter 9 'Appraising the chief executive'.

If there isn't a budget for your professional development and support, don't be afraid of asking your trustees for it. It is important to show to the organisation that however good a chief executive is, you need to keep learning and developing in order to do an even better job. This will send out a powerful message to your staff and hopefully will also encourage the board to consider its own development.

6.7 | Softer issues: working effectively with the chair and the trustees continued

Understanding the role of the chair

Chairing is an undervalued skill. Few of us are born with chairing skills. Instead we learn and develop the expertise needed to do a really sound job. A successful chair does not just chair board meetings skilfully. The role is a much wider one. The trustees will expect the chair with your help to ensure that they fulfil their responsibilities. They will expect the chair to support, supervise and act as a 'critical' friend to you. They will expect the chair to ensure that you provide the board with the information that they need for the proper discharge of their duties. They will expect the chair to lead the way in setting up mechanisms, structures and systems to ensure that governance is strong. They will expect the chair to support you in making management strong.

A role decription is an important tool for bringing clarity to the chair's role, which will help not only the chair but also you and the board. There are a number of model role descriptions available from organisations like NCVO and others. However, as governance and the role of the chair of trustees has evolved over the last decade, it is important to use a role description which has kept up-to-date with these changes and which reflects the greater emphasis on strategy, risk, accountability and performance. All model documents need to be modified to the needs of your organisation. A model role decription for the chair can be found at Resource 3.2 and 5.1.

The key responsibilities of the chair are:
- to provide leadership to the board and to ensure that trustees fulfil their duties and responsibilities for the proper governance of the organisation
- to support, and where appropriate, to challenge the chief executive and to ensure that the board as a whole works in partnership with executive staff.

You should also carefully read Chapter 5 'The role of the chair in good governance'.

It is vital that the chair and the board not only support you but constructively challenge you. You are advised to read section 5.4 'Balancing support with constructive challenge' and section 5.5 Julia Unwin's five modes of board behaviour. These may also be a useful tool for your relationship with senior management/leadership team.

6.8 | Dealing with problems with the chair and/or trustees

The chair with too much time

Chairing a charity effectively takes time and anyone taking on the role must expect to give you, the board and the charity sufficient time. Yet we all know of chairs who, either because they are retired or because they have already made enough money not to work, decide that their presence is needed virtually full-time at the charity. They have an office in the charity and probably even a secretary. They start to interfere in management, issuing instructions not just to you but also to other staff without your knowledge. Employees and volunteers become confused and no longer know to whom they are responsible; and are unclear about how to deal with the situation when they are given conflicting instructions from the chair and the chief executive.

The chair quickly takes credit when things are going well and even more rapidly blames the chief executive when things go wrong. Soon the chair forgets that he or she is responsible to the board and that authority resides collectively with the board and not with the chair. The board usually starts by being pleased with the commitment of the chair but ends up disempowered and marginalised. In this situation, the chief executive tends to move on.

There are a number of approaches to take in this situation
- Work hard to build up a relationship with the chair and build his/her confidence in, and respect for, you. Use all your people skills and charm in order to find common ground from where you can start to alter the chair's behaviour. Try to identify the chair's strengths and encourage the chair to move into areas that he/she can do well but which keep him/her out of management.
- Flatter the chair into getting involved in activities that are unrelated to the charity so that there are more external demands on his/her time.
- Persuade the board to have a briefing session or seminar facilitated by an outsider who, can remind the trustees of their role, responsibilities and personal liabilities and who can strongly remind them that ultimate authority and responsibility lies with the trustees collectively and nowhere else.
- Make sure that through the agenda and briefing papers that the trustees are aware of the big issues and how they are being addressed by you and your executive team. Where appropriate and whenever possible try to arrange the need for major decisions to coincide with the times of board meetings. At board meetings, ask directly for trustees' advice and ensure that decisions are made by the board.
- Explain to the chair the difficulties faced by staff getting contradictory instructions and persuade the chair that except for you, his/her secretary and the company secretary, instructions should be given through you. Together, let staff know about this decision.
- Build strong relations with key trustees such as the vice-chair or treasurer, so that at an appropriate stage you can discuss the issue with them and seek their advice.
- Build good relationships on a one-to-one basis with each trustee and make sure that they know of the charity's successes and the part you and your senior management team played in each success and, how you are tackling any challenges. You need to develop trust, confidence and mutual respect and should not be tempted to be economical with the truth or to give everything an unmerited positive spin.
- Try to identify a chief executive who has had similar experiences and who lived to tell the tale. Learn from his/her experiences.
- Try and be as patient and as calm as possible reminding yourself that this is going to be a long haul.
- If everything fails, seek a comparable post elsewhere.

6.8 | Dealing with problems with the chair and/or trustees continued

The chair with no time

A less likely scenario is one where the chair is rarely available and appears to have lost interest in the charity. Often this is because of changed circumstances such as their 'day-job' becoming more demanding, or there are family or health problems. Sometimes, it is because they want to do something remarkable, such as sailing round the world, but don't want to give up roles that give them status.

Naturally if it is a temporary situation such as poor health, a senior trustee can step in as interim chair until the situation is resolved. If the situation is more permanent and the chair shows absolutely no realisation that his or her unavailability is causing problems, despite various conversations with you about the matter, then you should discuss the situation with the vice-chair or another senior trustee. It will be their responsibility to consider the circumstances with fellow trustees and address the problem.

The trustee with undue influence

The situation where one or two trustees have undue influence can develop in one of two ways in my experience. The first is that trustees collectively and often subconsciously begin to develop huge confidence in the judgement of one or two trustees and as a result suspend their own judgement and sometimes even common sense, and will unquestioningly accept the views or judgement of these trustees. This is an unhealthy situation as no one is right all the time and trustees are expected to use their own judgement on issues put before them. However, it is not an easy situation to deal with. Often this can be tackled tactfully by the chair in one-to-one discussions with trustees. A training session by an independent outsider can also address the issue in a non-confrontational way.

The more dangerous situation is where a trustee deliberately goes about ensuring that he/she wields a great deal of power. They often make an impressive start as a trustee by getting the board out of a tricky situation. Trustees are so relieved that the new trustee is soon serving on most major decision-making committees or is invited to attend meetings where key decisions are being made. This situation is often exacerbated by a weak or ineffectual chair and/or by a weak, ineffectual board.

Getting the board to agree to having a governance review led by an independent expert in governance is probably the most effective way forward. Ensure that the independent outsider carries out one-to-one conversations under Chatham House Rules[1] with each trustee and other key people. Further ensure that the report of the governance review addresses the issue and that there is training for trustees on the dangers of individuals or groups of individuals wielding a great deal of power which undermines the collective responsibility and authority of trustees.

The chair who refuses to take on a leadership role

Occasionally a chair believes that his/her role is purely to chair meetings and perhaps represent the charity to external agencies from time to time. Apart from this the chair does little. For example the chair leaves the chief executive or company secretary to set board and committee agendas; the chair refuses to deal with trustees who are ineffectual, destructive or just nuisances and expects the chief executive to take on this role; the chair takes little interest in ensuring that the board is refreshed by ensuring regular intake of new trustees etc.

[1] The Chatham House Rule: *'When a meeting, or part thereof, is held under the Chatham House Rule, participants are free to use the information received, but neither the identity nor the affiliation of the speaker(s), nor that of any other participant, may be revealed'.*

There are a number of approaches to take in this situation

- Talk to the chair about the value of mentors and how much you and other key people have benefited by having mentors. Gradually suggest the chair should consider a more experienced chair of trustees to act as his/her mentor. Carefully arrange an appropriate mentor ensuring that the mentor recognises and practices a leadership role as chair.
- Try to get the chair to join a networking group of chairs of trustees. Charity Trustee Networks should be able to help you with this.
- Remind trustees that authority delegated by the board of trustees must be in writing and reviewed regularly. Persuade the board that a review of delegated authority is now due. As part of this process, delegated authority to key individuals will come up for review. Ensure that all honorary officers including the chair have a role description that spells out their role and especially the chair's leadership role.
- Emphasise the importance of the charity's culture of reviewing and improving performance and gently encourage the chair to get the board to collectively review its own performance and that of other key people, such as the honorary officers. Make sure that your views are fed into the review of the chair's performance.
- If none of the above seem to work, seek advice and help from the vice-chair or another senior trustee whom the chair respects.

More specific advice on dealing with some of the issues that a chair who does not understand his/her leadership role may fail to address:

- If the chair shows no inclination to participate in the setting of board agendas, make sure that during your regular meetings with the chair, and as part of the natural flow of conversation, you start talking about which issues the board will need to address. Note these down and then point out that you have in effect got an outline agenda. Explain that this was an enormously helpful process and get the chair to agree to doing it again. After a couple of meetings be more direct and put drafting the board agenda on the agenda for your meeting with the chair. After a while you will find the chair will slip into the role of thinking about and probably even drafting agendas.
- If the chair is reluctant is to take on the responsibility of ensuring new trustees are recruited, refrain from taking on this task yourself. Instead, suggest that the board sets up either a nominations committee with this specific task or that the board regularly sets up ad-hoc search committees to find new trustees. If necessary, remind the board that they have to report annually on how the board recruits, inducts and trains trustees. Facilitate the process of recruitment of trustees and make it easy for the chair and trustees to take control of the process.
- If you have a difficult, destructive, bullying, ineffective or problem trustee whom the chair refuses to deal with, draft codes of conduct for trustees, yourself and members of your senior management team. Put codes of conduct on the board's agenda and get the trustees to agree to a trustee code of conduct. If you are in the process of reviewing your governing instruments, you may wish to advise the board to add a power to remove a trustee if a trustee commits a breach of the trustee code of conduct and the board passes a resolution that he/she is removed from office. Persuade the board to reflect regularly on its own performance and on the performance of individual trustees. If all this fails or the matter needs to be addressed more urgently, make it clear to the chair that it is the chair's, not your, responsibility to deal with the problem of ineffective trustees and suggest that he/she should involve another senior trustee whom he/she respects in this matter.

6.9 | Relationships with the board

We live in an age of greater scrutiny and much greater accountability. If disaster strikes, trustees will have to bear the brunt of any consequences of mismanagement. While you may lose your job, you will not suffer the same level of consequences as trustees who carry full legal responsibility for the organisation.

The boards that do best in strategically maximising the impact and effectiveness of their organisation are those who combine a high degree of support for the chief executive with a high level of constructive challenge when appropriate. Naturally, this does not mean that chief executives need to be constantly challenged but only when appropriate and always constructively. Although many chief executives would rather not be challenged, the best welcome it as long as it is done helpfully. Constructive challenges lift most of us to a higher level of performance. You are advised to read sections 5.4 and 5.5 for further information on this topic.

Meetings without you

Most chief executives hate their boards meeting without them and argue that important discussions and decisions should not be made without their presence. Normally, your contract will state your entitlement to attend board meetings and to raise issues directly with the board. It will almost certainly also state the right of the board to meet formally without you as long as you are informed in advance. Meetings without the executive are often and curiously called 'executive sessions'.

Trustees are likely to want to meet without you for reasons such as discussing:
- your remuneration
- your performance
- appointing your successor
- a request for significant investment in your professional development
- a sabbatical for you.

When this happens, do not worry if they appear to take a long time coming to a conclusion. My experience is that they usually sort the matter out quite quickly but then go on to talk about things that they feel they could not discuss with the executive present. These topics are almost certainly nothing to do with you so don't get paranoid while you wait outside to be called back in!

Boards sometimes want to meet by themselves to talk about sensitive issues. Topics under discussion may include:
- expressing unhappiness with the chair generally or on a particular issue
- collectively wanting to tackle a difficult trustee
- dealing with conflicts between two trustees
- considering a serious complaint about a trustee
- considering a confidential matter relating to a trustee and the trustee does not want staff to be present
- considering an issue that is troubling a trustee who cannot gauge whether it constitutes a serious problem or not
- meeting with the internal auditor
- meeting with the external auditor.

The stronger the bond of mutual trust, respect and confidence between you and the board, the less likely you and your staff will feel threatened by an 'executive session'. The advantage of having regular 'executive sessions' is that it becomes 'normal' and isn't interpreted by you or your senior team as a threatening action.

Occasionally the board may want to meet with you but without the rest of the executive team. This may include discussing:
- remuneration of senior staff

- your assessment of individual members of your senior team
- worries that the board may have which they would like to share with you alone
- worries that you may have that you prefer to discuss directly with your board without other executives present
- ideas that you have that may be risky or contentious and which you feel you need to sound out your board before you raise it with your senior team
- ideas for mergers or acquisitions that need to be kept confidential from your senior team during the initial, tentative stages.

When meetings like these happen, it is important that you reassure your team that it is quite natural and understandable for trustees to want occasionally to meet alone with you and without them.

Some boards like to have an annual dinner with their chief executive to develop the very special relationship between them and you and to discuss some of the issues above.

Campaigning and the chief executive

A potentially contentious area is the chief executive's role in campaigning. Should the chief executive have a free hand or is this a matter for the trustees?

Some chief executives believe that they have the freedom to decide on the themes and key messages of any campaign undertaken by their charity and that these are not matters for their trustees. Charity Commission guidance disagrees.

Campaigning and Political Activities by Charities (CC9) http://www.charity-commission.gov.uk/publications/cc9.asp issued by the Charity Commission advises:

'When planning or considering a campaign or political activity, trustees need to be clear about how the campaign or activity will further or support the work of the charity and, with that in mind, set clear and measurable objectives. A political activity might be highly successful in achieving the objective of raising public awareness, or of encouraging the public to support the work of the charity, even if it does not lead to an immediate change of law or government policy. Not all political activity will be successful. It is therefore important for trustees to be able to explain their charity's decision to engage in campaigning or political activity, and to set objectives for the campaign which have a reasonable likelihood of success, as well as making sure that they have monitored progress towards them during the implementation phase of the campaign.

When developing objectives, trustees should be aware of and, where appropriate, follow good practice.

Evaluating and managing risks: Trustees are responsible for identifying and reviewing the major risks to which a charity is exposed, and for putting in place systems to mitigate these risks. Some types of campaigning and political activity, particularly those that have a high public profile, have the potential both to enhance and to damage the charity's reputation, and also to compromise its independence. This means that charities need to identify and manage the possible risks involved; it does not mean that they have to avoid all risks.

As part of its assessment of the overall risks and benefits of the activity, a charity should consider:
- the risk that the activity may not be effective, or that the charity will be drawn into activities that are outside its purposes;
- the costs and benefits of engaging in a particular campaign;
- ways of approaching the campaign;
- the risks attached to the campaign, and how these might best be managed; these include public perceptions of the charity's independence, for example if a charity is supporting or opposing a policy that is also advocated by a political party;
- the strategy for delivering the campaign; and

6.9 | Relationships with the board continued

• *how best to evaluate the campaign's success and impact.*

Trustees must not allow the charity to be used as a vehicle for the expression of the political views of any individual trustee or staff member (in this context we mean personal or party political views).

Trustees should also ensure that they have an adequate level of knowledge about their donors. Trustees should be alert to the risk that, very occasionally, a donor may have an ulterior motive for giving money to their charity that could be unconnected with the charity's work, and which could adversely affect the charity's reputation. Ultimately, it is the responsibility of trustees to be satisfied that a donation is in the best interests of the charity.

Reputational risk: Trustees will also need to consider the impact of the proposed campaigning or political activity for the charity's reputation. A charity's independence and reputation must be protected, and trustees will need, as part of their overall campaign strategy, to consider arrangements to protect the charity's reputation.

Balance of risks and benefits: Overall, trustees need to be reasonably convinced that the likely benefits of campaigning outweigh the costs and risks. That involves assessing the likelihood of a successful outcome. The trustees must ask themselves:

• *Will this really further or support the work of the charity?*
• *Is it worth the effort and resources involved?*

If they can answer yes to both questions, they can confidently go ahead.

Monitoring impact and success: Monitoring and evaluating the success of a campaign should be built into a campaign strategy from the outset. They are a key means of ensuring that resources are being used wisely, and of contributing to the effectiveness of future campaigns.

Consultation: In seeking to influence legislation or public policy a charity may consider consulting with its key stakeholders, and possibly with members of the public. It might, for example, arrange consultative meetings in order to test the views of its beneficiaries before supporting changes to legislation and public policy. Such consultation is not, however, a formal requirement. The main consideration for charity trustees is that they have a clear understanding of the ways in which the activity will further or support the work of the charity.'

Trustees set and are responsible for vision, mission, strategic direction, performance, reputation and risk; therefore, boards of trustees need to approve new campaigns and their key messages before they are launched.

With your help, trustees should consider not only the purpose of any new campaign and its key messages but also the style of the campaign, especially if either content or style might result in controversy; by doing so they protect both the charity and the chief executive. Risk should be proportionate to benefits.

Trustees may wish to delegate, consciously and not by default, these decisions to a smaller group of trustees or indeed to you as the chief executive. As with all delegated powers this should be recorded in writing, have proper reporting mechanisms and should be reviewed regularly.

There will be times when a decision on campaigning needs to be made between meetings of trustees or the group delegated to consider these matters. This should be covered by clear, general, written guidelines from trustees on decision-making between meetings.

Campaigning outside charitable objects

Under charity law, charities can only work within their charitable objects; therefore campaigning outside one's charitable objects could be seen as a breach of trust by the trustees who are ultimately responsible for the charity. However many feel that larger charities have a responsibility to provide leadership to the sector. This could lead them to campaign outside their charitable objects.

It would be particularly advisable for you as chief executive to seek clearance from your trustees before the charity, or you as the charity's representative, campaigns outside charitable objects that are on issues of relevance to the wellbeing of the charitable sector. It is advisable also to consult the Charity Commission.

Campaigning in a personal capacity

There are of course some situations in which it would be inappropriate for senior figures in a charity to voice their private views publicly: for example, the chair of a hospice whose public policy is adamantly opposed to euthanasia but who personally believes in assisted dying, should not publicly air his or her private views on the subject.

If you feel strongly about an issue about which your charity cannot, or does not wish to, campaign, then you must obtain and accept guidance from their trustees before speaking up in a public forum. Common sense should prevail: if a chief executive would like to campaign about the plans for a park near his home, he should not be expected to get his trustees' consent to do so.

If permission to express private views in a public forum is granted, chief executives should make it abundantly clear that they are speaking or writing in a personal capacity and are not necessarily voicing the views of their charity. If they do not, it could potentially damage the charity or be interpreted as an abuse of their position.

6.10 | Conclusion

Good governance is about a partnership based on mutual trust, respect and honesty. Good governance recognises the complementary but different roles played by those who govern and those who manage. Good governance is a partnership between strong, effective management and strong, effective governance.

Good governance isn't just about finances and compliance but also about planning for the future together and ensuring the maximum beneficial impact on those the charity is set up to serve.

Good governance isn't just based on putting in good systems, policies and procedures. It is based on team work and on nurturing and developing trustees. As with good management, this relies heavily on good two-way communication.

Good governance isn't about trustees agreeing constantly with the chief executive but about appropriate and constructive challenge. Good governance is a mixture of supporting, stretching, scrutinising, stewardship and strategy.

Good governance cannot be achieved without the support and help of the chief executive. Good governance needs the chief executive, in partnership with the chair, to put energy into making it happen.

Sometimes, despite all the efforts of a chief executive, governance remains weak, troubled and ineffective. If this happens, it might be time for you to move on. Let us hope it never comes to this. If it does, learn from your experiences and when applying for your next chief executive post, remember it is a two-way process and that you are selecting whether or not to work with a particular group of trustees.

Finally, enjoy your trustees and enjoy your role of being a chief executive.

Chapter 7
Recruiting trustees

7.1| Refreshing the board – limited terms of office

Small charities that have few if any employees, would probably cease to exist if they brought in limited terms of office for their trustees as trustees not only govern the charity but also deliver the work of the charity with other volunteers. Finding people who can give this level of commitment can be difficult.

On the other hand professionally managed charities should develop ways of attracting a good flow of suitable trustees. In order to ensure that the board is regularly refreshed by new trustees who can look at the governance and the charity with fresh eyes, limited terms of office are ideal. There is no ideal limit. Common limits are 2x3years, 3x3years, 2x4 years, 2x5years etc. Some charities allow trustees who have reached the limit to return after a year's break from the charity and the clock then starts again or they return for one additional term of office. Other charities have the power to reappoint a trustee if he or she has skills and expertise that aren't easily replaced but need to do so by having a 75% majority on a resolution to offer the particular an additional term of 1, 2, 3 or 4 years.

In order to overcome problems of new trustees not being suitable despite careful recruitment (for example the new trustee fails to attend after their first meeting or the new trustee feels he/she must dominate all discussions and decision-making), some boards introduce a one-year initial appointment e.g. instead of two three-year terms, they have 1+3+2 year terms.

If the board is planning to introduce limited terms of office for trustees or honorary officers, trustees will need to modify the governing documents and take legal advice. The board will also need to think about how it stages the departure of current trustees who might have been trustees for quite a while. The board does not want a large number of trustees to depart together unless they are particularly poor trustees. Generally the board should stagger their departure over a number of years (say three), based upon the time each has served as a trustee.

7.2 | Due diligence

Surprisingly, charities still provide very little hard information for potential trustees and, even more surprisingly, potential trustees rarely demand sufficient information, ie rarely apply 'due diligence' prior to accepting an invitation to become a trustee.

At the very least a charity should provide an information pack (now usually available on the charity's website) for prospective trustees containing:

- statement of the charity's vision, mission and values
- most recent annual report & accounts *(these can be obtained from the Charity Commission website but it is better to have them available on the charity's website as well)*
- current strategic plan
- copy of the most up-to-date assessment of the charity's performance against its strategic plan
- major risks currently facing the charity
- person specification (see Resource 7.2 for an outline person specification),
- role description (see Resource 2.1 for a model role description of a trustee),
- expected commitment of trustees and the charity's commitment to trustees. See Resource 7.3 for an example outline of commitments
- copy of or link to Charity Commission's publication *'CC3 - The Essential Trustee: What you need to know'*
- details of trustee liability insurance
- details of the policy regarding trustee expenses and how trustees can claim expenses.

Potential trustees should not be reluctant to ask for further information about the charity or to ask challenging questions about the charity's plans, assets and liabilities.

7.3 | Nomination committees and skills audits

Many trustee boards just add friends, acquaintances and colleagues to the board in the hope that some might turn out to be quite helpful. A growing number of boards now realise that they need to have a mechanism for identifying people who not only have appropriate skills, experience and working styles (board members need to be team players, as trustees need to make decisions collectively), but also those who share the vision and values of the charity. Effective boards should try to test the commitment and capabilities of potential trustees prior to them being invited to join the board. Often potential trustees are invited to various charity events and to attend a couple of board meetings prior to a decision being taken by the board as to their suitability to take on the responsibilities of trusteeship.

A strong healthy board is built by having a thorough process for the recruitment and selection of trustees followed by a programme of induction as well as on-going support and development. A driving force in the process of developing a strong and effective board should be the nominations committee. The nominations committee, perhaps with a few additional responsibilities, is sometimes called the board development committee or governance committee. See Resource 7.4 for model terms of reference for a nominations committee.

If the charity's governing instruments allow non-trustees to sit on board committees, I would encourage the board to include the chief executive as a full member of the nominations committee when it is advising on potential trustees; or, at the very least to have the chief executive in attendance. Some people feel strongly that the chief executive should not be involved in any ways in recruiting trustees – I disagree. When looking for a new chair, clearly the chief executive will need to be involved in some way as the chair/chief executive relationship is a crucial one.

Instead of having a standing committee, some organisations may prefer to use an ad-hoc nominations committee. The advantage of having an ad-hoc committee is that, over time, most trustees will have the opportunity of being involved in identifying future board members and in the process of their induction and development.

A formal or informal audit, of the skills, experience and diversity of existing trustees should be carried out regularly. A skills audit will highlight gaps in the collective experience and expertise of the trustee board.

Charities can use (if they have one) their annual skills audit form and potential trustees' skills audit form as an opportunity to get trustees to reaffirm (and potential trustees to affirm) their commitment to their role and to the charity. See Resource 7.6 for possible wording of affirmation.

7.4 | Identifying potential trustees

Looking for trustees among one's friends, acquaintances and colleagues is not wrong if it is done as part of a wider strategy. For example, one American not-for-profit organisation identifies suitable board members by inviting 20 well-connected, respected people in fields related to the work of the charity, to join a 'one-meeting committee'. At this meeting they are told about the organisation, its current successes and challenges, and the qualities and skills that are needed on the board. Each attendee is asked to nominate an individual who fits the bill. Within 24 hours, meetings are arranged for the 20 people nominated to meet the chief executive and chair. The members of the 'one-meeting committee' leave with a greater knowledge and understanding of the charity, often going on to become supporters and sometimes even trustees.

Other methods of identifying potential trustees include looking among the charity's volunteers, committee members or members of various advisory forums such as user forum or young people's forum. This method allows the charity to see people in action and to test commitment to the charity prior to an approach being made by the nominations committee. Other charities identify key organisations that the charity would like to develop stronger links with, and set up mechanisms for assessing their key people as possible trustees.

Trustee vacancies, with the skills and expertise required, can be advertised not just among supporters and members via mailings, newsletters and the website, but more widely such as in local or national newspapers or journals. Advertising in external publications needs to be carefully targeted otherwise it can be costly and bring little response. For example, if a trustee with PR skills is needed it is wise to advertise in a PR journal.

Membership organisations often complain that they cannot develop balanced and diverse boards as they are at the mercy of their members' nominating and voting whims. However, membership organisations can take proactive steps to develop balanced boards that have the skills needed to govern well. Co-option has often been used to obtain trustees with relevant skills and backgrounds. In addition, membership organisations should advertise to their members the skills needed on the board. This should be done both at the time of seeking nominations as well as to voters prior to the election. Some membership charities not only advertise the skills, experience and backgrounds needed on the board but also have a shortlisting committee that scrutinises the nominations received and only shortlists for election those who have one or more of the skills needed and who satisfy the nomination criteria or person specification.

Head hunters are occasionally used by charities that can either afford to pay their fees or if the head hunter can be persuade to work on a 'pro-bono' or reduced fee basis. Methods used by head hunters include search and open competition through advertisements.

Interviews and reference

It is important to have a fair and open process for the recruitment of trustees. Trustees are taking on a crucial role and will collectively with other trustees have ultimate authority over the charity and ultimate responsibility for the charity. The process therefore needs to be thorough.

At the very least, potential trustees should be asked to provide a CV with the names and full contact details of two referees. Ideally one should be from the chair of a board on which they have served. A brief statement explaining why they would like to become a trustee is also helpful.

Potential trustees should be interviewed and references taken up. Apart from judging shortlisted candidates against the person specification, also look for getting a range of personalities and backgrounds on the board.

Checks on potential trustees

First take up references on chosen candidates. Ask for proof of identity, eg a passport. Surprisingly, the Charity Commission reports discovering trustees with more than one identity!

Check that the candidate does in fact have the qualifications that are needed on the board. As a chief executive, I recall recommending an owner of a firm of surveyors (a property trustee had been identified on the skills audit) only to discover that he owned the firm but had no knowledge of surveying or property!

If your charity deals with children or vulnerable adults, Criminal Record Bureau (CRB) checks are required. As most trustees should be encouraged to meet beneficiaries, I would recommend getting an enhanced check done.

Some charities also check with the Charity Commission to see if the potential trustees is listed as a removed or disqualified trustee. Similar checks can be done through Companies House to find out if a potential trustee has been disqualified from serving as a company director. Check to see if the person is disqualified on the grounds of being bankrupt. Ask the potential trustee to fill in a disclosure form. See Resource 7.5 for an example declaration form.

Useful websites:
- Criminal Record Bureau www.crb.homeoffice.gov.uk
- Charity Commission www.charity-commission.gov.uk
- Companies House www.companieshouse.gov.uk
- Insolvency Service www.insolvency.gov.uk

Making the appointment

Governing documents state clearly how trustees are appointed. Make sure that the procedures laid down are followed.

7.5 | Induction, support and training

All new trustees need to receive a handbook/manual or be able to access it via the charity's website, (see Resource 7.4 for model contents of a trustee induction pack) and have briefing sessions (some of these can be fairly informal) on:

- the vision, mission and strategic plans of the charity (chief executive)
- the charity's big issues and how they are being addressed (chief executive and chair)
- major risks facing the charity and how they are being managed (chair and chief executive)
- the governance structure of the charity and how the structure helps the trustees comply with their legal, regulatory and moral responsibilities (chair)
- charity finance and how to read the financial information provided to trustees (finance director)
- the board's policies and the mechanisms used to review these regularly (chair)
- how the board assesses the performance of its chief executive, measures the performance of the charity and reflects on its own performance (chair)
- the generic role, responsibilities and personal liabilities of trustees.[1]

In addition new trustees need to visit the charity and have the opportunity to:

- meet and get to know members of the senior management team, especially the chief executive and finance director, who may provide some of the briefings
- visit at least one centre providing services
- walk around the charity and talk to staff, volunteers, beneficiaries etc
- attend charity functions and events.

Other ideas to add to an induction programme include:

- a more experienced trustee acting as mentor to a new trustee
- an away-day for trustees soon after an annual general meeting (AGM) to help new trustees to get to know fellow trustees in a more informal environment, and to help develop the trustees into a team
- a one-to-one meeting with the chair of trustees after the new trustee has attended a couple of board meetings. This will
  - enable the trustee and the chair to get to know each other better
  - give the new trustee the opportunity to clarify their understanding of the charity and its governance
  - identify any support needs as well as to identify how the new trustee can use their skills, interests and experience to become more involved in the charity
  - give the new trustee the opportunity to use their 'fresh eye' to comment on how the governance of the charity could be strengthened.

Further development of trustees

As part of the board's annual session on reflecting on the quality of governance, board members need to identify both their individual and collective training needs for the coming twelve months, and to identify which skills or expertise are needed either within the board or which need to be made available to the board by the retention of appropriate additional professional advisers.

Governance should appear as a budget heading on the annual budget. This will signal the importance the charity places on good governance and will recognise formally that the charity needs to invest in developing better governance.

---

[1] Numerous courses are run by firms of solicitors and auditors. **Governance** magazine runs one-day courses throughout England and Scotland for trustees, chairs and chief executives. www.civilsociety.co.uk

It would help governance to move up the charity's agenda if trusts, foundations and other funders insist, when making large grants (in excess of £10,000), that the charity receiving the grant must spend a given percentage (say in the region of 5–10%) on developing its governance.

Resources for Chapter 7

Resource 7.1 Sample, formal skills and diversity audit for trustees/governors

	Existing trustees								Potential trustees			
	1	2	3	4	5	6	7	8	A	B	C	D
Professional expertise												
In the area of the charity's work eg residential care												
Finance/accountancy												
Business acumen												
Governance of charities												
Legislation in relation to charity's work												
Monitoring and evaluating performance of organisations												
Marketing												
Property and estate management												
Pensions												
Other												
Gender												
Ethnic background												
Age												
Location												

After existing trustees have completed the form, gaps and weak areas will become clear and a person specification based on these can be developed and the search for suitable people can begin.

As with all sample and model documents, these should be adapted to the needs of your charity.

Resource 7.2 Sample person specification for trustees

You will need to demonstrate in your application/at interview that you possess the essential criteria for the post as detailed below. In addition demonstration of some of the desirable criteria will greatly assist you in your application.

The Nolan Committee identified seven principles to which those in public life should adhere: selflessness; integrity; objectivity; accountability; openness; honesty; leadership.

Personal qualities	Essential	Desirable
Commitment to the ethos and values of the charity	✓	
Commitment to equal opportunities and the promotion of diversity	✓	
Independence of thought and judgement	✓	
Ability to work as part of a team	✓	
Willingness to devote time, enthusiasm and effort to the duties and responsibilities of a trustee	✓	
Aptitude and skills	Essential	Desirable
An understanding and acceptance of the legal duties, responsibilities and liabilities of trusteeship	✓	
Ability to evaluate and interpret information	✓	
An understanding of issues affecting the voluntary sector		✓
Ability to play a strategic role to successfully effect change and meet objectives of the charity	✓	
Eagerness to reflect and learn even in the role of trustee	✓	

Resources for Chapter 7 continued

Resource 7.2 continued

Knowledge and experience	Essential	Desirable
Senior management experience in a medium/large public/voluntary sector organisation		✓
Specific professional knowledge, experience and skills in at **least one** of the following areas: Note these are just examples, normally there are only three or four listed. • charity law • legislation, especially in relation to the area of the charity's work • business acumen • professional expertise in the main areas of the charity's work eg care of the elderly • finance/accountancy • the management of change • monitoring and evaluating performance in commercial and non profit organisations • marketing, media and PR • lobbying and campaigning • recruitment and human resources issues, including employment legislation • property and estate management • pensions issues	✓	
Other requirements	Essential	Desirable
Willingness to attend meetings of the board and other meetings as required, mostly in	✓	
Willingness to undertake visits and other trustee responsibilities as required	✓	
Willingness to undertake training and participate in evaluation of board's work	✓	

Trustees CEO Chairs

Resource 7.3 Sample outline of commitments required by trustees

Commitment of trustees to the charity

- to act solely in the interests of the charity
- to declare all actual or potential conflicts of interest
- to act collectively
- to respect confidentiality
- to make available skills and experience to the charity
- to attend regularly board and committee meetings having prepared fully for these meetings. (proposed minimum commitment of ... out of ... board meetings)
- ideally to serve on at least one committee
- to gain a better understanding of the charity by attending at least one event each year
- to support the chief executive and the management of the charity
- where appropriate, to challenge current thinking, the method of governance and management of the charity but always to do so constructively and always acting solely in the best interest of the charity
- to work in partnership with the staff to achieve the mission of the charity, understanding and respecting the different but complementary roles of trustees and staff
- to regularly and collectively reflect on how the board fulfils its responsibilities as trustees and directors of the charity and how the board brings added value to the achievement of the charity's objectives.

Commitment of the charity to the trustees

- to provide the board with timely, high-quality information in order to allow the board to govern well
- to provide the board with timely advice ensuring that external professional advisors are available as and when needed
- to work in partnership with the board to ensure that the board fulfils all its statutory and legal responsibilities
- to invest time, money and other resources in order to help develop good governance
- to ensure that a trustees handbook is available and regularly updated
- to work in partnership with the honorary officers and the nominations committee to ensure that new trustees receive induction and support, and that appropriate briefings and/or training are available to all trustees
- to provide the honorary officers and trustees with the necessary administrative and other support that they will need to govern well
- to reimburse trustees' out-of-pocket expenses incurred in the course of their duties as trustees, trustees and directors.

Resources for Chapter 7 continued

Resource 7.4 The nominations (or governance) committee

Terms of reference for a nominations committee

Approved by the board of trustees on _____ 20_____

Composition, attendees, quorum and reporting

- The nominations committee will consist of not less than .... trustees appointed by the board, and the chief executive. The chair of trustees is normally a member of the nominations committee.

  There are difference of views as to whether the chief executive should be on the nominations committee or not. I advise that he/she should. Others disagree.

  Whether the chair of trustees should be the chair of the nominations committee is very much a matter for the individual charity. With a significant growth in the duties and responsibilities of chairs of professionally managed charities, it may be wise to allocate the chairing of this committee to another trustee although the chair of trustees is likely to be an active member of this committee. However, the chair should not be involved in selecting his/her successor.

  It is important to have people with a range of backgrounds on the nominations committee. Committee members also need to be good judges of character.

- The board will appoint the chair of the nominations committee.

  The chair of the nominations committee needs to be both fair and impartial, needs to be a skilled board member and knowledgeable about the charity. If external advertising or external agents (eg head-hunters/search agents) are not being used, the chair and members of the committee will need to have access to extensive networks.

- Members of the nominations committee may serve for not more than ... years.

- The nominations committee will report back regularly and at least annually to the board of trustees.

Overall responsibility

Take delegated responsibility on behalf of the board of trustees for identifying, recruiting and proposing new members of the board, and for their induction, support and development.

Main duties

1 To carry out regular skills audits of the trustee board and identify the skills, experience, characteristics and backgrounds that are needed to provide high quality effective governance

Membership organisations that elect trustees at AGMs should inform members of the skills and experience needed on the board and should ask prospective board members to explain briefly in the election literature how they fit the profile.

2 To prepare role descriptions, person specifications and an information pack for prospective board members

It is important to be very open about the time commitments involved and what is expected of each trustee. It is also essential that prospective board members share the charity's mission and values, are team players, can be constructively challenging and independently minded. It is also important to be honest (on a confidential basis) about the challenges facing the charity.

3 To prepare a recruitment plan and timetable

Consideration needs to be given as to whether vacancies should be advertised internally (eg through the website, newsletters, the intranet, etc), advertised externally (eg locally, nationally, in specialist journals if specialist skills are needed such as PR, on the web, etc) and/or whether a recruitment or search agency is used.

4 To identify a list of prospective board members and honorary officers

It is important to draw these names from a wide variety of sources. Obtain a written CV. Check CVs against the skills, expertise and experience needed. Produce a short list

5 To develop the interest of the prospective board members in the work of the charity.

If at all possible, invite prospective board members to some of the charity's events. This will give other people within the charity an opportunity to meet them informally. It also tests the candidates interest in the work of the charity as well as giving some indication as to whether (s)he has time available to become involved in the charity.

6 To meet the prospective board members and to scrutinise their suitability.

Ideally arrange for each prospective trustee to meet the chair of the nominations committee, the chair of trustees and the chief executive. This can be formal or informal meeting(s) but either way be clear about what you wish to achieve, what information you need to get and what information you need to give to the prospective trustee. Invite prospective board members to complete the skills audit form or use the skills audit form as a basis of discussion at which the prospective trustee's commitment to the mission and values of the charity should also be assessed. Take up references. Cross-check suitability by talking to different people who know the prospective trustee.

7 To invite chosen prospective trustees to allow their names to go forward to the board and to recommend them to the board.

Provide trustees with potted biographies as well as fit with the skills identified through the skills audit. Similarly, if trustees are elected by members at an AGM or by postal votes, provide potted biographies and fit with the skills profile.

8 To inform successful and unsuccessful candidates.

It is important to confirm that successful candidates still have the time needed to be trustees of the charity. It is also important to debrief unsuccessful candidates and to maintain their interest in the work of the charity in some way.

Resources for Chapter 7 continued

9 To induct, mentor and involve new board members.

Ensure that the new trustees also receive an induction pack (Contents of a model induction pack can be found on page ....), list of dates of trustees' meetings, date of the trustee away-day, date of AGM as well as other key events in the charity's diary. Organise induction sessions as well as a programme of visits to head office and other offices/centres/branches. If possible after six months as a trustee, the chair of trustees should have a confidential one-to-one chat with the new trustee to see how (s)he is settling in, whether there are any issues that (s)he has spotted and would like to raise, whether (s)he requires any further information, briefings, etc.

10 To ensure that the board has time to reflect on its own performance, on how it can govern the charity better, future training, support and development needs.

11 To ensure that there is an annual programme of board development including technical and other briefing sessions, away-day, etc.

Resource 7.5 New trustee: sample declaration of eligibility

All charities should, but most charities do not, ask potential trustees to sign a declaration about their eligibility for the post of trustee. This sample declaration form is an adapted from a more detailed declaration form for trustees, which can be found on the NCVO website.

I declare that:

☐ I am over age 18. (Note: This is a general rule for charities although the Charity Commission has allowed trustees under 18, but specific permission must be sought. Company directors do not have to be 18.)

☐ I am not an undischarged bankrupt.

☐ I have not previously been removed or disqualified, on the grounds of misconduct or mismanagement in the administration of a charity, from trusteeship of a charity by a court or the Charity Commission. (Note : The Charity Commission can remove trustees on a purely administrative reason – this does not bar them from becoming a trustee elsewhere.)

☐ I am not under a disqualification order under the Company Directors' Disqualification Act 1986.

☐ I have not been convicted of an offence involving deception or dishonesty (unless the conviction is spent).

☐ I am, in the light of the above, not disqualified by the Charities Act 1993 (section 72) from acting as a charity trustee.

☐ I am not disqualified from working with children.

☐ I give my consent for the charity to carry out relevant checks on me including, if necessary, identity checks, Criminal Record Bureau (CRB) checks and checks against the Charity Commission's lists of removed or disqualified trustees.

☐ If appointed, I undertake to fulfil my responsibilities and duties as a trustee of (name of organisation) in good faith and in accordance with the law and within (name of organisation)'s objectives / mission.

☐ I do not have any financial interests in conflict with those of (name of organisation) (either in person or through family or business connections) except those which I have formally notified in a conflict of interest statement. I will specifically notify any such interest at any meeting where trustees are required to make a decision which affects my personal interests, and I will absent myself entirely from any decision on the matter and not vote on it.

Signed: _____   Name of trustee _____

Date _____

Further guidance:
Disqualification for acting as a charity trustee (Operational guidance OG41)
http://www.charity-commission.gov.uk/About_us/Ogs/index041.aspx

Helpdesk for NCVO members can be found online at www.ncvo-vol.org.uk/helpdesk

Resources for Chapter 7 continued

Resource 7.6 Affirmation statement for trustees

Affirmation

1 I continue to be fully supportive of our mission, vision, purposes, goals and values.

2 I understand that attendance at, and preparation for, board and committee meetings and board away-days will take the equivalent of .... days of my time. I am able to give this time during the coming year and expect to attend most if not all board and committee meetings. If for good reason I am unable to attend a meeting, I will inform the relevant chair in good time.

3 Early in each meeting, I will notify the board if I find myself in a conflict of interest position with any item on the agenda.

4 I will abide by the code of conduct for trustees.

Signed: _____   Date _____

For potential trustees only

Agreement

1 I agree to be nominated for election as a trustee.

2 I am fully supportive of the mission, vision, purposes, goals and values.

3 I understand that attendance at, and preparation for, board and committee meetings and board away-days will take the equivalent of ....days of my time. If elected, I am able to give this time during the coming year and expect to attend virtually all board and committee meetings. If for good reason I am unable to attend a meeting, I will inform the relevant chair in good time.

4 If elected, early in each board or committee meeting, I will notify the board if I find myself in a conflict of interest position with any item on the agenda.

5 If elected, I will abide by the code of conduct for trustees.

Signed: _____   Date _____

Resource 7.7 A trustee handbook/manual or induction pack

All new trustees need to receive a trustee handbook/manual. This can either be an electronic version (easier to keep up-to-date) or the traditional loose-leaf folder version. Model contents of a trustee handbook are:

Model contents of a trustee handbook are:

1 The charity
- vision, mission and values
- most recent annual report and accounts
- strategic and business plans
- key policies (for example: health and safety, safeguarding, investment, reserves)
- report of annual risk audit

2 Legal status and regulatory guidance
- copy of governing instruments
- copy of Charity Commission booklet on The Essential Trustee: What you need to know (CC3), Hallmarks of an Effective Charity (CC60), and Good Governance: A Code for the Voluntary and Community Sectors
- companies charity booklet on Directors and Secretaries Guide, if the charity is a company

3 Governance
- role descriptions for trustees, chair of the board, treasurer etc
- code of conduct for trustees and other relevant policies eg, anti-bullying, confidentiality, grievance procedures, whistle-blowing by trustees
- governance structure diagram and/or list of board committees together with details of membership of these
- terms of reference for board committees
- document recording levels of the board's delegated authority including financial delegation and controls
- list of current trustees and contact details
- annual list of dates of board meetings, annual general meeting, board away-day, etc
- details of travelling and subsistence allowances for trustees with a copy of a claims form

4 Management
- contact details for chief executive, finance director and other members of senior management/leadership team
- diagram showing management structure
- role description of chief executive and finance director

Chapter 8

Reflecting on and improving board effectiveness

8.1 | Introduction: the need

Companies, public bodies and charities now face much greater scrutiny about their effectiveness and about the quality of both management and governance. A long list of corporate disasters has put much greater emphasis on the role and responsibilities of those who govern organisations. More accountability is expected; there is greater enforcement of laws and regulations and a higher likelihood that directors, trustees and governors will be personally and collectively answerable for their actions, decisions and in some cases for their inaction.

Appraisal of staff performance is now the norm, tools for measuring the performance of organisations are now commonly used; but boards of trustees, directors and governors who reflect on their own performance and effectiveness, are still not commonplace.

Reasons given by some boards of trustees for introducing board appraisal:
- *'We want all staff and volunteers to be appraised. We want to measure the performance of the charity. We have to lead by example and show that we are a learning organisation truly committed to improving performance throughout the charity and as an organisation as a whole.'*
- *'Organisations can survive reasonably well with good management and weak governance but strong, effective management teamed with strong, effective governance is a winning combination.'*
- *'Poor governance undermines organisational performance.'*
- *'Charities that are at risk of failure are usually poorly governed.'*
- *'Would you like anyone to say that the board is holding back the growth and success of the charity?'*
- *'An opportunity for the board to assess and reflect on its strengths and weaknesses.'*
- *'By considering our performance, we as trustees are reminded of our roles and responsibilities'*
- *'An opportunity to prioritise our activities for the future and gain the commitment of all trustees to the board's future priorities.'*
- *'It gives all trustees an opportunity to voice their frustrations and to share ideas on how the board can be more effective'*
- *'An opportunity to learn and develop.'*
- *'An opportunity to develop as a team and ensure that all trustees contribute to setting board goals and to effective governance.'*
- *'To show that trustees and management are a team working together to achieve the charity's vision and mission.'*

Developing and maintaining an effective board is a journey not a destination. The success of the journey depends very much on trustees working together to ensure that the board fulfils its duties and responsibilities. Taking time out regularly to reflect on how well the board is progressing will help the board to keep focused and to deliver high-quality governance.

Once the decision is made to review regularly the performance of the board, many boards jump in at the deep end by bringing in the 'experts' or spending significant sums of money on resource-hungry options. Often this leads to no further attempts to review the performance of the board for several years. A more gentle, evolutionary approach is recommended therefore.

8.2 | The first steps

Rather than go straight into suggesting a review of board performance or a formal board appraisal, chairs would be better off introducing the idea very gently by not mentioning the words 'board appraisal' or 'review of board performance' but just starting the process of the board informally reflecting on its performance at the end of each meeting.

Reviewing board meetings

At the end of each meeting, the chair should lead a short discussion on how the meeting was run. A general question, 'How did you find today's meeting?' is not recommended. Most trustees, eager to leave, are most likely to say 'fine' even if they feel unhappy with the meeting. It is important that the chair guides the short discussion with a *couple* (no more!) of pertinent questions such as:

- Did the right agenda items come to the board?
- Did the board papers arrive in good time and serve their purpose to inform and enable the trustees to make enlightened decisions?
- How can the papers be improved?
- Did we concentrate on making policy decisions and discussing issues that are truly the board's responsibility or did we drift into discussing management issues or matters of detail?
- Did the chief executive have an opportunity to openly discuss current and likely future major issues with us?
- How did we work as a team on the issues before us?
- Did we remember to recognise and celebrate success?
- Was the meeting too long or too short?
- Was there sufficient time to discuss issues?
- Did we spend too long discussing issues?
- How can we make the next meeting more effective?

At the same time the chair and chief executive should be working together to ensure that the trustees have a real understanding of their role and responsibilities and that they understand the difference between management and governance.

Gradually the topic of reviewing the performance of the board can be introduced and hopefully it will be seen as the next, natural step in an evolutionary process. It is less threatening to start with reviewing the effectiveness of the board. Ultimate authority and responsibility lies collectively with the board. It therefore makes sense to start with the collective effectiveness of the board. Once this is embedded into the board's way of working, it can be extended to looking at the effectiveness of individual trustees.

8.3 | More formal ways of reviewing board performance

When should formal appraisal or reviews of board performance be introduced?

It is easiest to answer this question with a negative. The wrong time to introduce board appraisal is during, or immediately after, a major crisis especially if the board carries some responsibility for the crisis occurring. In this situation the trustees are likely to be defensive and are unlikely to be totally objective in assessing their own performance. However, a good question to ask board members during any review of performance is, 'What do you consider to be the most significant mistake made by the board in the last year/two years and with hindsight where do you think we went wrong?' It would also be interesting to discover whether the board recognised it had made a mistake and discussed what it, and the charity, had learnt from the experience.

Introducing board appraisal is never easy. Even when times are good, many trustees will take the line, 'Why fix something that isn't broke?', and there will be a strong tendency to stick to the status quo. Often a new chair or a new chief executive is the catalyst for introducing board appraisal. Not all trustees will be immediately in favour of the board reviewing its performance. The chair should be prepared to take on board some of the concerns of those who are against any form of board appraisal and will need to spend time making the case for reviewing board performance. However, improving board performance is too vital to the future effectiveness of the organisation for the chair to give up on the idea, even in the face of initial, possibly vocal opposition.

How do we go about reviewing the performance of the board?

There are no hard and fast rules about how board appraisal should be carried out although many people will say there are. There are certainly no blueprints for the procedure although there are several sample board appraisal forms available; some of which are published here. If you are considering board appraisal there are a number of factors that need to be considered before you start:

- It is vital to remember that reviewing board performance is about an attitude of mind and not an exercise in ticking boxes: it needs to be a continuing process and a genuine journey of learning and improvement.
- It is important for each board to evolve a process that is right for it; that reflects the board's and the charity's current stage of development and future plans as well as its complexity. However, if you feel that for the first appraisal you want to try a standard questionnaire do so, but put time aside later to consider how the standard questionnaire can be tailored for future use or whether, next time, you are confident enough to develop your own questionnaire and process.
- Consider whether you want your chief executive to be an active part of the appraisal process or only brought in informally towards the end of the process to discuss how the board's performance impacts on the management of the charity. I personally prefer to actively involve the chief executive from the beginning: not only because governance and management are a partnership but also because the chief executive will have a unique perspective on the effectiveness of the board. Again, trustees need to decide what is right for their charity. It might be that initially the chief executive only comes in at the end but, as mutual trust and respect grow, the chief executive begins to play a much greater part.

8.3 | More formal ways of reviewing board performance

Who should carry out the board appraisal?

There are several options including:

1 Board self-assessment or self-evaluation

In my view no appraisal is worth doing unless it has a strong element of self-appraisal. Most boards opt for self-evaluation because it involves every member of the board; because the board is likely to know its own strengths and weaknesses far better than someone who has only limited exposure to the board and its practices; and because the board is more likely to take on board the learning points that come out of such a process if all trustees feel ownership of the process and its outcomes.

2 A board committee

If board members are feeling overworked, they can opt for a board committee to carry out the formal evaluation with the whole board coming in at the end to discuss the evaluation and to agree on what needs to change and how this can be achieved.

3 A non-board committee

Boards sometimes feel that a non-board committee that brings together people connected with the charity (eg, service users, former trustees, presidents or vice presidents) and independent outsiders (eg, chair of trustees or chair of a governance committee of another charity; experts on governance or team performance; or people who bring a different perspective and a large dose of common sense), can give a more complete and objective assessment of the board's performance.

4 An outside consultant

Outside consultants are particularly useful if there are a number of emotionally charged board issues or if the board wants to introduce board evaluation but does not have the time to develop its own process and criteria.

Whichever method is chosen, it is wise to remember that developing and maintaining a high performing board is a journey and not a destination. Lifelong learning is not just for individuals but also for boards of trustees.

What else do we need to do?

Board or governance objectives

Ideally, as with all appraisals, it is easier to measure board performance if the board has clear annual objectives. Often a chair of trustees will know what (s)he wants to achieve during the year but may not have articulated them in any way or discussed these objectives with the whole board. Not having governance objectives for the year should not deter boards from starting the process of formally reviewing their performance. My experience has been that board objectives for the following year emerge quite naturally at the end of the review process.

Examples of board objectives arising from some boards of trustees with which I have worked include:
- improving the quality of board papers
- develop a more open process for identifying potential trustees
- set up a programme for the induction of new trustees
- have a board away day to discuss governance and management and their interface
- have a board away-day to start the strategic planning cycle
- simplify the financial reports that come to the full board
- clarify and record in writing powers/authority delegated by the board
- organise a social event for trustees to get to know each other
- review the governance structure
- circulate potted biographies of trustees
- bring in limited terms of office for all trustees and especially for honorary officers
- clarify the commitments that we are asking trustees to make to the charity and vice-versa
- spend more board time on looking at achieving our vision and mission and a little less time on finance
- work with the chief executive to find appropriate tools to measure the performance of the charity
- reduce board meetings from four to two hours.

Possible questionnaires for the board to review its performance.

Most reviews of board performance use either a questionnaire or a series of face-to-face interviews with individual trustees or both. Even with interviews, questions need to be prepared in advance. There are various different approaches to producing questionnaires. The most effective questionnaires manage to incorporate the best features of the various types illustrated in the next few pages. However the real value of a questionnaire (or of one-to-one interviews) is not the completion of the forms, or the report that analyses the completed questionnaires; but the quality of the discussion that follows and ultimately the improvement in the quality of governance.

Having looked at various board appraisal questionnaires, it is my experience that they generally fall into six different categories based on:
1 desired behaviours and practices
2 competencies needed to govern well
3 key areas of trustee responsibility
4 code of good governance
5 hallmarks of an effective charity
6 a mixture of all five or none of them!

Examples of the first 5 types can be found in the resource sections of the chapter.

8.5 | Reflecting on the effectiveness of the chair

Everyone needs feedback on their performance including chairs of trustees. Quite often the vice or deputy chair leads the review by gathering feedback under Chatham House Rules from each trustee and the chief executive. This can be done formally by means of a form or more informally, although as rigorously, by meeting on a one-to-one basis or speaking on the phone. Self-evaluation should also be an important part of the review.

If there isn't a vice chair or if the vice chair does not feel sufficiently confident to take on the task, I have found it helpful to invite a former trustee who was highly regarded by the trustees, to carry out the review.

Sometimes, a chair of another charity is brought in to carry out the review or a consultant (who needs to understand charity governance and who has expertise in carrying out performance appraisal) is used instead.

Various forms can easily be constructed on a similar basis to the forms for reviewing the performance of the board. These forms could be based on:
- the chair's role description
- desired behaviours of an effective chair
- tailored to a particular aspect of the chair's work, eg running meetings
- competencies of trustees etc.

8.6 | Conclusion

Many boards err on the side of setting out on the road to continuous development and learning by initially bringing in very cumbersome and resource-hungry methods of measuring board performance and then by never repeating the process because no one has the energy or the time to continue the process. A gentle start followed by a process which grows more sophisticated as the charity matures and as the board becomes more effective are better options. After a period of time, board evaluation will become a completely natural and enormously valuable part of the life of your board and of your charity.

How do you know if the process of the board reflecting on its own performance is helping?
A successful review of board performance usually leads to the following:

- trustees feeling more involved
- trustees feeling part of a team
- trustees, both individually and collectively, having a better understanding of their roles and responsibilities
- trustees and staff having a clearer idea of what are board policies
- a clearer idea of how the trustees can hold the chief executive to account for the management of the charity without feeling that they need to know everything and to micro-manage
- quality of board papers improves
- the business of the board is done more effectively
- better and stronger partnership with the chief executive and senior staff with the trustees governing and staff managing
- a clearer focus on the strategic priorities and on achieving these
- a more successful charity!

Resources for Chapter 8

Resource 8.1 Questionnaire Type 1 – based on desired behaviours and practices

This tends to be the simplest questionnaire. The board identifies desired behaviours and practices for the board, and builds a questionnaire around these. For example:

ITEM	Strongly agree	Agree	Disagree	Strongly disagree	Comments Ideally giving examples to illustrate
The board works together as a team					
The board understands its role as policy-maker					
The board understands its stewardship role					
Individually and collectively, trustees understand their roles and responsibilities					
Trustees communicate effectively with each other					
Trustees communicate effectively with senior management					
Trustees contribute to board effectiveness by attending meetings, reading papers and participating in discussions					
Board papers help trustees to make informed decisions and arrive in good time.					
Board agendas are pertinent, well-structured and aid effective governance					
The board and chief executive work well together					
The board and staff understand their different but complementary roles					

Resource 8.2 Questionnaire Type 2 – based on competencies

The second type of questionnaire identifies the competencies needed to govern well and builds a questionnaire around these competencies. Again these will vary according to the needs of each charity. I prefer to use the six competencies identified by Holland, Chait and Taylor, who are experts in the field of governance of non-profit organisations in the USA These competencies capture the essential elements of effective governance:

1 **Contextual:** the board understands the charity, its values, culture and philosophy.

2 **Educational:** the board takes steps to ensure that trustees are well informed about the charity, their roles and responsibility and how the performance of the charity and key individuals are measured.

3 **Interpersonal:** the board puts energy into developing as a team which although comprising of very individual personalities manages to develop a sense of shared purpose and group decision-making. It shares the sense of inclusivity and fellowship with the staff and stakeholders.

4 **Analytical:** no matter how passionately committed individual board members are, as a board they have the capacity to look at situations dispassionately and analytically, drawing on multiple perspectives.

5 **Political:** the board respects the board governance process, never allowing individuals or small groups to undermine the board's essential stewardship role. At the same time the board respects the authority of its staff at all levels.

6 **Strategic:** the board helps to envision and shape the charity and steers it towards its future, taking responsibility for the charity's long-term success or failure.

Douglas Jackson and Thomas Holland developed a board evaluation process which uses a coding system for structured interview responses – eg 1 point for any recognition or description of a competence; 3 points for a particular or comprehensive set of actions. Generally charities wanting to use this very thorough method will need to bring in experts to carry out this work.

A simple form can be designed that allows each trustees to consider each competency; to intuitively give a score on how (s)he feels the board rates on each competency; and to use these six essential competencies as a basis for board discussion, which leads to agreement on future board priorities and objectives.

Resources for Chapter 8 continued

Essential competencies	Score [0-poor to 5-excellent]	Comments on current position [Give examples]	Suggestions on how we can develop this competency [Make practical suggestions]
1 Contextual: the board understands the charity, its values, culture and philosophy.			
2 Educational: the board takes steps to ensure that trustees are well informed about the charity, their roles and responsibility and how the performance of the charity and key individuals are measured.			
3 Interpersonal: the board puts energy into developing as a team which although comprising of very individual personalities manages to develop a sense of shared purpose and group decision-making. It shares the sense of inclusivity and fellowship with the staff and stakeholders.			
4 Analytical: no matter how passionately committed individual board members are, as a board they have the capacity to look at situations dispassionately and analytically, drawing on multiple perspectives.			
5 Political: the board respects the board governance process, never allowing individuals or small groups to undermine the board's essential stewardship role. At the same time the board respects the authority of its staff at all levels.			
6 Strategic: the board helps to envision and shape the charity and steers it towards its future, taking responsibility for the charity's long-term success or failure.			

Resource 8.3 Questionnaire Type 3 – based on the five key areas of trustee responsibility

The final type of questionnaire is almost a checklist, based on the role and responsibilities of trustees. The key responsibilities of trustees are to hold the charity 'in trust' for current and future beneficiaries by:

1 ensuring that the charity has a clear vision, mission and strategic direction and is focused on achieving these
2 being responsible for the performance of the charity and for its culture
3 ensuring that the charity complies with all legal and regulatory requirements
4 being guardians of the charity's assets, both tangible and intangible, taking all due care over their security, deployment and proper application
5 ensuring that the charity's governance is of the highest possible standard.

Vision, mission and strategic direction	Strongly agree	Agree	Disagree	Strongly disagree
The charity has a clear vision, mission and strategic plan that have been agreed by the board, and that there is a common understanding of these by trustees and the senior management team.				
The business, annual and other plans support the vision, mission and strategic priorities.				
The chief executive's annual and longer-term objectives and targets support the achievement of the vision, mission and strategic priorities.				
Board policies support the vision, mission and strategic priorities.				
The board ensures that there are effective mechanisms to listen to the views of current and future beneficiaries.				
The board ensures that there are effective mechanisms to review the external environment for changes that might affect the charity.				

Resources for Chapter 8 continued

Performance and corporate behaviour	Strongly agree	Agree	Disagree	Strongly disagree
There are effective mechanisms for measuring objectively the progress of the charity in relation to its vision, mission, strategic objectives/priorities, business plans and annual targets.				
The trustees receive regularly reports on the performance of the charity.				
The chief executive reports regularly on progress towards agreed strategic priorities.				
The trustees hold the chief executive to account for the management and administration of the charity.				
The trustees ensure that the chief executive receives regular, constructive feedback on his/her performance in managing the charity and in meeting his/her annual and longer-term targets and objectives.				
The trustees ensure that the chief executive develops a learning organisation and that all staff, both paid and unpaid, review their own performance and regularly receive feedback.				
The trustees articulate, with the help of the staff and others, the values of the charity.				
Board policies are reviewed regularly.				
Trustees and management are fully aware of which policies are board policies and those which are the direct responsibility of management.				
The board ensures that there are mechanisms for beneficiaries, employees, volunteers, other individuals, groups or organisations to bring to the attention of the trustees any activity that threatens the probity of the charity.				

Legal and regulatory compliance	Strongly agree	Agree	Disagree	Strongly disagree
The board of trustees has set up mechanisms to ensure it is aware of all current or new legal, statutory and regulatory requirements and that it is confident that the charity complies with, all legal, regulatory and statutory requirements.				
The trustees maintain familiarity and comply with the rules and constitution that govern the charity, and review the constitution regularly.				
The board's delegated authority is recorded in writing by means of minutes, terms of reference for board committees and sub-committees, role descriptions for honorary officers, trustees and key staff, etc, and there are clear reporting procedures back to the board, which are recorded in writing and complied with.				
The responsibilities delegated to the chief executive are clearly expressed and understood, and directions given to him/her come from the board as a whole.				
The major risks to which the charity is exposed are reviewed annually and systems have been established to mitigate or minimise these risks.				

Resources for Chapter 8 continued

Guardian of the charity's assets	Strongly agree	Agree	Disagree	Strongly disagree
The charity has satisfactory control systems and procedures for holding in trust for the beneficiaries all monies, properties and other assets.				
All monies are invested to the maximum benefit of the charity, within the constraints of the law and ethical and other policies laid down by the board.				
Income and property of the charity are applied for the purposes set out in the governing document and for no other purpose, and with complete fairness between persons who are properly qualified to benefit.				
The trustees act reasonably and prudently in all matters relating to the charity and always bear in mind the interests of the charity.				
The board accepts accountability for the solvency and continuing effectiveness of the charity and the preservation of its endowments.				
The board exercises effective overall control of the charity's financial affairs and ensures that the way in which the charity is administered is not open to abuse by unscrupulous associates or employees; and that the systems of control are rigorous and constantly maintained through regular evaluation and improvement in the light of experience.				
The board ensures that intangible assets such as organisational knowledge and expertise, intellectual property, the charity's good name and reputation etc are properly valued, utilised and safeguarded.				
For land owned by the charity, the trustees know on a continuing basis what condition it is in, if its boundaries are being encroached upon, what can be done with it and how it is or should be used. In particular, the trustees are able to ensure that any property which is a permanent endowment, is preserved and invested in such a way as to produce a good income while at the same time safeguarding the real value of the capital.				
The trustees have systems to ensure that all income due to the charity is received and that all tax benefits are obtained and all rating relief due is claimed.				

Capacity to govern	Strongly agree	Agree	Disagree	Strongly disagree
The trustees ensure that the charity has a governance structure that is appropriate to a charity of its size/complexity, stage of development, and its charitable objects, and that enables the trustees to fulfil their responsibilities.				
The board of trustees annually reviews the charity's governance structure and the board's own performance.				
The trustees work closely with the chief executive to ensure that the board has on it the skills it requires to govern the charity well, and that the board has access to relevant external professional advice and expertise.				
The trustees ensure that there is a systematic, open and fair procedure for the recruitment or co-option of trustees, future chairs of the board and future chief executives (with a view to succession).				
The board ensures that all trustees receive appropriate induction on their appointment and that they continue to receive appropriate advice, information and training (both individually and collectively).				
The board ensures that trustees have a code of conduct and comply with it, and that there are mechanisms for the removal of trustees who do not abide by the trustee code of conduct.				
The trustees ensure that major decisions and board policies are made by the trustees acting collectively.				

Resources for Chapter 8 continued

Resource 8.4 Questionnaire Type 4 Based on the Code (version 2.0 October 2010 version)

It is easy to develop a questionnaire based on the Good Governance: A Code for the Voluntary and Community sector (the Code). For example:

	Comments on current position	Suggestions on how we can develop this further
Principle 1: an effective board will provide good governance and leadership by understanding their role. Members of the board will understand their role and responsibilities collectively as a board and as individual trustees in relation to: • their legal duties • the provisions of the governing document • the external environment • the total structure of the organisation and in terms of • setting and safeguarding the vision, values and reputation of the organisation • overseeing the work of the organisation and • managing and supporting staff and volunteers where applicable.		
Principle 2: an effective board will provide good governance and leadership by ensuring delivery of organisational purpose. The board will ensure that the organisation delivers its stated purposes or aims by: • ensuring organisational purposes remain relevant and valid • developing and agreeing a long-term strategy • agreeing operational plans and budgets • monitoring progress and spending against plan and budget • evaluating results • reviewing and/or amending the plan and budget as appropriate.		

	Comments on current position	Suggestions on how we can develop this further
Principle 3: an effective board will provide good governance and leadership by working effectively both as individuals and as a team. The board will have a range of appropriate policies and procedures, knowledge, attitudes and behaviours to enable both individuals and the board to work effectively. These will include: • finding and recruiting new board members to meet the organisation's changing needs in relation to skills, experience and diversity • providing suitable induction for new board members • providing all board members with opportunities for training and development according to their needs • periodically reviewing their performance both as individuals and as a team.		
Principle 4: an effective board will provide good governance and leadership by exercising effective control. As the accountable body, the board will ensure that: • the organisation understands and complies with all legal and regulatory requirements that apply to it • the organisation continues to have good internal financial, management controls • the board regularly reviews and identifies the major risks to which the organisation is exposed and puts in place systems to manage those risks • delegation to sub-committees, staff and volunteers (as applicable) works effectively and the use of delegated authority is properly supervised.		

Resources for Chapter 8 continued

	Comments on current position	Suggestions on how we can develop this further
Principle 5: an effective board will provide good governance and leadership by behaving with integrity. The board will: • safeguard and promote the organisation's reputation • act according to high ethical standards • understand and manage conflicts of interest and loyalty • maintain independence of decision making; • deliver impact that best meets the needs of beneficiaries.		
Principle 6: an effective board will provide good governance and leadership by being open and accountable. The board will lead the organisation in being open and accountable, both internally and externally. This will include: • open communications, informing people about the organisation and its work • appropriate consultation on significant changes to the organisation's services or policies • listening and responding to the views of supporters, funders, beneficiaries, service users and others with an interest in the organisation's work • handling complaints constructively and effectively considering the organisation's responsibilities to the wider community, for example, its environmental impact.		

Resource 8.5 Questionnaire Type 5 – Based on Hallmarks of an Effective Charity (Charity Commission Publication CC10)

www.charity-commission.gov.uk/publications/cc10.asp

	Comments on current position	Suggestions on how we can develop this further
Hallmark 1: Clear about its purposes and direction *An effective charity is clear about its purposes, mission and values, and uses them to direct all aspects of its work.* In order to demonstrate this, the charity: • ensures that its mission and planned activities are within the purposes set out in its governing document; • has a clear idea of its mission, and the strategies and steps that it will take to achieve it, set out in written documents that are regularly reviewed, giving the charity focus, direction and clarity; • is able to explain how all of its activities relate to and support its purposes, strategy and mission, and benefit the public; • regularly reviews whether the charity's purposes as set out in its governing document are up to date and relevant to the needs of its beneficiaries; • is independent and recognises that it exists to pursue its own purposes and not to carry out the policies or directions of any other body; • considers future sustainability – balancing what is needed now with what will be needed in the future.		

Resources for Chapter 8 continued

	Comments on current position	Suggestions on how we can develop this further
Hallmark 2: A strong board *An effective charity is run by a clearly identifiable board or trustee body that has the right balance of skills and experience, acts in the best interests of the charity and its beneficiaries, understands its responsibilities and has systems in place to exercise them properly.* In order to demonstrate this, the charity: • ensures that the trustee body is constituted in accordance with the governing document; • identifies the mix of skills, knowledge and experience necessary for the efficient and effective administration of the charity and ensures that the recruitment and appointment of new trustees provides adequate opportunities for re-assessing and achieving that mix; • has a trustee body that is the right size for the charity – large enough to include the skills and experience needed to run the charity effectively, but small enough to allow effective discussion and decision making; • has a clear understanding of the respective roles of the trustee body and staff with role descriptions for trustees and charity officers (such as the chair and treasurer); • ensures that the charity's committees, staff and agents have clear and appropriate delegated authority to carry out their designated roles in delivering the charity's purposes. It also has systems in place to monitor and oversee the way in which delegated powers are exercised; • undertakes all appropriate checks to ensure that a prospective trustee is both eligible and suitable to act in that capacity. (For some charities there may be a legal requirement to seek CRB disclosures for potential (and serving) trustees); • identifies and meets the individual induction, training and development needs of trustees and has in place a framework for evaluating board and trustee performance; • ensures its trustees understand that they must act only in the charity's interests and that any conflicts of interest are identified and managed; • identifies and complies with relevant legislation and takes professional advice where necessary		

	Comments on current position	Suggestions on how we can develop this further
Hallmark 3: Fit for purpose *The structure, policies and procedures of an effective charity enable it to achieve its purposes and mission and deliver its services efficiently.* In order to demonstrate this, the charity: • regularly reviews its governing document to ensure that it is up to date and that the trustees have the powers that they need in order to achieve the charity's purposes and to manage its resources effectively; • takes appropriate steps to protect its reputation in all aspects of its work, especially in its dealings with beneficiaries and others with an interest in the charity; • implements policies and procedures to ensure that all vulnerable beneficiaries are protected from abuse; • regularly reviews and assesses the risks faced by the charity in all areas of its work and plans for the management of those risks; • regularly reviews its structures, policies and procedures to ensure that they continue to support, and are adequate for, the delivery of the charity's purposes and mission; this includes policies and procedures dealing with board strategies, functions and responsibilities; good employment practices and the encouragement and use of volunteers; • recognises, promotes and values equality and diversity in beneficiaries, staff and volunteers, and in all aspects of its activity; • considers whether collaborations and partnerships (including the possibility of a merger) with other organisations could improve efficiency, the use of funds and the better delivery of benefits and services to beneficiaries		

Resources for Chapter 8 continued

	Comments on current position	Suggestions on how we can develop this further
Hallmark 4: Learning and improving *An effective charity is always seeking to improve its performance and efficiency, and to learn new and better ways of delivering its purposes. A charity's assessment of its performance, and of the impact and outcomes of its work, will inform its planning processes and will influence its future direction.* In order to demonstrate this, the charity: • has considered how to identify, measure and learn from the charity's achievements, impacts and outcomes, including the positive and negative effects that it has on beneficiaries, others with an interest in the charity and the wider community; • sets achievable targets and indicators against which success and improvement is measured and evaluated based on the purposes of the charity, the needs of its beneficiaries, the quality of its services and the resources available; • welcomes and acts upon feedback (positive as well as challenging) from its beneficiaries and other people with an interest in the charity about the services it provides and the areas where improvements could be made; • looks at and assesses innovative and imaginative ways of working towards achieving its purpose and aims; • identifies emerging trends in the environment in which it operates and uses this information as part of its planning processes; • identifies and uses opportunities to influence the environment in which it works to be more conducive to its mission and purposes, following the law and good practice when campaigning or lobbying; • is not complacent but is engaged in a process of continual improvement, using techniques and tools best suited to its size and activities, such as recognised quality systems and benchmarking, in order to improve its own future performance; • is ready to share good practice with others.		

	Comments on current position	Suggestions on how we can develop this further
Hallmark 5: Financially sound and prudent *An effective charity has the financial and other resources needed to deliver its purposes and mission, and controls and uses them to achieve its full potential.* In order to demonstrate this, the charity: • has policies to control and manage its reserves, investments and borrowing, taking professional advice where needed; • integrates financial planning with wider organisational planning and management, ensuring that funds are available when the charity needs them and are used in the most effective way to the benefit of the charity; • ensures financial sustainability by managing cash flow and monitoring and reviewing financial performance during the year, taking timely corrective action where needed; • considers the sources of its income and has a strategy in place to raise the funds it needs - diversifying its sources of income as far as possible; • reviews its fundraising strategies and activities to ensure that they comply with good-practice standards, taking account of any relevant ethical issues; • is aware of the financial risks involved with existing and new ventures and manages the risk of loss, waste and fraud by having robust financial controls and procedures in place; • structures the charity's activities in a tax efficient way and minimises the operational risk to the charity from trading activities; • prepares its annual report and accounts in accordance with good practice requirements, and fulfils the legal requirements for filing in a timely fashion.		

Resources for Chapter 8 continued

	Comments on current position	Suggestions on how we can develop this further
Hallmark 6: Accountable and transparent *An effective charity is accountable to the public and others with an interest in the charity (stakeholders) in a way that is transparent and understandable.* In order to demonstrate this, the charity: • complies with its legal obligations (and best practice), as set out in the Statement of Recommended Practice (SORP), to produce annual accounts and a report which includes an explanation of what the charity has done for the public benefit during the year; • explains in its annual report the extent to which it has achieved its charitable purposes in a way that people with an interest in the charity can understand; • has well-publicised, effective and timely procedures for dealing with complaints about the charity and its activities. These should explain how complaints and appeals can be made, and give details of the process and likely timescales; • can show how it involves beneficiaries and service users in the development and improvement of its services; the contribution may have been by way of the appointment of beneficiaries as trustees or their involvement through discussion, consultation or user group input; • has a communications plan which ensures that accurate and timely information is given to everyone with an interest in the work of the charity, including the media, donors and beneficiaries		

Resource 8.6 Other ideas for reflecting on board effectiveness: Board appraisal based on 'Exceptional governance'

Extract with permission from *The Source: Twelve Principles of Governance That Power Exceptional Boards,* a publication of BoardSource www.boardsource.org Article published July 2007 issue of *Governance: essential information for effective trustees*

	Comments on current position	Suggestions on how we can develop this further
1 Constructive partnership Exceptional boards govern in constructive partnership with the chief executive, recognizing that the effectiveness of the board and chief executive are interdependent. They build this partnership through trust, candor, respect, and honest communication.		

	Comments on current position	Suggestions on how we can develop this further
2 Mission driven Exceptional boards shape and uphold the mission, articulate a compelling vision, and ensure the congruence between decisions and core values. They treat questions of mission, vision, and core values not as exercises to be done once, but as statements of crucial importance to be drilled down and folded into deliberations.		

	Comments on current position	Suggestions on how we can develop this further
3 Strategic thinking Exceptional boards allocate time to what matters most and continuously engage in strategic thinking to hone the organisation's direction. They not only align agendas and goals with strategic priorities, but also use them for assessing the chief executive, driving meeting agendas, and shaping board recruitment.		

Resources for Chapter 8 continued

	Comments on current position	Suggestions on how we can develop this further
4 Culture of enquiry Exceptional boards institutionalize a culture of inquiry, mutual respect, and constructive debate that leads to sound and shared decision making. They seek more information, question assumptions, and challenge conclusions so that they may advocate for solutions based on analysis.		

	Comments on current position	Suggestions on how we can develop this further
5 Independent-mindedness Exceptional boards are independent-minded. They apply rigorous conflict-of-interest procedures, and their board members put the interests of the organisation above all else when making decisions. They do not allow their votes to be unduly influenced by loyalty to the chief executive or by seniority, position, or reputation of fellow board members, staff, or donors		

	Comments on current position	Suggestions on how we can develop this further
6 Ethos of transparency Exceptional boards promote an ethos of transparency by ensuring that donors, stakeholders, and interested members of the public have access to appropriate and accurate information regarding finances, operations, and results. They also extend transparency internally, ensuring that every board member has equal access to relevant materials when making decisions		

	Comments on current position	Suggestions on how we can develop this further
7 Compliance with integrity Exceptional boards promote strong ethical values and disciplined compliance by establishing appropriate mechanisms for active oversight. They use these mechanisms, such as independent audits, to ensure accountability and sufficient controls; to deepen their understanding of the organisation; and to reduce the risk of waste, fraud, and abuse		

	Comments on current position	Suggestions on how we can develop this further
8 Sustaining resources Exceptional boards link bold visions and ambitious plans to financial support, expertise, and networks of influence. Linking budgeting to strategic planning, they approve activities that can be realistically financed with existing or attainable resources, while ensuring that the organisation has the infrastructure and internal capacity it needs		

	Comments on current position	Suggestions on how we can develop this further
9 Results-orientated Exceptional boards are results-orientated. They measure the organisation's progress towards mission and evaluate the performance of major programs and services. They gauge efficiency, effectiveness, and impact, while simultaneously assessing the quality of service delivery, integrating benchmarks against peers, and calculating return on investment.		

Resources for Chapter 8 continued

	Comments on current position	Suggestions on how we can develop this further
10 Intentional board practices Exceptional boards purposefully structure themselves to fulfill essential governance duties and to support organisational priorities. Making governance intentional, not incidental, exceptional boards invest in structures and practices that can be thoughtfully adapted to changing circumstances.		

	Comments on current position	Suggestions on how we can develop this further
11 Continuous learning Exceptional boards embrace the qualities of a continuous learning organisation, evaluating their own performance and assessing the value they add to the organisation. They embed learning opportunities into routine governance work and in activities outside of the boardroom.		

	Comments on current position	Suggestions on how we can develop this further
12 Revitalization Exceptional boards energize themselves through planned turnover, thoughtful recruitment, and inclusiveness. They see the correlation between mission, strategy, and board composition, and they understand the importance of fresh perspectives and the risks of closed groups. They revitalize themselves through diversity of experience and through continuous recruitment.		

Resource 8.7 Other ideas for reflecting on board effectiveness
The Sir Nicholas Fenn and Sibford School methods for reviewing board and individual trustee effectiveness

When Sir Nicholas Fenn was chair of Marie Curie Cancer Care (MCCC), he arranged to meet each trustee on a one-to-one basis each year. The purpose of the meeting was to discuss:
- how the effectiveness of the governance of MCCC can be strengthened
- how the effectiveness of the trustee in question can be increased
- what Nick, as chair, should do to be a more effective chair.

If we preferred to discuss Sir Nicholas's performance as chair with someone else, we were at liberty to speak to the treasurer (as there was no vice chair).

Sir Nicholas would then write a paper based on the feedback from these meetings. Time would be put aside at a 'council' (name given to the board of trustees of MCCC) meeting to discuss the paper and to agree changes.

If chairs can afford the time to carry out one-to-one meetings with each trustee, this is an excellent method of reviewing the effectiveness of the board, of individual trustees and of the chair. It is also an opportunity for chairs to develop further their relationship with each trustee.

Another chair of trustees (Sibford School), who has less time than Sir Nicholas, uses a similar scheme. She circulates a questionnaire to each trustee which covers the same three areas. Completed questionnaires are analysed by her and she subsequently arranges one-to-one conversations by telephone with each trustee to discuss their personal views plus the collective views of the board. She then amends her paper, which is discussed at a board meeting at which changes in the way the board operates are agreed.

Some of the questions she asks are:
- Which board subcommittees are you on?
- When does your term of office come to an end?
- How have you enjoyed the last year on board?

Board meetings
In your opinion
- Is the business well conducted?
- Are we covering issues that are important?
- Are we wasting time on any issues?
- Is there a more efficient way of dealing with business?
- Are you receiving sufficient information with the agenda?
- Are you playing a full part in decision making?

Relationship with school
- Do you understand the difference between governance and management? Do you find this difficult?
- Do you feel that you know enough about the school?
- How many school functions have you managed to attend this year?
- How could we make it easier for you to get to know the staff?

Resources for Chapter 8 continued

Your role on the board
- What do you think you bring to board?
- What has been your most important contribution this year?
- In what ways would you like to add to your current input?
- Do you have any duties you would like to relinquish?
- Do you feel well supported in your role?
- Do you have any training needs?

Resource 8.8 Other ideas for reflecting on board effectiveness: Review of performance based on Higgs Report

The discussions (the whole board or in one-to-one discussions between the chair and each trustee) can be structured around the recommendations of the Higgs Report: Review of the role of non-executive directors, published in 2003:

- How well has the board performed against any performance objectives (eg role description; the board's objectives for the year) that have been set?
- What has been the board 's contribution to the testing and development of strategy?
- What has been the board's contribution to ensuring robust and effective risk management?
- Is the composition of the board and its committees appropriate, with the right mix of knowledge and skills to maximise performance in the light of future strategy?
- Are inside and outside the board relationships working effectively?
- How has the board responded to any problems or crises that have emerged and could or should these have been foreseen?
- How well does the board communicate with the chief executive, employees and others?
- Is the board as a whole up-to-date with latest developments in the regulatory environment, the charity sector and in the sub-sectors within which the charity operates?
- How effective is the board committees? [Specific questions on should be included such as, for example, finance or audit committees' role, their composition and their interaction with the board.]
- How clear is the board about delegated authority and how effective is it in holding those with delegated authority to account?

The processes that help underpin the board 's effectiveness should also be evaluated, for example:

- Is appropriate, timely information of the right length and quality provided to the board and is the chief executive responsive to reasonable requests for clarification or amplification? Does the board provide helpful feedback to the chief executive on its requirements?
- Are sufficient board and board committee meetings of appropriate length held to enable proper consideration of issues? Is time used effectively?
- Are the board's procedures conducive to effective performance and flexible enough to deal with all eventualities?

In addition, there are some specific issues relating to the chair of the board which should be included as part of an evaluation of the board 's performance, eg:

- Is the chair of the board demonstrating effective leadership of the board?
- Are relationships and communications with major stakeholders well managed?
- Are relationships and communications within the board constructive?
- Are the trustees acting collectively and taking collective responsibility? Does ultimate authority remain collectively with the board?
- Are the processes for setting the agenda working? Do they enable trustees to raise issues and concerns?

Resources for Chapter 8 continued

The chair and trustees should consider the following issues and the individual concerned should also be asked to assess themselves. For each trustee:

- How well prepared and informed are you for board meetings and is your meeting attendance satisfactory?
- Do you demonstrate a willingness to devote time and effort to understand the charity and its business and a readiness to participate in events outside the board?
- What has been the quality and value of your contributions at board meetings?
- What has been your contribution to development of strategy and to risk management?
- How successfully have you brought your knowledge and experience to bear in the consideration of strategy and other matters brought to the board?
- How effectively have you probed to test information and assumptions?
- How effectively and proactively have you followed up your areas of concern?
- How effective and successful are your relationships with fellow trustees and the chief executive?
- Does your performance and behaviour engender mutual trust and respect within the board and between the board and the chief executive?
- How actively and successfully do you refresh your knowledge and skills and are you up-to-date with: the latest developments in areas such as governance, financial reporting, the voluntary sector and issues relating to the work of your charity?
- How well do you communicate with fellow trustees and the chief executive? Are you able to present your views convincingly yet diplomatically and do you listen and take on board the views of others?

Resource 8.9 Other ideas for reflecting on board effectiveness

Another example of good practice comes from the Scout Association. Each year trustees complete the following questionnaires, a paper is written and discussed by the trustee. Changes are agreed and are introduced.

The Scout Association TRUSTEE SELF-EVALUATION
PERSONAL TRUSTEESHIP

		Always	Sometimes	Rarely	Never
1	I understand the charity's mission				
2	I support the charity's mission				
3	I am knowledgeable about the charity's major programmes and services				
4	I follow external trends and important developments in areas related to the work of the charity				
5	I read the charity's financial statements				
6	I understand the charity's financial statements				
7	I act with knowledge and prudence				
8	I have a good working relationship with other trustees				
9	I advise and assist the Chair when asked				
10	I have a good working relationship with the Chief Executive				
11	I prepare for and participate fully in Board meetings				
12	I willingly volunteer and use my special skills to further the charity's mission				
13	I complete all my trustee assignments in a responsible and timely manner				
14	I respect the confidentiality of the Board's sessions				
15	I focus my attention on long-term policy rather than short-term operations				
16	I avoid burdening staff with requests for special favours				
17	I avoid conflicts of interest				
18	My opinions are heard and considered in the Board				
19	I find serving as a Trustee a satisfying experience				
20	I give/set-aside time for my training and development as a Trustee				

Resources for Chapter 8 continued

**TRUSTEE SELF-EVALUATION
CORPORATE TRUSTEESHIP**

Each Trustee to complete the self-evaluation check-list individually prior to discussion.

Score: **3** = very satisfied
2 = satisfied
1 = not satisfied
0 = very dissatisfied
N = not enough information to make a decision

		Score	Notes
1	The Board is familiar with the charity's Vision		
2	The Board is knowledgeable about the charity's current activities and services		
3	The Board fully understands the external environment in which it is operating		
4	The Board has a strategic plan		
5	The Board is preparing for the charity's future		
6	The Board focuses on long-term policy rather than short-term operations		
7	The Board has a risk-management process in place		
8	The Board has robust systems for financial planning		
9	The Board reviews the Annual Budget and its implications		
10	The Board has approved an effective marketing and public relations strategy		
11	The Board contains sufficient range of high calibre expertise across skill-sets required		
12	The Board understands and operates to respective roles of Trustees and staff		
13	The Board supports the Chief Executive and key staff in their roles		
14	The Board holds effective meetings		
15	Board members attend regularly and prepare thoroughly		
16	The Board does not allow a few individuals to dominate meetings		
17	The Board acts as a single body rather than as a collection of individuals		
18	The Board's size and structure is appropriate		
19	The Board implements clear Trustee development procedures (induction, Trustee training, etc)		
20	The Board adds value to the charity		

Chapter 9
Appraising the chief executive

9.1 | Introduction

All of us, and chief executives are no exception, need candid and constructive feedback on our performance. This is not only to provide reassurance that we are doing well, but also to learn and to develop professionally. During my many years working with chief executives, they have expressed, frequently and sometimes privately, the need for honest, objective feedback as to whether or not they are doing a good job. They often get mixed messages from their trustees.

The chief executive, who is so crucial to the success of an organisation, probably needs performance feedback more than anyone else in the organisation. This is because the more senior you are, it is proportionately less likely that staff or volunteers will tell you honestly if they feel that you can do things better. In addition, the extraordinary demands on a chief executive's time, means that he/she has less time than most to reflect on their own performance and how it can be improved unless time is regularly put aside for their appraisal. Often, because chief executives may work very long hours, no one feels they want to fault them in any way. The need for the chief executive to provide leadership and to act as a role model to staff, volunteers, etc, can sometimes make it more difficult for them to receive less than fulsome praise.

Chief executives need and want their performance reviewed but why should boards of trustees be interested in appraising the performance of their chief executive? Trustees have five key responsibilities. These are:
- ensuring that the charity has a clear vision, mission and strategic direction and is focused on achieving these
- being responsible for the performance of the charity and for its culture
- ensuring that the charity complies with all legal and regulatory requirements
- acting as guardians of the charity's assets, both tangible and intangible, taking all due care over their security, deployment and proper application
- ensuring that the charity's governance is of the highest possible standard.

Being responsible for the charity's performance, its fundamental values, its ethos and culture is not an easy task, especially as trustees are not directly involved in managing and running the charity. The only way therefore to keep a finger on the pulse of performance is to ensure there is:
- a good relationship with the chief executive based on mutual trust, respect, honesty and openness
- mechanisms in place to measure the performance of the charity against clear strategic objectives
- the chief executive is committed to his/her own professional development and that of the staff
- the trustees are committed to the chief executive's professional development and that of the staff
- a performance management policy for the whole charity
- the chief executive's performance is reviewed regularly
- the board's performance is reviewed regularly and the board too is committed to learning and development.

Surveys show that about 70% of professionally managed charities review the performance of their chief executive, yet some boards only start to consider evaluating their chief executive when there are concerns about his/her performance. This is exactly the wrong time and the wrong reason for reviewing the performance of a chief executive, and a one-off, last-minute, antagonistic appraisal will not, in any way, help the board if it is faced with a legal challenge.

9.2 | Key messages

This chapter has five key messages:

- Performance appraisal should be part of the culture of the organisation and should include the appraisal of the board.
- The main purpose of appraising the chief executive should be to maximise his/her effectiveness by providing appropriate support and professional development.
- Appraisal must be a continuous process with informal and ongoing feedback culminating in a more formal, usually annual, appraisal process.
- Appraisal is a tool to build mutual trust, understanding, respect, honesty and openness, and should concentrate on the future rather than the past.
- If anyone who is playing a significant part in the appraisal does not have professional experience of carrying out appraisals, training will need to be provided before the process begins.

Planning and preparation

The quality of performance appraisal is often inversely proportional to the seniority of the person being appraised. Therefore planning, ongoing consultation with the chief executive, and a great deal of thought needs to go into developing or improving the process that is right for appraising your chief executive. Although this chapter will give you various models for appraising your chief executive, it is important that the chair and the chief executive develop one which is right for your organisation, your chief executive and your board.

Agreement on why the chief executive's performance should be appraised

Clarity and mutual understanding of the reasons for appraisal are very much the starting point. Reasons can include:

- to ensure that the trustees are meeting their duty of care for the charity
- to ensure that the trustees are meeting their responsibility for the performance of the charity and for ensuring that strategic and annual goals are being achieved
- to ensure clarity about what the charity, the board and the chief executive are expected to achieve
- an opportunity to formally recognise a job being well done
- an opportunity to give regular feedback and thus avoid surprises
- to ensure learning, as appraising the chief executive is an educational process for both the chief executive and the board
- to improve the performance of the chief executive through professional development and support, make him/her even more effective, sustain excellence and maximise his/her potential
- to improve management of the charity
- to improve the performance of the whole charity
- to clarify the different but complementary roles of the chief executive and the board
- to obtain a longer-term assessment of the chief executive's performance against agreed objectives
- to develop a more honest, candid and open relationship based on mutual respect between chief executive and the board.

Agreement on the purpose of chief executive appraisal

Some argue that the purpose of appraisal is either to ensure that the chief executive and the organisation achieve key results or to maximise the effectiveness of the chief executive through professional development. I disagree. The purpose of appraisal needs to include both and much more.

It is easy to go into chief executive appraisal with the appraiser and appraisee having differing views on the purpose of the appraisal. It is therefore important to agree the purpose of the appraisal before the planning begins.

Ideally the broad purpose of appraising the chief executive should be:

- to build a strong relationship between the board and the chief executive based on mutual trust, respect, honesty and openness
- to foster the development of the chief executive and ensure the chief executive receives the support he/she needs
- to build upon and improve the performance of the chief executive and ultimately of the charity
- to clarify expectations between the board and the chief executive and to agree what is to be achieved by the chief executive, the board and the organisation in the near future and in the longer term.

Appraisal and remuneration

Some organisations use appraisal to set the remuneration of the chief executive. If this happens it is vitally important that any discussions of salary, bonuses or performance-related pay occur at a completely different meeting and several weeks after the completion of the appraisal. In the longer term, the performance of the chief executive is likely to impact, consciously or unconsciously, on the chief executive's remuneration, as boards will not only want to retain the services of a very successful chief executive but also to show him/her that he/she is valued. However boards should be aware there are other ways of rewarding those who serve the charity well, such as investing significantly in their professional development. Perhaps encouraging them to play a more prominent role on a much wider stage or offering a short sabbatical to longer-serving successful chief executives to give them room to stand back and think more creatively and strategically.

Some charities have introduced performance-related pay or a system of bonuses – methods that are more commonly used by commercial companies. There is growing evidence that performance-related pay, especially at chief executive level, in for-profit companies is not having the impact it was expected to do on either the performance of the chief executive or the company. We can all recall examples of companies that have paid massive performance payments just before the company slides into disaster. Linking remuneration to share value and the 'bottom line' may be relatively straightforward in a commercial company, but linking remuneration to performance is far more complex in a voluntary organisation.

9.3 | Developing the ongoing appraisal process

Good appraisal comes in two parts. It is a continuous process with both informal and ongoing feedback, as well as a more formal, usually annual, appraisal process.

Ongoing informal feedback

The ongoing informal feedback is usually given by the chair of trustees on behalf of the board. The chair and the chief executive need to arrange to meet regularly, usually every two or three months, to discuss specifically developments since their last meeting and plans for the next two/three months. It is an opportunity for the chief executive candidly to:

- discuss his/her achievements since the last meeting
- discuss issues that might be worrying him/her
- discuss issues that might be troubling the chair of trustees
- bring to the chair's attention and gain his/her support for any difficult, contentious or potentially risky decisions that the chief executive may wish to make
- brief the chair on possible future events or developments that may have an impact, for better or worse, on the charity
- give the chair of trustees advance warning of any objectives/goals, personal or organisational, that may not be achieved or those that are likely to be achieved sooner than expected
- consider the chief executive's whole job and not just one or two specific issues
- ask for additional support or training that will assist the chief executive
- comment on the impact of the board, honorary officers or trustees on his/her work.

Although these meetings should be informal, it is useful to structure these meetings and to make short notes (not more than one page of A4) on key points. Always end the meeting by arranging the date, time and place of the next meeting. However frantically busy both the chair and the chief executive are, both should see these meetings as a priority.

The purpose of these meetings is not to discuss routine matters such as papers for the next board meeting or how a major appeal is going. The meeting needs to focus on the chief executive and the type of topics listed above. The success of these meetings is dependent on mutual trust, respect and openness between the chief executive and chair.

If the current relationship between the chair and the chief executive is difficult and antagonistic, they should agree steps to try to improve their relationship and in the meantime agree who (vice chair? treasurer? another trustee?) should carry out these regular one-to-one feedback sessions.

If the problems between the chair and chief executive result from confusion about each other's role, role descriptions for both (See Resource 3.1 and Resouce 3.2 for model role descriptions) should help and so should carrying out a role analysis exercise.

Although the chair of trustees usually line manages the chief executive on behalf of the board, this responsibility is occasionally delegated to another trustee who has greater experience of providing professional support to, and appraising, senior staff.

Formal, usually annual, appraisal process

The regular one-to-one meetings between the chair of trustees and the chief executive where performance feedback has been discussed should culminate in the formal, usually annual, appraisal. There are a number of formal appraisal models. Whichever model is selected, and you may wish to use different models at different times, **self-appraisal** has to be an essential, not optional, part of every appraisal.

Some organisations develop a special questionnaire for the chief executive to complete as part of the self-appraisal. Others use the same questionnaire given to the trustees or others. Whichever method or model is used, self appraisal will only be valuable if the chief executive trusts and respects his/her appraisers.

The chief executive needs to be as honest and open as possible when considering his/her own performance. Most people tend to be much harder when assessing their own performance than they are on other people's performances. Interestingly, I have found that some of my weaknesses, such as my poor memory for names, have appeared to others to be strengths because I work so hard trying to compensate for this weakness. Similarly, our strengths can also be our weaknesses. For example, the chief executive's total commitment to the charity might mean that he/she works incredibly long hours, which might not be good for the chief executive or the charity.

Appraisers must not take undue or unfair advantage of the chief executive's honest self-appraisal but should ensure that support and training are offered for any areas of the chief executive's performance that needs development.

When deciding on the model for the formal appraisal, clearly the chief executive and chair of trustees must play a major part in the discussion and the decision.

9.4 | Types of appraisal

Standard appraisal

The most common model of appraisal is 'standard' or 'downward' appraisal. This is where the chief executive is appraised by one or more trustees. It would be unusual if the chair of trustees was not involved. In some charities the appraisal is carried out by the chair alone, or by the honorary officers, or by a current or ad-hoc committee set up by the board for this purpose. The trustees carrying out the formal appraisal may wish to involve the whole board by seeking their individual views through completion of a questionnaire of some kind, or they may not. It is important to remember that the chief executive is responsible to the whole board and not just to the chair of trustees or any sub-group of the board.

Standard appraisal generally works well. Its weakness is that trustees only see a limited side to the chief executive's performance. To overcome this, some boards utilise feedback from staff or go even further by going outside the organisation to key stakeholders such as funders, agencies with which the charity works in partnership, beneficiaries, volunteers etc. (See also the section later on 360 degree appraisal).

Upward appraisal

A few chief executives prefer to be appraised by their staff, either because they have a much fuller view of the chief executive's performance than the trustees have or because the trustees are reluctant, perhaps not having sufficient confidence in their ability, to carry out an appraisal. Sometimes only the views of the senior management team are sought and, at other times, a much wider range of opinions are canvassed, quite often through anonymous questionnaires. This model is called upward appraisal.

Upward appraisal is rarely used. However having experienced it myself through choice, I found it worked wonderfully well. I was introducing appraisal throughout the organisation and wanted to lead by example. My senior management team, whose views I greatly respected, obtained the opinions, under Chatham House rules (comments can be repeated but not attributed), of any member of staff who wished to participate and of course this included the views of the senior management team. The appraisal was thorough, enormously helpful and professionally invaluable. It was complemented by self-appraisal and contributed to my ongoing professional development. Our view was that if it was carried out each year, the staff would not put as much thought and effort into the process. We agreed to use upward appraisal every two years.

Another method of upward appraisal of the chief executive is to carry out an attitude survey of all employees. Included in the questionnaire can be questions on issues such as communications, management style of the chief executive, management style of the senior management team as a whole, and of the employee's line manager. A picture of the strengths and weaknesses of the chief executive as seen by the staff can be distilled from the mass of information collected. However, these surveys should not be taken lightly. They are expensive and create expectations that something will happen as a result of the exercise. Surveys such as these should only be carried out if there is a commitment to follow up on results and a willingness to confront possible unforeseen or unwelcome findings.

The weakness of upward appraisal is that it does not include the views of the trustees, nor does it involve goal setting for the coming year, which remains a task for the board in partnership with the chief executive.

Peer appraisal

Rather than be appraised by trustees or staff directly, peer appraisal involves bringing in a serving or recently retired charity chief executive to carry out the review. This can be done in a number of ways.

Either the appraiser can make his/her own assessment by a series of questions put to the chief executive and which are based on the chief executive's role description, his/her annual goals and objectives, and the charity's strategic plan.

Or, the chief executive and chair agree who the appraiser will interview as part of the evidence-gathering process. This usually includes the chair, a selection of trustees, staff, volunteers, beneficiaries, etc. A report is written on the basis of these interviews which he/she discusses first with the chief executive. The second draft goes to the chair before it is finalised.

Understandably, as the performance of the charity is inextricably linked to the performance of the chief executive, there is a danger that external reviewers' reports read more like a report on the performance of the charity than an analysis of the evidence relating to the chief executive's performance.

Another form of peer appraisal is for the board to seek the views of a number of charity chief executives who have had the opportunity to see the work of the chief executive and are able to make an assessment of his/her performance. The disadvantage of this model is it does not obtain any input from trustees or staff, who are the people who work most closely with the chief executive.

360-degree appraisal

360-degree appraisal combines some or all of the previously mentioned methods of appraisal: upward, downward, peer, external, self.

Its advantages are that:
- it covers areas of performance that are not observed by trustees or by staff
- it demonstrates the chief executive's commitment to developing an open, learning organisation
- it makes staff feel they have a part to play in organisational decision-making
- it emphasis the organisation's commitment to performance management and professional development

Over the last decade 360-degree appraisal of chief executives has become increasingly popular. It does, however, involve a great deal of time and can be expensive. I have participated in a number of 360-degree appraisals of chief executives and find the whole process is often undermined by poor-quality questionnaires for external assessors, which are written by people who have no real understanding of others' perceptions and therefore do not ask the right questions. Open questions are more likely to elicit a more enlightening response rather than information gleaned from ticked boxes next to badly designed questions. An example of 360-degree questionnaires written by Nathan Garber can be found in Resource 9.2.

When done well, 360-degree appraisal can be brilliant. However, I would recommend that this model is not used each year but perhaps every two or three years. One of the other models, standard or upward, could be used in the intervening years.

9.5 | Prerequisite agreement on who will be involved

Once the decision has been made on which model is to be used for the formal appraisal of the chief executive, a decision can be made as to who will be involved in the appraisal. Again this should ideally be a decision made jointly by the chair and the chief executive. For upward or 360-degree appraisal, it is important to ensure that the chief executive does not just select people who will give him/her a glowing report. This will defeat the purpose of appraisal as a professional tool for development. This rarely happens but it is important to be aware that it might. On the other hand, do not get paranoid!

The model has been chosen and the appraisers have been selected. What next? Before rushing into producing questionnaires or organising face-to-face interviews, pause for a moment. There are still several steps to be taken before the more detailed work of the production of the questionnaires should begin.

Clarity

First there should be:
- clarity on what the trustees hope the organisation will achieve (strategic plans and priorities)
- clarity on the goals the chief executive has been asked to achieve since his/her last appraisal
- clarity on how success is to be measured (success criteria) [Remember not every type of success can be easily measured!]
- a clear job description for the chief executive.

All of the above should be provided for, and studied by, everyone involved in the appraisal.

If the board has not yet agreed a strategic plan or set annual goals for the chief executive or the charity, they should start the process for developing a strategic plan and the resulting business/corporate/annual plans will follow. While this is being done, and it will take time to do well, the appraisal of the chief executive can still go ahead, based on competencies needed for the role, or on the role description (if it is a recent one), rather than on strategic priorities and the chief executive's annual objectives.

If anyone who is playing a significant part in the appraisal does not have professional experience of carrying out appraisals, training will need to be provided before the process begins.

Principles underpinning the appraisal process

The board and the chief executive need to agree on the principles underpinning the appraisal process. A successful appraisal process which is acceptable to the board and the chief executive needs to be based on:

- Collaboration
  It is vitally important that developing the appraisal process is seen as a partnership between the board and the chief executive. This means the board and the chief executive must discuss and agree all aspects of the appraisal process including who sees the final report.

- Confidentiality
  If the appraisal is to be a true learning exercise for the chief executive and the board, in which appraisee and appraisers can be honest, open and sensitive to each other, then the process must provide for confidentiality of documents. Agreement must be reached in advance as to who will receive the final report. Will it be just the chief executive and the chair? Will it be the chief executive and all the trustees involved in the appraisal? Will it be the chief executive and the whole board?

Some chief executives, to emphasise the charity's culture of openness and learning, like to share their appraisal report with their senior management team. Very occasionally the chief executive shares the appraisal report with all his/her staff. However, if the chief executive decides on either of these courses of action then he/she needs to discuss this first with the chair and the board. The board will also need to consider whether it will want to share the report on the board's performance with a wider group as well and if they do not, what will this imply to the staff?

The chief executive should also consider the consequences of showing or discussing his/her appraisal report with some or all of his/her staff. Expectations will be raised and he/she will need to continue sharing appraisal reports or face the possibility that people will come to the conclusion that the report is only circulated when it is good. Also, if the chief executive shares his/her appraisal report with the senior management team, will the senior management team be expected to share their appraisal report with each other? If it is circulated to all staff, will it mean that all appraisal reports of all staff will be available to all?

• Impartiality
None of the appraisers must allow their personal views of the chief executive to impact on their professional, dispassionate and objective assessment of his/her performance. Being clear about goals and priorities and having clear criteria for success will help enormously. However it should be recognised that, in a charity, success criteria for some aspects of the chief executive's or the charity's work might be difficult to define, especially where a charity's mission is very wide, for example: 'to rid the world of poverty' or 'to end child cruelty' or 'to campaign for a more just and fairer society'. Similarly, some aspects of the chief executive and his/her work will be difficult to quantify precisely, for example: integrity, flexibility, creativity, initiative.

9.6 | Deciding the basis of the formal appraisal and producing the questionnaires

Once the groundwork has been done, consideration needs to be given as to the basis of the performance review. A study of chief executive appraisal questionnaires show that these are either based on:

- competencies needed by charity chief executives
- performance against the charity's strategic priorities and the chief executive's annual goals/objectives/targets
- the chief executive's role description

or a combination of two or more of the above.

9.7 | Competencies needed by chief executives

Much work has been carried out in many parts of the world looking at competencies needed by those who lead organisations. Rather than reinventing the wheel, boards of trustees are advised to adapt work already done to the needs of their own organisation.

Example 1 Not surprisingly, the work carried out by the British senior civil service on competencies for top civil servants is particularly relevant to charity chief executives, as both groups of leaders work in the not-for-profit sector. ACEVO's (Association of Chief Executives of Voluntary Organisations) model chief executive appraisal form uses the work done by the senior civil service. This framework covers nine key competencies.

Direction	Management and communication	Personal contribution
• Leadership • Strategic thinking and planning • Delivery of results	• Management of people • Communication • Management of financial and other resources	• Personal effectiveness • Expertise • Intellect, creativity and judgement

The senior civil service also produced a very helpful prompt sheet for use by appraisers and this is shown in Resource 9.3.

Example 2 The State Services Commission of New Zealand (SSCNZ) has developed a list of core competencies for public service chief executives and the personal attributes and skills that lie behind them. SSCNZ also provides indicators of highly effective behaviour behind each competency, as well as indicators of ineffective behaviour. These may be of interest to trustees, although not all will be relevant to every charity (ISBN 0-478-24403-7).

Only the 'headline' competencies are given here:

Personal attributes	General management	Leadership
• Commitment to achievement • Honesty and integrity • Intellectual capability	• Management of people • Managerial expertise • Effective communication	• Building and sustaining relationships • Strategic leadership • Managing in political-cultural context

9.7 | Competencies needed by chief executives continued

Example 3 One of my favourite competency frameworks was produced by Business Psychology Wales Ltd for the NHS and their framework is particularly pertinent to service delivery organisations. The framework includes a very helpful checklist of competencies, under the following broad headings:

Communicating purpose and direction Creating expectations and communicating vision
Harnessing innovation and strategic thinking Capturing new ideas, analysing and solving complex problems
Modelling standards of personal performance Setting the highest standards and principles of behaviours
Cultivates partnerships and team-working Motivating and developing people and relationships toward the achievement of mutually beneficial goals
Learning and continuous performance development Drawing on experience, new ideas and learning to improve results
Improving service delivery Focusing money toward achieving value for money and results
Sharing knowledge and expertise Developing understanding of and influencing a wider knowledge base

See Resource 9.5 for the checklist.

Creating a questionnaire based on competencies

Having decided which competencies you wish to use, it is very easy to design a questionnaire around these for appraiser and appraisee to complete. Put each competency as a heading and leave a space for observations and comments below.

Sections on professional development and agreed actions with dates should also be added. Once agreed, the chief executive's goals for the next twelve months should be added to an appropriate section on the form. It is vitally important the board has ensured that there are funds available for the chief executive's professional development. See Resource 9.6 for a sample appraisal form based on these competencies.

The chief executive, as part of his/her self-appraisal, completes each section using the checklist or prompt sheet as an aid. The appraisers do the same. Forms are exchanged prior to the appraisal meeting at which the various views are shared and a consensus view agreed. Alternatively, having given the matter thought before the meeting, the chair and chief executive can discuss and then jointly complete the form.

Instead of open-ended questions such as the comment boxes, appraisers and the chief executive can be asked to score each competency from 1–4 (an even number is best, otherwise people are likely to tick the middle number with very little deep thinking). The form should make it clear exactly what each of the scores represents. For example, 1 could mean 'excellent' or 'far exceeds expectation' and 4 could be 'unsatisfactory' or 'needs significant improvement'. There should be an opportunity for the appraiser to tick a box saying 'not sure' or 'appraiser has no experience'. Even if a scoring system is used, it is important to leave space for comments and observations. Appraisers should be asked to give examples to support their remarks.

If specific questions are asked then the questions need to be very carefully crafted so that they seek to measure quality and not just quantity.

The development of any questionnaire should be done in close consultation with the chief executive.

9.8 | Questionnaires based on strategic priorities and the chief executive's annual goals

Strategic priorities

The first stage for developing this method of appraisal is to be clear about the organisation's strategic priorities and, from the strategic plan, to develop a business/corporate plan from which the annual plans for the organisation have evolved.

The aim should be not only to agree what the chief executive is expected to accomplish but also what is important in his/her performance. In other words, they should establish annual performance standards for the chief executive.

The strategic, business/corporate and annual plans will not necessarily address everything that a chief executive needs to do, for example, his/her responsibility to enable the board to fulfil its governance responsibilities. This is why an up-to-date job description and the statement on the charity's values, ethos and philosophy play an important part in developing these performance objectives and standards.

Annual performance goals and standards

The annual performance standards will need to be developed collaboratively and the chief executive will probably want to work in partnership with the senior management team during the development stage of the standards.

Effective performance standards need to be:
- suitable to the requirements of the job
- reflect the realities of the work environment including external factors that might affect the achievement of the standards
- be written in clear language and should be clearly understood by the chief executive and the board
- should be acceptable to both the chief executive and the board.

You need to bear in mind that quantifiable measures may not always be appropriate. If they are appropriate, do the reporting mechanisms provide the information you need?

Your checklist when developing standards will need to include:
- Are they consistent with the charity's goals?
- Are they realistic?
- Are they specific?
- Are they based on quantifiable data or surveillance or other verifiable information?
- Are they challenging?
- Are they understandable and clear?
- Can they evolve as circumstances change or are they too rigid?

Some examples of goals and annual performance standards:

Goal: Raise the profile of the charity with central and local government
Performance standard: Produce, in collaboration with all relevant staff, a strategy and action plan (with costings) and gain the approval of the board for these.

Goal: Reduce the annual financial deficit, currently £654,321, within three years
Performance standard: Produce a revised strategy and action plan involving both income generation and cutbacks. Reduce the deficit by at least 25% in the first year and a further 50% in the second year, with a surplus being generated by year 4.

Goal: Work in partnership with other organisation(s) to better achieve our strategic objectives
Performance standard: To obtain funding for at least one of the three projects already under development and to produce detailed implementation plans for the funded project(s).

Goal: To give the chief executive a better work/life balance
Performance standard: By the next review period, the chief executive will achieve a pattern of working which only requires work at weekends in exceptional circumstances and, in two year's time, the chief executive will have reduced his/her average working week to 48 hours.

Having decided on goals and standards, a simple questionnaire can then be drawn up. See Resource 9.7 for a sample questionnaire based on goals and performance standards.

As with questionnaires based on competencies, those completing the questionnaires can also be asked to give a score for each goal. I do not recommend scoring without commentary of some kind.

Some model questionnaires, such as the one produced by Board Source (see Further Reading in Further Help and Support.), go on to produce average scores for each category. I personally would advise against using scoring in this way but you might feel that it is a helpful model for your organisation. If a scoring scheme is used and averages calculated, it is important to bear in mind that not all the goals and standards will have equal importance. This means that to make the most of a scoring scheme you need to assign specific weighting factors to each of the standards. For example if you were a trustee of the charity whose chief executive goals are given above, you may want to give most weighting to the reduction of the annual deficit (goal 2) and least weighting to partnership working (goal 3) so the weighting might be: Goal 1 – 15%; Goal 2 – 30%; Goal 3- 10%; Goal 4 – 10%; Goal 5 – 15%; Goal 6 - 20%. Multiply the average score for each goal by the weighting factor, add them together and you then finish up with a score for the whole review! If you use the scales suggested in section 9.7 on creating questionnaires based on competences and Resource 9.5 , a final score over 2.5 would indicate the chief executive's performance is causing concern.

The questionnaire will also need to have sections on professional development requirements, goals for the next review period and actions agreed. Any changes to the chief executive's role description should also be considered and agreed.

Many chief executives prefer appraisal based on strategic priorities and clearly defined goals because expectations of them as chief executives are very clear. The disadvantage is that it can be a method that concentrates mainly on the past rather than the present and the future. It can also concentrate on the achievement of the operational plan rather than asking questions about the skills and competencies that are needed to deliver that plan.

9.9 | Questionnaires based on job descriptions

Once you have an up-to-date job description it is relatively easy to develop an appraisal form based on the job description. The sample job description in Resource 9.8, is used by its author, Simone Joyaux, to produce an appraisal questionnaire for those carrying out the appraisal (see Resource 9.9).

9.10 | Self-evaluation

Instead of completing the same questionnaire as part of self-appraisal, Simone Joyaux recommends that the appraisal committee asks the chief executive several open-ended questions.

This can be found at http://simonejoyaux.com/e107_files/downloads/CEOSelfEvaluation.pdf. An extract is below:

Self-evaluation for the chief executive

1 Please review the chief executive performance appraisal form and be prepared to comment on your performance, with specific examples.

2 Please prepare a memo that responds to the following items:
   a) your performance compared to the accountabilities in your job description
   b) the overall health of the charity and your role in its health
   c) your major contributions to the charity during the year
   d) progress on the charity's goals / direction and your role in its progress
   e) your working relationship with the board of trustees, its officers and committees
   f) your working relationship with your staff
   g) your effectiveness as an enabler of the board
   h) your own performance areas that require improvement and strategies that you plan to utilize for improvement
   i) any problems or special concerns related to your job that need to be addressed in order to enhance your performance, and strategies that you recommend.

Please provide your responses to the appraisal committee chair prior to their deliberations meeting. Please be prepared to discuss your comments in your performance appraisal meeting.

As with the competency framework, sections on professional development, goals for the next year and actions agreed should be added. The job description should also be reviewed and any mutually agreed changes made.

9.11 | Interpreting the results

Once the completed questionnaires are gathered in, they will be discussed at the appraisal meeting. In preparation for this meeting the lead appraiser, who is likely to be the chair of trustees or chair of the committee set up to carry out the appraisal, should spend time prior to the meeting, analysing the responses. He/she should draw out areas of greatest capability and greatest weakness, and see if other evidence, such as the review of the charity's performance supports or contradicts the views of the appraisers. He/she needs to examine areas where there is a significant difference between the self-appraisal assessment and those of the appraisers. Are these differences caused by misunderstandings of what was expected of the chief executive? Finally, the lead appraiser also needs to see if there are any themes running through the responses.

The lead appraiser is responsible for ensuring that the appraisal meeting is open, honest, supportive, constructive and a positive learning experience for the chief executive, for the appraisers and eventually for the board.

Things that can go wrong

The quality of the questionnaire, the attitude of the chief executive and the appraisers, a very open and honest discussion, and the skills of the lead appraiser should ensure a successful appraisal. However, things can go wrong. Reasons for this can include:

- the appraisers think the chief executive is wonderful and can walk on water, and are therefore blinded to his/her weaknesses – the chief executive is thrilled but is being denied any professional development or learning experience
- one or more of the appraisers believe the chief executive is incompetent and only draws out evidence to support their view and refuses to accept evidence to the contrary
- there is a general propensity to rate positively and to avoid saying anything unfavourable
- there is a general propensity to rate negatively and to avoid saying anything favourable
- views are based on the chief executive's personality rather than his/her achievements; [the chief executive's personality will have an impact on his/her performance but this should be considered separately]
- the appraisers have a limited view of the chief executive's performance and draw conclusions on very little evidence or one specific event
- further professional development is promised but never delivered.

Conclusion

Reviewing the performance of the chief executive should be a rewarding exercise for all those concerned and for the charity. Planning and preparation, openness and honesty and a genuine desire to learn and to be constructive will ensure the success of the ongoing review of your chief executive's performance. Do not seek perfection in your chief executive – we all have our strengths and weaknesses. Finally, do not forget to take time out to celebrate the achievements of your chief executive, of the board and of the charity.

Resources for Chapter 9

Resource 9.1 Role analysis exercise

A role analysis exercise is worth carrying out when either the chair of trustees or chief executive have just been appointed or are relatively new in post. It is also worth doing if either the chief executive or the trustees feel that they are unclear of the different but complementary roles of governance and management. Periods of rapid growth or significant change can also affect the roles of key people and board committees. This is therefore a good time to go through a role analysis exercise.

- The role analysis exercise should be used as a basis for discussion in order to clarify roles.
- It is suggested that the chair and chief executive adapt the form adding and removing some of the subject areas and then work through the exercise together having previously and separately thought through the issues.
- Columns should **NOT** be completed by a series of ticks. Instead descriptions need to be used. For example: no role; carries out; full authority; proposes action; suggests options; informs; if within budget approved by the board; etc ....
- A discussion with the whole board should follow.
- Roles need to be reviewed regularly because organisations develop and change. Personnel change too – the previous chair may have been a brilliant public speaker and an excellent spokesperson for the organisation; the new chair may have different skills and may prefer to leave this role to others.
- The process of discussing respective roles should in itself contribute much to a good, strong partnership between the chair and chief executive. Often, when a good relationship is established, there is little further need to refer to role descriptions. However, if an organisation is growing rapidly and roles are changing, role descriptions should be regularly reviewed and, if appropriate, changed by mutual agreement.

Chief executive's role	Subject area	Chair's role	Board's role	Delegated to .... committee
	Functioning effectively at trustee level			
	Structuring the board			
	Recruiting new trustees			
	Ensuring trustees understand their responsibilities			
	Induction, briefings, training, support of trustees			
	Board meetings, board papers, board agendas			
	Dealing with difficult or 'rogue' trustees			
	Succession planning			
	Information needs of trustees			
	Reviewing the constitution			

Resources for Chapter 9 continued

Chief executive's role	Subject area	Chair's role	Board's role	Delegated to .... committee
	Planning strategically			
	Defining the mission			
	Defining the vision			
	Leading strategic planning			
	Producing and agreeing the strategic plan			
	Producing and agreeing the corporate or business plan			
	Producing and agreeing the annual plan and targets			
	Policy			
	Deciding which policies are board policies			
	Developing a timetable to review board policies			
	Policy recommendation and development			
	Identifying and managing risk			
	Evaluation			
	Agreeing key performance indicators			
	Monitoring key performance indicators			
	Measuring the performance of the organisation			
	Monitoring the performance of the organisation			
	Appraising the chief executive			
	Reviewing the performance of the board			
	Reviewing the performance of board committees			
	Staff appraisal			

Chief executive's role	Subject area	Chair's role	Board's role	Delegated to .... committee
	Financial			
	Budget preparation			
	Budget approval			
	Capital purchase (major equipment, cars, buildings)			
	Building renovation/ refurbishment decision			
	Expansion decisions			
	Leasing decisions			
	Purchase of major items			
	Major repairs (more than £............)			
	Minor repairs (less than £............)			
	Emergency repairs			
	Monthly financial reporting			
	Monthly financial approvals			
	Staff salaries			
	Signing of contracts above £....			
	External relationships			
	Chief spokesperson			
	Spearheads lobbying			
	Spearheads fundraising			
	Media policy			
	Personnel			
	Hiring of staff			
	Dismissing staff			
	Allocating work/projects to staff			
	Staff grievances			
	Staff disciplinary procedure			
	Staff appeals (grievance, discipline, appraisal)			
	Appointing the chief executive			

Resources for Chapter 9 continued

Resource 9.2 Self-assessment instrument

Reprinted with permission from the Saskatchewan School Boards Association, Regina, Saskatchewan: admin@saskschoolboards.ca

Ask yourself these questions about your responsibilities and performance Chief Executive.
Circle the appropriate response.

A. Personal/professional

	Usually			Rarely
Do you have a clear understanding of the expectations the board has for your role?	1	2	3	4
Do you communicate openly and effectively with your trustees?	1	2	3	4
Do you exercise fair-mindedness in your dealings with the employees?	1	2	3	4
Do you openly respect and trust your board?	1	2	3	4
Are you reliable in meeting the commitments made to your board?	1	2	3	4
Are you flexible and creative in your approach to change?	1	2	3	4
Do you demonstrate effective skills of conflict management?	1	2	3	4

B. Purpose and direction

	Usually			Rarely
Are you aware of the goals and priorities of the charity?	1	2	3	4
Do you communicate expectations of the board and of the charity clearly to employees?	1	2	3	4
Can you identify the issue, problem or project that most concerns this board at this time?	1	2	3	4
Do you have a clear idea as to your priorities and goals for your work in the charity?	1	2	3	4
Do you have means and criteria for knowing when these priorities and goals are being met?	1	2	3	4

C. Technical/managerial

	Usually			Rarely
Do you manage the paperwork associated with your position effectively?	1	2	3	4
Do you effectively monitor and respond to the changing human resources needs in the charity?	1	2	3	4
Can you understand and effectively direct the financial and business affairs of the charity?	1	2	3	4
Do you delegate appropriately in your approach to your decision-making functions?	1	2	3	4

D. leadership

	Usually			Rarely
Do you devote serious attention to creating and maintaining a high level of morale and a positive climate in the charity?	1	2	3	4
Do you exercise effective supervision of professional staff?	1	2	3	4
Do you regularly monitor the effectiveness of the charity and work of the charity?	1	2	3	4
Do you keep adequately informed of recent developments?	1	2	3	4

E. Political skills

	Usually			Rarely
Do you communicate effectively with beneficiaries and other groups of key stakeholders?	1	2	3	4
Do you keep abreast of changes in regulation and compliance which have implications for the charity?	1	2	3	4
Do you work to improve the image of the charity in the broader community?	1	2	3	4
Do you seek to influence government concerning the emerging needs of your beneficiaries?	1	2	3	4

Resources for Chapter 9 continued

F. What were the most significant successes of the charity during the past year?

_____

_____

_____

_____

G. What are the most pressing problems faced by the charity?

_____

_____

_____

_____

H. What are your own most significant and pressing professional development needs?

_____

_____

_____

_____

Reprinted with permission from the Saskatchewan School Boards Association – Regina, Saskatchewan – admin@saskschoolboards.ca

Resource 9.3 360-degree performance appraisal templates

This template was written by, and is published here with the kind permission of, Nathan Garber of Nathan Garber & Associates

This document provides a list of questions for three questionnaires or interviews the appraisal committee might use to gather information on the Chief Executive's performance from selected partner organisations, from board members, and from employees. If mailed, the questionnaires should be sent with a covering letter from the chair of the committee with stamped self-addressed envelopes and returned directly to the chair to ensure privacy. The preferred is by interview rather than by the completion of forms.

QUESTIONS TO OBTAIN FEEDBACK FROM PARTNER ORGANISATION
(sent at least every 3 years to selected CEs of partner organisations.)

In preparation for the CE's upcoming performance appraisal, would you please comment in the following areas and return to *(name)* before *(date)*

1 You will find enclosed, our mission statement, a statement of our organisational goals, and a statement of the values and beliefs which underlie our organisation. Please read them and give your views on the following questions. Our committee would appreciate it if you would explain your opinions by providing examples of things the CE has done.

a) In your opinion, to what extent is the organisation making progress towards the stated mission and goals?

_____

_____

b) In your opinion, to what extent is the CE responsible for progress or the lack of it?

_____

_____

c) In your opinion, to what extent are the actions of the CE consistent with our stated values and beliefs?

_____

_____

2 a) Please place a mark on the scale below to indicate how you would characterize your relationship with our organisation?

unsatisfactory ├──────────────────┤ satisfactory

unproductive ├──────────────────┤ productive

uncooperative ├──────────────────┤ cooperative

b) How might it be improved?

_____

_____

Resources for Chapter 9 continued

QUESTIONS TO OBTAIN FEEDBACK FROM PARTNER ORGANISATION continued

3 Outline any accomplishments or strengths of the CE which have been notable for you.

_____

_____

4 What improvements would you like to see in the CE's performance?

_____

_____

5 Any other comments?

_____

_____

QUESTIONS TO OBTAIN FEEDBACK FROM PARTNER ORGANISATION
(sent at least every 3 years to selected CEs of partner organisations.)

In preparation for the CE's upcoming performance appraisal, would you please comment in the following areas and return to *(name)* before *(date)*

1 You will find enclosed, our mission statement, a statement of our organisational goals, and a statement of the values and beliefs which underlie our organisation. Please read them and give your views on the following questions. Our committee would appreciate it if you would explain your opinions by providing examples of things the CE has done.

a) In your opinion, to what extent is the organisation making progress towards the stated mission and goals?

_____

_____

b) In your opinion, to what extent is the CE responsible for progress or the lack of it?

_____

_____

c) In your opinion, to what extent are the actions of the CE consistent with our stated values and beliefs?

_____

_____

2 a) Please place a mark on the scale below to indicate how you would characterize your relationship with our organisation?

unsatisfactory ⊢————————————⊣ satisfactory

unproductive ⊢————————————⊣ productive

uncooperative ⊢————————————⊣ cooperative

b) How might it be improved?

_____

3 Outline any accomplishments or strengths of the CE which have been notable for you.

_____

_____

4 What improvements would you like to see in the CE's performance?

_____

_____

5 Any other comments?

_____

Resources for Chapter 9 continued

QUESTIONS TO OBTAIN FEEDBACK FROM STAFF
(sent at least every 3 years to direct reports of CE depending upon turnover)

In preparation for the CE's upcoming performance appraisal, would you please comment in the following areas and return to *(name)* before *(date)*

1 Please review the board's policies/documents which state our mission, goals, values and beliefs and give your views on the following questions. Please provide examples and reasons to support your view.
   a) To what extent is the organisation making progress towards the stated mission and goals?

   _____

   _____

   b) To what extent is the CE responsible for progress or the lack of it?

   _____

   _____

   c) In your opinion, to what extent are the actions of the CE consistent with our stated values and beliefs?

   _____

   _____

2 Please review the employee handbook which states the board's employment policies.
   Please comment on the CE's compliance with these policies. If you are not completely satisfied that organisational practices are in compliance with these policies, please indicate your reasons.

   _____

   _____

3 Outline any accomplishments or strengths of the CE which have been notable for you.

   _____

   _____

4 What improvements would you like to see in the CE's performance?

   _____

   _____

5 Any other comments?

   _____

   _____

QUESTIONS TO OBTAIN FEEDBACK FROM BOARD MEMBERS
(sent annually to board members)

In preparation for the CE's upcoming performance appraisal, would you please comment in the following areas and return to *(name)* before *(date)*

1 Please review the board's policies/documents which state our mission, goals, values and beliefs and give your views on the following questions. We would appreciate it if you would explain your opinions by providing examples of things the CE has done.

a) In your opinion, to what extent is the organisation making progress towards our stated mission and goals?

_____

_____

b) In your opinion, to what extent is the CE responsible for progress or the lack of it?

_____

_____

c) In your opinion, to what extent are the actions of the CE consistent with our stated values and beliefs?

_____

_____

2 Please review the board documents which state our expectations for CE's performance.
Please comment on the CE's compliance with these documents. If you are not completely satisfied that organisational practices are in compliance with board policies, please indicate your reasons.

_____

_____

3 Outline any accomplishments or strengths of the CE which have been notable for you.

_____

_____

4 What improvements would you like to see in the CE's performance?

_____

_____

5 Any other comments?

_____

_____

Resources for Chapter 9 continued

Resource 9.4 Competencies prompt sheet – senior civil service model

The table below was originally developed by the British civil service for senior civil servants and is very similar to competencies needed by charity chief executives.

DIRECTION	MANAGEMENT AND COMMUNICATION	PERSONAL CONTRIBUTION
Leadership • creates and conveys a clear vision • initiates and drives through change • is visible, approachable and earns respect. • inspires and shows loyalty • builds a high performing team • acts decisively having assessed the risks • takes final responsibility for the actions of the team • demonstrates the high standards of integrity, honesty and fairness expected	**Management of People** • establishes and communicates clear standards and expectations • gives recognition and helps all staff develop full potential • addresses poor performance • builds trust, good morale and cooperation within the team • delegates effectively, making best use of skills and resources within the team • seeks face to face contact and responds to feedback from staff • manages the change process perceptively • manages relationships with trustees and between staff and trustees	**Personal Effectiveness** • show resilience, stamina and reliability under heavy pressure • takes a firm stance when circumstances warrant • is aware of personal strengths and weaknesses and their impact on others • offers objective advice to trustees without fear or favour • pursues adopted strategies with energy and commitment • adapts quickly and flexibly to new demands and change • manages own time well to meet competing priorities
Strategic Thinking and Planning • identifies strategic aims, anticipating future demands, opportunities and constraints • demonstrates sensitivity to stakeholders' needs • makes choices between options which take into account their long term impact • translates strategic aims into practical and achievable plans • takes decisions on time, even in uncertain circumstances	**Communication** • negotiates effectively and can handle hostility • is concise and persuasive orally and in writing • listens to what is said and is sensitive to other's reactions • demonstrates presentational and media skills • chooses the methods of communication most likely to secure effective results	**Expertise** • earns credibility through depth of knowledge/experience • knows how to find and use other sources of expertise (including IT) • understands parliamentary and political processes and how to operate within them • applies best practice from other sectors and organisations • understands how policy impacts on operations, staff, users and volunteers

DIRECTION	MANAGEMENT AND COMMUNICATION	PERSONAL CONTRIBUTION
Delivery of Results • defines results taking account of users or other stakeholder's needs • delivers results on time, on budget and to agreed quality standards • demonstrates high-level project and contract management skills • ensures that others organise their work to achieve objectives • knows when to step in and when not to • encourages feedback on performance and learns for the future	**Management of Financial and other Resources** • negotiates for the resources to do the job, in the light of wider priorities • commits and realigns resources to meet key priorities • leads initiatives for new and more efficient use of resources • ensures management information systems are used to monitor/control resources • manages contracts and relationships with suppliers effectively	**Intellect, Creativity and Judgement** • generates original ideas with practical application • homes in on key issues and principles • analyses ambiguous data and concepts rigorously • defends logic of own position robustly but responds positively to reasoned alternatives • encourages creative thinking in others • delegates decisions

Resources for Chapter 9 continued

Resources 9.5 CPD leadership competence framework

This framework was written by, and is published here with the kind permission of, Business Psychology Wales Ltd. It was developed originally for use in the NHS.

	COMMUNICATING PURPOSE AND DIRECTION (Creating Expectations, and Communicating vision)		CPD 360°
Competencies	Use a wide range of communication methods, skills and language to match the needs of the audience?		
	Prioritise for achieving goals?		
	Involve relevant people in deciding what needs to be done?		
	Influence and contribute to the policy making process?		
	Clarify roles and responsibilities in line with short and long term objectives?		
	Develop practical and achievable plans?		
	Emphasise the link between local/personal objectives to that of the broader organisation?		

	HARNESSING INNOVATIVE AND STRATEGIC THINKING (Capturing new ideas, analysing and solving complex problems)		CPD 360°
Competencies	Show sensitivity to wider political and organisational priorities?		
	Quickly assimilate and identify key issues in complex, or conflicting data?		
	Develop new ideas, opportunities, or ways for solving complex problems?		
	Show ability to turn ideas into action		
	Consider the potential and impact of new technology for example, for analysing data, benchmarking or problem solving?		
	Analyse problems from different points of view?		
	Influence or develop strategies to sustain cultural change?		
	Establish systems to ensure effective use of resources and delivery?		
	Demonstrate forward thinking in managing risks and planning for consequences?		
	Offer objective advice or guidance based on in-depth analysis of evidence		

Trademark **CPD 360°**

MODELLING STANDARDS OF PERSONAL PERFORMANCE (Setting the highest standards and principles of behaviour)		CPD 360°
Competencies	Show respect and value for diversity and equality of opportunity?	
	Maintain visibility and availability at all levels?	
	Act with honesty and integrity?	
	Add value through openness and sharing of knowledge and expertise?	
	Promote and stimulate development opportunities for all?	
	Maintain highest standards and commitment through stages of planning, implementation and communication of results?	
	Show preparedness to challenge, and to be challenged?	
	Take responsibility for own decisions and promote accountability in others?	
	Shares credit and recognition for achievements and successes?	

CULTIVATES PARTNERSHIPS AND TEAM-WORKING (Motivating and developing people and relationships toward the achievement of mutually beneficial goals)		CPD 360°
Competencies	Cultivate effective partnership working, through alignment of mutually beneficial goals?	
	Share the lead, knowing when to delegate and involve others?	
	Promote team working across boundaries to achieve goals?	
	Give and ask for regular constructive (positive and negative) feedback?	
	Quickly tackle poor performance or inappropriate behaviours?	
	Promote the values of diversity of ideas, backgrounds, methods of approach?	
	Motivate by showing interest, enthusiasm and involvement	

Trademark **CPD 360°**

Resources for Chapter 9 continued

LEARNING AND CONTINUOUS PERFORMANCE DEVELOPMENT (CPD) (Drawing on experience, new ideas and learning to improve results)		CPD 360°
Competencies	Lead from the front – showing consistency in commitments to learning, development and change objectives?	
	Show awareness of own strengths and weaknesses?	
	Act as coach, questioning to encourage development through self-reflection?	
	Involve others' in planning, setting priorities for their own learning needs?	
	Clearly communicate the links between personal, team and organisational objectives?	
	Actively seek new or different ideas and opportunities for own and others' learning?	
	Adopt a mentoring approach, sharing skills, knowledge and ideas?	
	Encourage feedback and evidence from a wide range of sources to monitor progress against planned personal and organisational objectives?	
	Deal quickly with lack of ownership or responsibility for continuous development?	
	Encourage learning through benchmarking and support group working, within and outside the voluntary sector?	

IMPROVING SERVICE DELIVERY (Focusing energy toward achieving value for money and results)		CPD 360°
Competencies	Show energy and drive for results, creating a climate of performance delivery and accountability?	
	Plan and organise work and resources to deliver on time, within budget and with high quality standards?	
	Clearly communicate goals and expected outcomes?	
	Critically review ongoing work processes, analysing operational and other data, and benchmarks to inform decision-making?	
	Use models to manage risks, making timely changes to affect continuous improvement in delivery?	
	Energise others in timely sharing, and involvement in the need for changes?	
	Show and encourage a shared approach to problem solving?	
	Know processes and people, and makes best use of diverse strengths, technology and resources to deliver results?	

Trademark **CPD 360°**

SHARING KNOWLEDGE AND EXPERTISE (Developing understanding of, and influencing a wider knowledge base)		CPD 360°
Competencies	Have the ability to represent the charity showing in-depth knowledge and expertise?	
	Provide advice and guidance on professional and statutory or social issues?	
	Show understanding of the charity, and its decision-making processes, in the context of partner organisations?	
	Build wide contact networks with relevant individual's to maintain a high knowledge base?	
	Encourage, and bring cross-disciplinary knowledge to bear on issues and opportunities?	
	Build understanding of the changing environment?	
	Use expertise to add value to the work of other organisations?	
	Coach and develop others with less knowledge or expertise?	
	Show interest in identifying and sharing understanding of differences within the sector and between sectors	

Trademark **CPD 360°**

Business Psychology Wales Ltd
Windsor House
4 Llantrisant Road
Pontyclun
Rhondda Cynon Taff
S Wales
CF72 9DQ
Tel : 01443 230555
Fax : 01443 230666
Email consultants@bpwales.co.uk
www.bpwales.co.uk

Resources for Chapter 9 continued

Resources 9.6 Sample appraisal form based on competencies

Name: _____ Date _____

Name of appraiser completing this questionnaire _____

Section 1 – to be completed by the chief executive and each appraiser independently

Using the checklist or the prompt sheet as an aid, please complete this questionnaire, without allowing your personal views of the chief executive to impact on your professional, dispassionate and objective assessment of his/her performance. Whenever possible, give examples to illustrate your conclusions.

**COMMUNICATING PURPOSE AND DIRECTION
(Creating expectations and communicating vision)**

Observations and conclusions:

**HARNESSING INNOVATION AND STRATEGIC THINKING
(Capturing new ideas, analysing and solving complex problems)**

Observations and conclusions:

**MODELLING STANDARDS OF PERSONAL PERFORMANCE
(Setting the highest standards and principles of behaviours)**

Observations and conclusions:

CULTIVATES PARTNERSHIPS AND TEAM-WORKING
(Motivating and developing people and relationships toward the achievement of mutually beneficial goals)

Observations and conclusions:

LEARNING AND CONTINUOUS PERFORMANCE DEVELOPMENT
(Drawing on experience, new ideas and learning to improve results)

Observations and conclusions:

IMPROVING SERVICE DELIVERY
(Focusing money toward achieving value for money and results)

Observations and conclusions:

SHARING KNOWLEDGE AND EXPERTISE
(Developing understanding of and influencing a wider knowledge base)

Observations and conclusions:

Resources for Chapter 9 continued

Section 2 - To be completed by the chief executive prior to these forms going out.
Chief executive's goals/objectives/targets arising out of previous appraisal
1
2
3
4
5

Section 3 – To be completed at the end of the appraisal meeting **Goals/objectives/targets**
Chief executive's goals/objectives/targets for the next 12 months with indication of success criteria
1
2
3
4
5

Professional development plan for the next 12 months		
Type of support or training	Who will organise?	Approximate cost
1		
2		
3		

Role description
Modifications if any to the chief executive's role description

Actions to be taken by the appraisers or the chief executive		
Action	**By whom?**	**By when?**

Signature of chief executive _____ Date _____

Signature of lead appraiser _____ Date _____

Resources for Chapter 9 continued

Resource 9.7 Sample appraisal form based on chief executive's goals and agreed performance standards

Name: _____ Date _____

Name of appraiser completing this questionnaire _____

Section 1 – to be completed by the chief executive and each appraiser independently

Please complete this questionnaire without allowing your personal views of the chief executive to impact on your professional, dispassionate and objective assessment of his/her performance. Whenever possible, give examples to illustrate your conclusions. [Note the actual goals and standards for the last 12 months should be typed in prior to circulation]

Goal 1:

Agreed performance standard:

Observations and conclusions:

Goal 2:

Agreed performance standard:

Observations and conclusions:

Goal 3:

Agreed performance standard:

Observations and conclusions:

Goal 4:

Agreed performance standard:

Observations and conclusions:

Goal 5:

Agreed performance standard:

Observations and conclusions:

Goal 6:

Agreed performance standard:

Observations and conclusions:

Resources for Chapter 9 continued

Section 2 – To be completed at the end of the appraisal meeting **Goals/objectives/targets**
Chief executive's goals for the next 12 months with agreed performance standards
Goal 1: Agreed performance standard:
Goal 2: Agreed performance standard:
Goal 3: Agreed performance standard:
Goal 4: Agreed performance standard:
Goal 5: Agreed performance standard:
Goal 6: Agreed performance standard:

Professional development plan for the next 12 months		
Type of support or training	**Who will organise?**	**Approximate cost**
1.		
2.		
3.		

Role description
Modifications if any to the chief executive's role description

Actions to be taken by the appraisers or the chief executive		
Action	**By whom?**	**By when?**

Signature of chief executive _____ Date _____

Signature of lead appraiser _____ Date _____

Resources for Chapter 9 continued

Resource 9.8 Sample job description for a chief executive

This job description for a chief executive was written by, and is published here with the kind permission of, Simone P. Joyaux of Joyaux Associates, USA. Simone is a consultant in fund development, board and organisational development, management, and strategic planning. Her contact details are given at the end of this form.

Position Title: Chief Executive

Reports to: Board of Directors

Reporting to this position: Finance Director, Director of Services...........

Job Summary

The chief executive, in partnership with the board, is responsible for the success of ABC Organisation. Together, the board and chief executive assure ABC Organisation's relevance to the community, the accomplishment of ABC Organisation's mission and vision, and the accountability of ABC Organisation to its diverse stakeholders.

The board delegates responsibility for management and day-to-day operations to the chief executive, and s/he has the authority to carry out these responsibilities, in accordance with the direction and policies established by the board. The chief executive provides direction and enabling to the board as it carries out its governance functions.

Accountabilities

1. Legal compliance
a) Assures the filing of all legal and regulatory documents and monitors compliance with relevant laws and regulations.

2. Mission, policy and planning
a) Helps the board determine ABC's values, mission, vision, and short- and long-term goals.

b) Helps the board monitor and evaluate ABC's relevancy to its beneficiaries, its effectiveness, and its results.

c) Keeps the board fully informed on the condition of ABC and on all the important factors influencing it.
  - Identifies problems and opportunities and addresses them; brings those which are appropriate to the board and/or its committees; and, facilitates discussion and deliberation.
  - Informs the board and its committees about trends, issues, problems and activities in order to facilitate policy-making. Recommends policy positions.

d) Keeps informed of developments in human services, not-for-profit management and governance and income generation.

3. Management and administration

a) Provides general oversight of all ABC activities, manages the day-to-day operations, and assures a smoothly functioning, efficient organisation.

b) Assures programme quality and organisational stability through development and implementation of standards and controls, systems and procedures, and regular evaluation.

c) Assures a work environment that recruits, retains and supports quality staff and volunteers. Assures process for selecting, development, motivating, and evaluating staff and volunteers.

d) Recommends staffing and financing to the board. In accordance with the board's policies and delegate authority, recruits personnel, negotiates professional contracts, and sees that appropriate salary structures are developed and maintained.

e) Specifies accountabilities for management (whether paid or volunteer) and evaluates performance regularly.

4. Governance

a) Helps the board articulate its own role and accountabilities and that of its committees and individual members, and helps evaluate performance regularly.

b) Works with the chair of trustees to enable the board to fulfil its governance functions and facilitates the optimum performance by the board, its committees and individual board members.

c) With the chair of trustees, focuses board attention on long-range strategic issues.

d) Manages the board's due diligence process to assure timely attention to core issues.

e) Works with the honorary officers and committee chairs to get the best thinking and involvement of each board member and to stimulate each board member to give of his or her best.

f) Recommends volunteers to participate on the board and its committees.

5. Financing

a) Promotes programmes, projects and services that are produced in a cost-effective manner, employing economy while maintaining an acceptable level of quality.

b) Oversees the fiscal activities of the organisation including budgeting, reporting and audit.

c) Works with the board to ensure financing to support short- and long-term goals.

d) Assures an effective income generating programme.

Resources for Chapter 9 continued

6. Community relations

a) Facilitates the integration of ABC into the fabric of the local and wider community by using effective marketing and communications activities.

b) Acts as an advocate, within the public and private sectors, for issues relevant to ABC, its services and constituencies.

c) Listens to stakeholders, especially beneficiaries in order to improve services.

d) Serves as chief spokesperson for ABC, assuring proper representation of ABC to the local and wider communities.

e) Initiates, develops, and maintains cooperative relationships with key stakeholder groups.

f) Works with members of parliament, civil servants, regulatory agencies, volunteers and representatives of the not-for-profit sector to promote legislative and regulatory policies that encourage and address the issues of relevance to ABC's work.

© Simone P. Joyaux, ACFRE
Joyaux Associates, USA
Consultant in fund development, board and organizational development, management, and strategic planning
www.simonejoyaux.com • spjoyaux@aol.com

Resource 9.9 Appraisal form based on sample job description

This performance appraisal form for a chief executive is based on the chief executive's job description (see Appendix .. and was written by, and published here with the kind permission of, Simone P. Joyaux of Joyaux Associates, USA. Simone is a consultant in fund development, board and organisational development, management, and strategic planning. Her contact details are given at the end of this form.

CE Name: _____ Date Hired: _____

Current evaluation period: _____

Please check one:

Response from individual Board member

☐ (Your name: _____ Date _____)

☐ Tabulated survey results from responding Board members   (for use by Appraisal Committee)

---

1. Mission, policy and planning

1.1 Ensures that the charity has a short- and long long-range strategy that achieves mission, and toward which the organisation makes consistent and timely progress.

☐ Needs much improvement   ☐ Needs slight improvement   ☐ Meets expectations   ☐ Exceeds expectations   ☐ Evaluator has no experience

Specific examples to support rating:

1.2 Provides leadership in developing business/corporate/annual plans with the board of trustees.

☐ Needs much improvement   ☐ Needs slight improvement   ☐ Meets expectations   ☐ Exceeds expectations   ☐ Evaluator has no experience

Specific examples to support rating:

Resources for Chapter 9 continued

1.3 Develops projects, programmes and services that are produced in a cost-effective manner, employing economy while maintaining quality.

☐ Needs much improvement ☐ Needs slight improvement ☐ Meets expectations ☐ Exceeds expectations ☐ Evaluator has no experience

Specific examples to support rating:

1.4 Evaluates programme relevancy, quality and effectiveness.

☐ Needs much improvement ☐ Needs slight improvement ☐ Meets expectations ☐ Exceeds expectations ☐ Evaluator has no experience

Specific examples to support rating:

---

2. Management and administration

2.1 Maintains a climate that attracts, keeps, and motivates a diverse group of top quality staff and volunteers. Recognizes and rewards staff and volunteers.

☐ Needs much improvement ☐ Needs slight improvement ☐ Meets expectations ☐ Exceeds expectations ☐ Evaluator has no experience

Specific examples to support rating:

2.2 Ensures that role descriptions for volunteers and staff are developed, and that regular performance evaluations are conducted and documented.

☐ Needs much improvement ☐ Needs slight improvement ☐ Meets expectations ☐ Exceeds expectations ☐ Evaluator has no experience

Specific examples to support rating:

Trustees CEO Chairs

2.3 Divides and assigns work effectively to staff and volunteers, delegating appropriate levels of freedom and authority, while maintaining adequate supervision and support.

☐ Needs much improvement ☐ Needs slight improvement ☐ Meets expectations ☐ Exceeds expectations ☐ Evaluator has no experience

Specific examples to support rating:

2.4 Ensures compliance with personnel policies and, legal and regulatory compliance on workplaces and employment.

☐ Needs much improvement ☐ Needs slight improvement ☐ Meets expectations ☐ Exceeds expectations ☐ Evaluator has no experience

Specific examples to support rating:

2.5 Provides a learning environment. Guides staff and volunteer development and training.

☐ Needs much improvement ☐ Needs slight improvement ☐ Meets expectations ☐ Exceeds expectations ☐ Evaluator has no experience

Specific examples to support rating:

2.6 Tactfully handles people-problems. Encourages a cooperative spirit and teamwork. Works well with others.

☐ Needs much improvement ☐ Needs slight improvement ☐ Meets expectations ☐ Exceeds expectations ☐ Evaluator has no experience

Specific examples to support rating:

Resources for Chapter 9 continued

---

3. Governance:

3.1 Works effectively with the board, honorary officers, committees, committee chairs and task forces.

☐ Needs much improvement   ☐ Needs slight improvement   ☐ Meets expectations   ☐ Exceeds expectations   ☐ Evaluator has no experience

Specific examples to support rating:

3.2 Provides appropriate, adequate, and timely information to the board, its officers, committees and task forces.

☐ Needs much improvement   ☐ Needs slight improvement   ☐ Meets expectations   ☐ Exceeds expectations   ☐ Evaluator has no experience

Specific examples to support rating:

3.3 Recommends and drafts policies to the board for review and action. Assures compliance.

☐ Needs much improvement   ☐ Needs slight improvement   ☐ Meets expectations   ☐ Exceeds expectations   ☐ Evaluator has no experience

Specific examples to support rating:

3.4 Effectively frames significant questions and complex issues in ways that facilitate board dialogue and action.

☐ Needs much improvement   ☐ Needs slight improvement   ☐ Meets expectations   ☐ Exceeds expectations   ☐ Evaluator has no experience

Specific examples to support rating:

3.5 Effectively communicates – orally and in writing – with the charity's diverse stakeholders.

☐ Needs much improvement   ☐ Needs slight improvement   ☐ Meets expectations   ☐ Exceeds expectations   ☐ Evaluator has no experience

Specific examples to support rating:

---

4. Leadership

4.1 Demonstrates initiative and creativity in identifying and addressing strategic issues facing the charity. Effectively manages continuity, change and transition.

☐ Needs much improvement   ☐ Needs slight improvement   ☐ Meets expectations   ☐ Exceeds expectations   ☐ Evaluator has no experience

Specific examples to support rating:

4.2 Bases plans and initiatives on thorough analysis of relevant facts. Sets and achieves clear and measurable goals and reasonable deadlines. Schedules work for the most efficient handling and elimination of unnecessary activities.

☐ Needs much improvement   ☐ Needs slight improvement   ☐ Meets expectations   ☐ Exceeds expectations   ☐ Evaluator has no experience

Specific examples to support rating:

4.3 Makes quality decisions in a timely manner and accepts responsibility for outcomes. Effectively solves problems.

☐ Needs much improvement   ☐ Needs slight improvement   ☐ Meets expectations   ☐ Exceeds expectations   ☐ Evaluator has no experience

Specific examples to support rating:

Resources for Chapter 9 continued

4.4 Provides information and recommendations regarding risk management to the board.

☐ Needs much improvement ☐ Needs slight improvement ☐ Meets expectations ☐ Exceeds expectations ☐ Evaluator has no experience

Specific examples to support rating:

4.5 Ensures development and implementation of realistic and ambitious income generating goals and plans to secure adequate funds to permit the charity to carry out its work.

☐ Needs much improvement ☐ Needs slight improvement ☐ Meets expectations ☐ Exceeds expectations ☐ Evaluator has no experience

Specific examples to support rating:

5. Stakeholder relations, marketing and communications

5.1 Serves as an effective spokesperson for the charity. Represents the work of the charity and its point of view to key constituencies including beneficiaries, government, donors and potential funders.

☐ Needs much improvement ☐ Needs slight improvement ☐ Meets expectations ☐ Exceeds expectations ☐ Evaluator has no experience

Specific examples to support rating:

5.2 Assures that sound working relationships are established and maintained with the charity's diverse stakeholders and participates in this important work.

☐ Needs much improvement ☐ Needs slight improvement ☐ Meets expectations ☐ Exceeds expectations ☐ Evaluator has no experience

Specific examples to support rating:

5.3 Effectively communicates – orally and in writing – with the charity's diverse stakeholders.

☐ Needs much improvement ☐ Needs slight improvement ☐ Meets expectations ☐ Exceeds expectations ☐ Evaluator has no experience

Specific examples to support rating:

6. Leadership

6.1 Demonstrates initiative and creativity in identifying and addressing strategic issues facing the charity. Effectively manages continuity, change and transition.

☐ Needs much improvement ☐ Needs slight improvement ☐ Meets expectations ☐ Exceeds expectations ☐ Evaluator has no experience

Specific examples to support rating:

6.2 Bases plans and initiatives on thorough analysis of relevant facts. Sets and achieves clear and measurable goals and reasonable deadlines. Schedules work for the most efficient handling and elimination of unnecessary activities.

☐ Needs much improvement ☐ Needs slight improvement ☐ Meets expectations ☐ Exceeds expectations ☐ Evaluator has no experience

Specific examples to support rating:

6.3 Makes quality decisions in a timely manner and accepts responsibility for outcomes. Effectively solves problems.

☐ Needs much improvement ☐ Needs slight improvement ☐ Meets expectations ☐ Exceeds expectations ☐ Evaluator has no experience

Specific examples to support rating:

Resources for Chapter 9 continued

6.4 Ensures high quality in all areas of operation including service delivery.

☐ Needs much improvement ☐ Needs slight improvement ☐ Meets expectations ☐ Exceeds expectations ☐ Evaluator has no experience

Specific examples to support rating:

6.5 Demonstrates proficiency in not-for-profit management and governance. Keeps abreast of developments in fundraising and income generation of all kinds and in the charity's field of work.

☐ Needs much improvement ☐ Needs slight improvement ☐ Meets expectations ☐ Exceeds expectations ☐ Evaluator has no experience

Specific examples to support rating:

6.6 Deals effectively with demanding situations and designs and implements actions.

☐ Needs much improvement ☐ Needs slight improvement ☐ Meets expectations ☐ Exceeds expectations ☐ Evaluator has no experience

Specific examples to support rating:

6.7 Consistently displays integrity and models the charity's values.

☐ Needs much improvement ☐ Needs slight improvement ☐ Meets expectations ☐ Exceeds expectations ☐ Evaluator has no experience

Specific examples to support rating:

Trustees CEO Chairs

7. Any other comments ?

© Simone P. Joyaux, ACFRE, Joyaux Associates, USA
Consultant in fund development, board and organisational development, management, and strategic planning
www.simonejoyaux.com spjoyaux@aol.com

Chapter 10
Recruiting a chief executive

10.1 | Introduction

One of the most crucial tasks carried out by a board of trustees is the identification, recruitment and induction of a new chief executive. Find the right person to lead and run the charity, and the positive impact on the charity and its work is huge. Get the wrong person and the negative impact on the whole organisation will be felt for years.

Yet it is not uncommon to see this crucial appointment poorly handled. Boards rush into placing advertisements and interviewing candidates before really considering what the charity is hoping to achieve in the long term and what sort of person it needs to get the charity there. Many boards fail to consider what their fundamental values, ethos and philosophy are. Nor do they seek to verify whether the shortlisted candidates share these. Problems subsequently arise when the new man or woman assumes a completely different set of values.

Giving time to prepare for the recruitment of a chief executive is essential and is time well spent. Boards also need to appreciate that the whole process of finding a new chief executive will take a great deal of energy and commitment by both the board, and doubly so, by members of the search committee. Because of their commitment, candidates from the voluntary sector usually want to work their full notice period and often want to get a short break before taking up a new appointment. As a result, the recruitment process can take anywhere between 6–12 months, and sometimes even longer, before the new chief executive is in post.

The recruitment process will be stressful at times, especially as most trustees also have challenging 'day' jobs, but it should be seen also as a time for positively promoting the charity. The whole process should be one that not only stretches the final shortlisted candidates (and the search committee!) but also one that woos the candidates. They are selecting you as much as you are selecting them.

There is no one process for chief executive recruitment that is best for all charities. Each charity needs to work out which process best matches its values and its needs.

10.2 | Agreement on broad strategic objectives

The basics

Every new chief executive will have ideas of his/her own as to where he/she would like to take the charity. Nevertheless it is important for trustees to consider and agree the general direction in which they want the charity to go. For example, if the charity has decided to extend its current adult services to children, the charity may need a chief executive who has experience of delivering services to children. Or if a charity plans to expand by merging or acquiring other charities, then the board may wish to appoint someone who has experience of mergers and acquisitions. Or if a charity intends to go into the delivery of public services, the next chief executive may need to be someone who has experience of either delivering or commissioning public services.

It is also worthwhile spending time considering the major challenges and risks that the charity is facing currently and those which it is likely to face in the future. The board will then have a much better picture of the sort of person it needs to lead the charity into the next decade and will be able to probe, by the questions they ask shortlisted candidates, how each candidate will deal with these challenges if he or she is appointed. Risk management is an essential part of the role of the chief executive and of the board.

It is not uncommon for boards of some medium-sized charities that are having difficulty generating income, to define fundraising as a significant part of the chief executive's role description and the person specification. This is usually a mistake. There is significantly more to a chief executive's role and he or she will not have time to run the fundraising function in addition to these duties except in very exceptional circumstances and then only on a shortterm basis. Chief executives expect to front meetings with potential major donors, to head up major appeals and to manage the director of fundraising but not to take responsibility for the day-to-day running of the fundraising function. Although not involved in the daily work of the fundraising department, the chief executive must always be fully aware of the need to bring in income and to be the driving force behind all the major departments including fundraising and income generation.

10.3 | Agreement on the charity's ethos, values and philosophy

There are many things that those of us who are involved in a charity take for granted: its ethos, values and philosophy. What makes your charity special and what are your fundamental values with which the new chief executive must be in agreement? We all think we know what the charity's ethos, values and philosophy are, but do all the trustees agree and do their assumptions coincide with those who work at the charity? Differing and strongly held views can be assumed and these views need to be aired, discussed and agreement reached. The senior management team under the current chief executive's guidance can start the process by trying to define succinctly the charity's ethos, values and philosophy, and can bring these to the board for discussion and approval.

The board or the search committee will need to decide how they test whether longlisted candidates' personal values and philosophy are compatible to those of the charity.

10.4 | Other initial considerations

The board will need to consider whether it will carry out the recruitment process in-house or whether it will engage a recruitment consultant or obtain some other form of external assistance. Will the hunt for the new chief executive be by advertisement only or by search as well? If the board undertakes the recruitment in-house, can they carry out a search themselves using all the contacts that they have in their sector and elsewhere? If they decide to use recruitment consultants, which one will best fulfil their needs?

Whatever you decide to do, who will drive the process? Will it be the whole board or will the board appoint a search committee? If the latter, who will chair the search committee and who will be on it? Will the whole board be involved at some stage and, if so, at what stage?

You need to consider very carefully whether or not internal candidates should be allowed to apply. Being an internal candidate can be an advantage as he or she has significantly greater insider knowledge. Or it can be a disadvantage as the search committee will be more aware of the internal candidate's weaknesses. Many boards feel, for internal political reasons, that internal candidates should be shortlisted for interview. This is a mistake. All shortlisted candidates should be there on merit only. If internal candidates do apply and are unsuccessful, it is vitally important that the chair of trustees, or the chair of the search committee, tells them that they are hugely valued in their current role and explains why they do not as yet have sufficient experience, expertise or skills for the post of chief executive.

All these questions and many more will need to be considered by the board. Finding time during a routine board meeting to consider the broad strategic objectives, the charity's ethos, values and philosophy and to give due consideration to the myriad of other related questions is nigh impossible if you want to give the issues sufficient and careful consideration. It is therefore strongly recommended that the trustee board have an additional meeting or take a half-day out to discuss issues solely relating to the recruitment of the next chief executive. Consideration will need to be given as to how, when and if you involve the current chief executive, the senior management team, other staff and/or other stakeholders in these discussions.

10.5 | Search committees

Fairly early in the process, the board will need to set up a search committee to supervise, plan and carry out the selection process. This might be the whole board but is more likely not to be. The search process will be time-consuming and it is essential that every member of the search committee is aware of and prepared to commit to the time that is needed. Every member will need to be present and actively involved in all aspects of the recruitment process. If they anticipate any difficulty with attendance or with involving themselves fully, they should not be included.

This is particularly important for the chair of the search committee as this role is especially demanding. He or she will be responsible for the week-to-week oversight of the recruitment process and acting as liaison between the board and the search committee. The chair of the search committee will also need to keep very closely in touch with the chair of trustees, if they are not one and the same person. The success of the process will depend to a large extent on the level of trust the board has in the chair of the search committee as the process unfolds.

The search committee must be reasonably small – ideally three and not more than six people. If you have too many people on a search committee there is a strong likelihood that not all members of the committee will be able to attend on all dates and the search committee will be unable to take a consistent approach through each stage of the selection process. You may wish to bring onto the search committee an independent professional adviser and/or representatives of other constituent groups (for example chair of regional committee, chair of the youth council, user representative).

Ideally each member of the search committee should bring relevant skills and experience to the search committee; must be able to approach the task objectively, professionally and in complete confidence; and must also be able to positively promote the charity to all those who apply. While the search committee must 'sell' the organisation to the candidates, they must also be honest, especially at the final interview stage, about the challenges facing the charity and its next chief executive.

10.6 | The search committee's remit

Having discussed and agreed the charity's values, ethos, philosophy, broad strategic priorities, key future risks, etc, the board needs to agree the remit of the search committee and the parameters within which the search committee must work. Listed below are some of the tasks that may be included in the search committee's remit (note: The board may prefer to reserve some of these to the board):

- keeping the board and especially the chair of trustees, if he/she is not on the search committee, informed of progress
- selecting, engaging, briefing, liaising and supervising the recruitment consultants, if they are being used, and agreeing the level of their services and their fee. See Resource 10.2
- deciding the outline remuneration package and main terms and conditions of the new chief executive's contract
- producing the person specification, job description and candidate information pack with the help of others such as the current chief executive or the recruitment consultant
- agreeing, in consultation with the board, the outline timetable for the process and the detailed project plan with the recruitment consultant if one is being used, and ensuring that this timetable is complied with
- deciding on the level of involvement of the search committee in long-listing and shortlisting if engaging a recruitment consultant
- deciding on the process to reduce the longlist to the shortlist (eg by interview only or a more detailed process, carried out by headhunter or search committee)
- deciding on the level of involvement of the current chief executive, the senior management team and other stakeholders
- deciding whether or not to use an independent external adviser
- agreeing the method for making the final selection from the shortlist, including at which stages the whole board will be involved, and carrying through this process
- deciding the timing of taking up references. Taking up references of shortlisted candidates or the final candidate in writing and by telephone or face-to-face. Carrying out all relevant checks including identity and qualification checks, CRB (if necessary) and medical checks on the chosen candidate after the offer is made
- informing the unsuccessful shortlisted candidates and providing them with feedback. [This is sometimes delegated to the recruitment consultant]
- thanking referees and those who nominated candidates during the search process
- negotiating the remuneration package and main terms and conditions of employment with the successful candidate (this is often done through the recruitment consultant)
- planning the timetable for announcing the new appointment both internally and externally
- organising, in partnership with the chair of trustees, induction, support, arrangements for the review of performance towards the end of the probationary period and arrangements for the ongoing appraisal of the chief executive
- outline planning of events to mark the achievements of the outgoing chief executive and expressing the charity's appreciation of his/her contribution.

The remit of the search committee should be sufficiently specific to ensure that the search committee takes the process in the right direction and sufficiently flexible to allow the search committee some creativity and extemporisation.

10.7 | The role of the chair of the search committee

Much is asked of the chair of the search committee, who not only has to provide weekly supervision of the whole recruitment process but also has to serve as a liaison between his/her fellow board members, especially the chair, and the search committee. Maintaining the trust and confidence of the board is a crucial part of his/her role. Frequent reports on progress to the board will be need, providing sufficient detail to show that the search programme is on schedule but nevertheless protecting confidentiality.

The chair of the search committee needs to be assisted by very committed search committee members and by sufficient secretarial and administrative support. Although being on a search committee is a very demanding role, it is also an enormously rewarding and enjoyable task. Certainly the search committee will deserve a celebratory lunch at the end of the recruitment process as a way of saying 'thank you' for all their hard work.

10.8 | Headhunters and recruitment consultants

Unless there are trustees on your board who are experienced in recruiting senior executives, ideally in the voluntary sector, and who can give the process significant amounts of their time, serious consideration should be given to using recruitment consultants or headhunters. There are enormous benefits in using recruitment consultants but lessening the search committee's workload is not one of them. The recruitment process will ask many hours of the members of the search committee and especially of its chair.

If you decide to get professional help with the recruitment process, it is worth doing some research by consulting other chairs of trustees who have recently used recruitment consultants. Not only will they be able to tell you how they rate the recruitment consultants they used but also give you some advice based on their own experiences. You should then draw up of a shortlist of two or three recruitment consultants, who should be invited to 'pitch' for the work.

Check that the person doing the presentation is actually going to be responsible for your recruitment. If he or she is not, make sure you meet the person who is. Try to gauge what proportion of time the lead person will spend on your assignment. Some of the larger headhunters will delegate most of the work to researchers. I would recommend someone who will take quite a personal interest in finding the right chief executive for you.

Once you have decided on your first choice, ask for and take up references ideally by telephone. See Resource 10.1 for a list of recruitment consultants and headhunters who work in the not-for-profit sector and Resource 10.2 for sample questions to put to recruitment consultants.

You will also need to decide whether you are going to recruit by advertising and by search or by advertising only or search only. Good practice, especially from an anti-discriminatory basis basis, requires that the post is advertised unless there are very exceptional circumstances why this cannot happen.

You would, of course, already have discussed the fees that your recruitment consultant will charge. Some recruitment consultants work mainly in the non-profit sector while others have strong specialisms in both the private and non-profit sectors. Generally fees charged by those who work mainly in the voluntary sector are lower than those who have a large proportion of their work in the private sector or who work for major government departments. The former can charge in the region of 25% to 30% of the first year's remuneration package or of the first year's salary. It is important to check which it is as it can make a significant difference to the final invoice. While the latter may charge in the region of 33%, some headhunters such will have a minimum fee and, if it is helpful to the client, will work for a fixed fee.

Most boards of trustees assume that because the organisation is a charity they will be able to negotiate a substantial reduction in fees. A few recruitment consultants do offer a reduction or discount but most do not, unless there is a very special reason for doing so. For example, if one of your trustees is a headhunter and persuades her firm to do the work on a reduced rate (care should be taken to check that your governing instruments allow you to pay trustees or trustees' businesses for non-trustee services) or if the charity has been a longstanding client of the headhunter.

There will be other charges in addition to the agreed fee – for example, the cost of advertising. Most if not all recruitment consultants have negotiated a specially reduced rate for advertising in newspapers (charges for advertising on the web tend to be fixed) because of the volume of business that they do with the newspapers and so you will pay less than you would if you placed advertisements directly in the same newspapers.

Once appointed, most good headhunters will want to talk to several of the trustees, especially the chair, and members of the senior management team, including the current chief executive. They will help you to assess what the organisation needs, what you are hoping to achieve and the person you need to get you there. However, a well-prepared board may have gone through this process already. Nevertheless, it is essential that the recruitment consultant has a real understanding of where the organisation is going, what challenges are likely to face the next chief executive and what sort of person is needed to lead the charity into the next decade.

You will also need to discuss whether the search committee will be involved in the longlisting or whether you will delegate this task to the headhunter. It is time-consuming but I prefer to see all applications after they have been graded by the headhunters. The search committee then meets to discuss the candidates and if necessary to regrade them and finally to produce the longlist. At this stage the headhunter will carry out one-to-one interviews with each person on the longlist or the search committee may decide to carry out the interviews instead. The headhunter should also check the authenticity of each longlisted candidate's CV, including qualifications and should probe the authenticity of the various achievements claimed by the candidate. If at the longlisting stage you discover you have at most six strong candidates, you will probably want to go straight to the shortlisting stage.

You will have to decide whether you are happy to agree the final shortlist by solely using the recommendations of the headhunter or whether the search group will make the decision after they have had feedback from the headhunter or by the interviews carried out by the search committee. Remember if the chair of trustees is not on the search committee it is vitally important to keep the chair fully informed at these critical stages.

If you do not wish to use a recruitment consultant to see you through the whole process, you may wish to use a consultant to assist you during some of the stages – for example, to take you through the key first phase of the planning and preparation.

10.9 | Independent professional advisers or assessors

Increasingly, whether or not a recruitment consultant has been engaged, charity boards are using an independent professional adviser either for the final interviews or as a full member of the search committee.

An external member of the search panel can:
- ensure that a dispassionate, objective outsider's view is brought to the decision-making
- where appropriate, be more challenging in their questioning of both the candidates and the other members of the search committee
- ask some of the questions that trustees would like to ask but feel they cannot because they might have to work with that candidate in the future
- probe possible areas of weakness
- more easily investigate the validity of claims made by applicants
- ensure that good practice and legal requirements are followed
- advise the panel against asking inappropriate questions
- ensure fairness
- advise trustees against appointing someone when none of the candidates are suitable.

If you decide to use an independent adviser, try to make it clear how much time you are asking of them, exactly what their remit is and, whether or not you are offering a fee.

A good independent assessor will want to spend at least a couple of hours on a one-to-one basis being briefed by the chair of the search committee and will need to be given a full information pack as well as details of relevant candidates.

10.10 | Developing a search timetable

Not only is the recruitment process much more time-consuming than can be expected but the length of time needed to carry out a thorough procedure for this crucial post will be normally longer than the board's initial expectations. The timetable can be shortened but there are risks attached to doing so. It is better to plan for an interim period after the current chief executive leaves rather than rush the whole process to ensure that there is a direct transfer from one chief executive to another. A typical time frame may be:

Week 1	Board meet to agree: • broad strategic objectives • the charity's ethos, values and philosophy • outline person specification • other initial considerations (eg budget for search process, • level of use of external help, level of involvement of whole board) • membership of search committee and appoint chair • remit of search committee
Week 3	Search committee meet to: • agree plan of action and outline process • plan timetable: members commit to attending at each stage • agree role description, person specification, where and how • the post is to be advertised, wording of advertisements, information pack for candidates, level of external assistance e.g. headhunters, consultant for early stages and/ or independent assessor • prepare draft contract for successful candidate
Week 6	• Headhunters are interviewed, selected and terms agreed • other external help identified and briefed • search phase begins
Week 8	• Information pack finalised and ready to be printed • advertisement goes to press
Week 9 & 10	• Advertisements appear
Week 13	• Closing date • applications acknowledged
Week 15	• First screening • longlist agreed
Week 17	• Longlist interviews begin • agree draft of contract of employment
Week 19	• Second screening • shortlist agreed • start taking up references and carrying out other checks
Week 22	• Third and final screening of shortlisted candidates • selection of new chief executive, including obtaining approval/endorsement by whole board • verbal offer of post • other candidates informed and unsuccessful candidates debriefed

10.10 | Developing a search timetable continued

Week 23	• Agree terms and conditions • offer the post in writing and wait for written acceptance • announce appointment internally • announce appointment externally
Week 24	• Thank referees and everyone who assisted in the process
Week 25	Meeting to • review the process and record lessons learned for the next • time a chief executive is appointed • plan induction, handover, first-year objectives, first year • review and ongoing appraisal • draw up outline plan of events to say farewell to outgoing chief executive
Week 36 or later	• New chief executive takes up appointment

Sometimes the order of each stage is different to the timetable above. For example, some boards appoint headhunters much earlier on and use them to assist the board and the search committee to cover the stages given in weeks 1 and 3 above. It is important to evolve the process and time-frame that is right for your charity, bearing in mind that a rushed process is unlikely to identify the best candidate and could leave an unfavourable impression on other applicants. However smoothly the recruitment process runs, there is no guarantee that a successful appointment will be made.

Communications and confidentiality

Communications

We have already discussed the importance of the board, and especially the chair of trustees, being kept informed throughout the recruitment process by the search committee. This is to ensure that the search committee retains the confidence and trust of the board and so that the board feels involved in the decisions that are being made by the search committee, within the board's agreed framework and with the board's delegated authority.

There are other stakeholders, such as staff and major funders, who may also need to be kept informed as to how the search is proceeding. A method of communicating with them, while still honouring the confidentiality of the applicants, needs to be given some consideration. First decide who needs to be kept informed then decide how this is to be done and at which stages during the process updates will be given. Some forward-thinking boards use their website to keep a wide range of stakeholders informed about the search process. Others send out regular newsletters and some have regular briefing sessions with staff.

What should be communicated if confidentiality of applicants needs to be respected? Some boards feel that the whole process needs to be shrouded in mystery. This is quite unnecessary. It is better to provide information willingly that stakeholders can easily, but surreptitiously, obtain by posing as possible applicants. If a search committee is to be appointed, let interested people know who will be on the search committee, what the committee's remit is, which headhunter, if any, has been appointed and what the planned timetable for the process is. The information pack including the person specification and role description should be made available on the charity's website. Putting all this information on the web probably makes communicating to wide audience easier but does not negate the need for some groups of stakeholders to hear the news straight from the chair of trustees, or in the case of staff, possibly from the chief executive.

Throughout this process the board and search committee should be sensitive to the feelings of the incumbent chief executive. As soon as a chief executive announces he or she is leaving an organisation, his or her sphere of influence diminishes virtually overnight as the board, staff and others immediately start wondering how things might be under a new chief executive and delay plans for the future until the new chief executive is in post. This is particularly noticeable if the outgoing chief executive has been there some time. Power and influence shift from the chief executive to the board, who until then may have been very dependent on the chief executive but who now feel very much in control. It is important to keep the chief executive part of the communication loop. Indeed, he or she should be the first to be briefed by the chair of trustees after the board has been brought up-to-date by the search committee. Do not rely on your recruitment consultant to keep the chief executive fully briefed. This is the task of the chair of trustees.

How the charity communicates with all applicants is a vital part of promoting your charity to a wide audience, who may later move into positions of influence. Enquiries about the post should be dealt with in a cheerful, helpful and informed manner. All applications should be acknowledged and the letter of acknowledgement should include information giving the dates by which key decisions will be made. This should be done even though it means repeating information available to all applicants. Unsuccessful candidates should be informed that they have not been long or shortlisted. Unsuccessful shortlisted candidates need to be debriefed by the chair of the search committee or by the recruitment consultant.

All referees should be thanked for providing references. Key people and groups of people need to hear about who has been appointed directly from the charity and not by an announcement in the voluntary sector or national press or on the charity's website. Remember this is a time for promoting a very positive image of your charity.

10.11 | Communications and confidentiality continued

Confidentiality

Throughout the process, the search committee, the board and anyone involved directly or indirectly with the search process must maintain the highest levels of confidentiality as to who has applied, who has been longlisted and who has been shortlisted. If the applications are being received by headhunters, the likelihood of information leaking is less than if the applications are being received by a member of the charity staff, such as the company secretary or the chief executive's secretary. If the applications are going directly to the charity, it is important to ensure that no one but the person charged with administering the applications catches sight, accidentally or otherwise, of any of the applications.

Search committee members should be particularly careful about maintaining confidentiality. It is not unknown for search committee members to get so excited about the high quality of applicants that they are tempted to boast about it.

At some stage before the final selection process, the shortlisted candidates will need to visit the charity's main offices and have the opportunity to meet various members of staff. All staff or trustees involved in showing the final candidates round, or in informal interviews with the candidates, should deal with the matter discretely and professionally. If their views are sought, these should be passed solely through the appropriate channels and not bandied around the office or elsewhere. Staff should be told that the visitors are on a fact-finding visit. This is particularly important if any of the shortlisted candidates have come through on the search process and have not applied for the post.

Consideration needs to be given as to whether the final shortlisted candidates are to be kept very carefully apart, whether they are to be invited to arrive at the same time or whether part of the final selection procedure will be a group discussion or a group exercise. The last option is uncommon as search candidates are unlikely to agree to participate in group discussions.

Candidates should be informed in advance when references are to be taken up, especially if their current employer is to be approached.

Breaches in confidentiality can cause embarrassment and has, in some cases, led to the withdrawal of some excellent candidates.

Trustees   CEO   Chairs

10.12 | Job description, person specification and information for candidates

Having completed the initial work of articulating the charity's broad, strategic objectives, its values, ethos and philosophy and the major risks that the charity may face in the years to come, the board or search committee now has a good understanding of what it is looking for and is in a position to agree a person specification and job description.

Job description

Rather than reinventing the wheel, one can adapt and tap into the best of various chief executive job descriptions that are readily available but all will need to be adapted to the particular needs of your charity at its present stage of development.

Your research for this task will probably start with your current chief executive's job description, followed by a look at job descriptions for chief executive that you have obtained from other charities and model job descriptions. Model descriptions can be found in Resource 3.1 and Resource 9.8. ACEVO (the Association of Chief Executives of Voluntary Organisations) produces a model job description which can be found on their website at http://www.acevo.org.uk/page.aspx?pid=1932. (See also useful contacts in Further Resources and Information section)

The key responsibilities of a chief executive are likely to include:
- advising and assisting the board to decide the strategic priorities and high-level board policies
- leading, directing and driving the organisation towards its strategic objectives
- managing the affairs of the organisation within the strategic, policy and reporting frameworks specified by the board and upholding its values, ethos and philosophy
- promoting the organisation both externally and internally
- managing either directly or indirectly all employees and volunteers, and ensuring that performance management systems for the staff, and for the organisation as a whole, are in place and being applied
- providing the board with accurate and honest feedback on the performance of the charity and the risks that it might be facing
- managing risk
- ensuring regulatory and legal compliance, and that there are proper systems of delegation and clearly defined limits of delegated authority
- assisting the chair to ensure that the board fulfils its responsibilities
- ensuring that the board receives timely advice and appropriate information on all relevant matters
- ensuring that matters requiring the attention of the board are brought to the board and are given proper consideration
- ensuring the proper management of all the charity's assets, tangible and intangible.

10.12 | Role description, person specification and information for candidates continued

Person specification

There is often a tendency to seek someone who can walk on water or someone who is a clone of the current, exceptionally successful chief executive; or to look for someone whose strengths are in the areas that coincide with the present chief executive's weaknesses. A person specification should evolve from the initial discussions about where the charity hopes to go, current major risks facing the charity and a methodical analysis of the qualifications, skills, expertise, experience and personal attributes that will be needed.

When the initial wish list is produced, it will almost certainly need to be pared down considerably and careful thought will need to be given as to which attributes are essential and which are desirable. You want someone who is talented in the essential aspects of the role but who may lack experience of some of the other less important skills and experience. For example, does the chief executive need to have a degree? Does the chief executive need to have experience of bringing about extensive change when you are looking for someone to consolidate after a period of rapid change or expansion? Does the chief executive need to have experience of running another organisation? Does the chief executive need to have previous experience of advising boards on strategy and implementing the board's strategic priorities? Does the chief executive need to have previous experience of working with the media or can you provide training? Does the chief executive need to be an accomplished communicator? Does the chief executive have to be an inspiring leader?..............

As part of your preparation for writing the person specification, you may wish to do some research on **chief executive competencies**. See Resource 10.5.

A possible structure for a person specification is:
- educational qualifications (For example, this section might purely ask for 'Evidence of significant and continuing professional development')
- relevant experience
- personal qualities
- knowledge and skills.

Do not forget to make clear which attributes are essential and which desirable.

The decisions you make about the person specification are crucial to the recruitment process and will need to be used as the basis of each stage of the screening process, so great care should be taken with its preparation.

The information pack

Remember the recruitment process is an opportunity to positively promote your organisation. Potential applicants' view of your charity will be influenced by the way in which their enquiries are handled.

Most charities now put all the information on the charity's website. If you prefer to provide a hard copy, remember that if at all possible, it is better to provide all the information that is needed in one bound issue rather than lots of loose bits of paper. If you cannot, or do not wish, to bind the information, then place it in an attractive folder but take care not include badly photocopied bits of paper, however overwhelmed you are with enquiries.

The information provided needs to include:
- a copy of the advertisement
- timetable for the recruitment process
- how to apply, including your policy regarding references and policy on confidentiality
- information about your organisation, including its mission and vision, its broad strategic objectives, its values and ethos (this should already be on your website)
- job description
- person specification
- outline terms and conditions for the post
- brief information about the management of the organisation, eg a chart showing the management structure with names of the key post holders
- brief information about the governance of the charity such as: number of trustees; name of chair; how trustees are elected, eg is it a membership organisation?
- equality policy and monitoring form.

The advertisement

Charity chief executive posts are sometimes advertised in *The Guardian* on Wednesdays, *The Times*, *The Observer* and *The Sunday Times*. Increasingly senior posts are being advertised on newspaper websites without advertisements appearing in newspapers. A recruitment consultant, if one is being used, will advise you as to where to advertise and will be able to purchase the advertising space at lower rate because of the volume of advertisements that they place in newspapers. If you are not using a headhunter you may still be able to obtain a discount if your charity is a member, for example, of NCVO. NCVO has negotiated a special discount advertising rate for its members with Charity Job http://www.charityjob.co.uk/ncvo/jobsearch.aspx .

It goes without saying that care needs to be taken with the wording of advertisements and when the newspaper sends you proofs for checking. If there is an error which is not your or your agent's fault, newspapers usually agree to rerun the advertisement without further charge.

10.12 | Job description, person specification and information for candidates continued

People are divided as to whether the salary should appear on the advertisement or in the information provided. I believe it should because as a potential applicant it gives me a feel for the level of experience that is being sought. If the salary is lower than I am seeking I will not apply. Certainly when I am approached by headhunters during a search to ask if I know of suitable candidates, I always start by asking about the person specification and then the remuneration package, before considering who might be appropriate. I know possible candidates who will be seeking, for example, a salary of £70,000–£80,000 while others would not consider anything less than £100,000. On the other hand, there are others who believe that advertising 'an attractive remuneration package' will appeal to a much wider range of candidates and this might well be the case. Your recruitment consultant will advise you about this and about how they will deal with subsequent enquiries about the remuneration package. Either way, you must have a clear idea of the salary range that you will consider.

It is important to give the closing date for applications on the advertisement. Always give at least a fortnight, or ideally longer, after the advertisement appears. Producing a good application is very time-consuming and most potential applicants are very busy people.

If you have statistics to prove underrepresentation, it is appropriate in an advertisement to say, if you wish, that applications from women, people with disabilities or from ethnic minorities will be especially welcomed.

You will have to state clearly how further information is to be obtained. Can information be downloaded from your website or the headhunter's website? Will applications have to be sent in by post or can they be emailed? Do you expect candidates to apply online? What do you want candidates to submit: a general covering letter or one that addresses specific issues? a completed application form? a CV of restricted length, eg not more than two pages? additional sheets providing evidence of how the applicant satisfies the essential criteria?.....

10.13 | Equality and diversity

When selecting members of the search committee, the board should give consideration to diversity. If all members of the search committee are from the private sector, they may select someone who is ideal as a chief executive of a private company but who may not be suitable for running your charity. A male-only search committee may discourage very able women from pursuing their application and vice versa. If all members of the search committee are over the age of 65, or if all are under the age of 25 (the less likely scenario), what does that say to applicants about your charity?

Similarly, examine the material that you are sending out to ensure that it does not inadvertently exclude disabled candidates. There are many highly successful disabled chief executives and chairs of trustees. For example, Geraldine Peacock, former chair of the Charity Commission and who was chief executive of Guide Dogs for the Blind Association has Parkinson's Disease; James Strachan, former chair of the Audit Commission and former chief executive of RNID, is deaf.

It is easy to exclude an exceptional candidate who has Parkinson's Disease or who is dyslexic by insisting on a handwritten letter. You may require a chief executive to travel around the country but is it essential for the chief executive to have a valid driving licence, which could exclude someone who has arthritis or a visual impairment? You need to be aware that the Disability Discrimination Act 1995 includes those with cancer, HIV or multiple sclerosis from the point of diagnosis, within the definition of a disability.

If you hold interviews or shortlisted candidates' visits to the charity on a Friday or a Saturday, you may exclude exceptional candidates just because of their religious beliefs.

Interviews need to be fair, consistent in approach and have objective criteria. Notes should be taken and kept. Information about race, age, colour, sexual orientation, religion (unless this is a specific requirement, eg a Christian charity that needs a committed Christian at the helm or the headteacher of a Muslim school who needs to be Muslim) or nationality (except to explain the rules regarding employment of non-EU citizens) should not be sought either through application forms (except through an anonymous, optional equal opportunities monitoring form) or at interview. Questions about health should not be asked prior to an offer being made (Equality Act 2010).

All employers should now be fully aware that at interview they must not ask, especially female candidates, about their marital status, their plans to have children, the ages of their children, what arrangements will be made to look after the children when they are ill and so on. It is equally inappropriate to ask similar questions or questions about race, age, religion, etc, during informal interviews or when the candidate is being shown round the charity. Staff or volunteers who are meeting candidates or showing them around the charity should be briefed accordingly.

If the charity works with children or vulnerable adults enhanced Criminal Record Bureau (CRB) checks must be carried out on the candidate who has been selected and any offer must be subject to clearance through these checks. However questions about arrests that did not lead to a prosecution or a conviction can rarely be justified and therefore should not be asked. Conversations with referees about the candidate's suitability for the post should provide information about the candidate's character and previous conduct without having to ask specific questions about arrests.

10.14 | Remuneration package and conditions of employment

Replacing a chief executive often leads to the review of the remuneration for this post, and possibly that of the whole leadership team. There are several remuneration surveys, for example ACEVO or Reward, which will allow you to do some benchmarking. If you are thinking about talking to similar charities to find out more about their chief executive's remuneration package, take care. Some independent schools were found guilty by the Office of Fair Trading over forming a cartel because they shared information about salaries and fees. Like mainstream charities, independent schools have a long tradition of helping each other and saw this exchange of information not as fee or salary fixing but as assisting fellow schools. The Office of Fair Trading permits the use of historic (ie last year's not current) remuneration information provided by independent bodies through surveys.

Consideration will need to be given to the outline terms and conditions such as:
- salary
- employer's contribution to pension scheme
- whether the following are offered as part of the package: car, health insurance; permanent health insurance, mobile phone; laptop or PC installed at home, other benefits in kind,
- holidays
- relocation expenses
- indication of length of working week and amount of flexibility including 'time off in lieu' if this is offered
- any policies, such as non-smoking policy or any requirement specific to your charity, for example, the Vegetarian Society is likely to require a chief executive who is vegetarian, which may influence a potential applicant's decision as to whether to apply or not
- notice (usually three months) and probationary periods (usually six months).

10.15 | References and verifying CVs and claims made by candidates

Before the information pack for candidates is prepared, you need to consider how many referees you want and at what stage you are likely to take up references. A minimum of two references is the norm but you may wish to give thought to who these referees need to be. Current or last employer is usually a requirement. Some boards of trustees and some headhunters ask for three referees. Sometimes boards ask applicants to provide contact details as referees of their current (or last) employer, someone who has worked with the applicant (peer reference) and someone who has worked for the applicant.

As the appointment of a chief executive is so crucial, you may wish to take up references on the final shortlisted candidates before the final interviews, but if you do this, the candidates should have been warned in advance in the information pack or you should seek their consent. In the educational sector, taking up references prior to interview is the norm but in virtually all other sectors, candidates expect references to be taken up after they have been offered the post. Any such offer made prior to taking up references should always be made subject to references being satisfactory to you. It is advisable to say to the chosen candidate 'You are the preferred candidate, subject to references'. For such a vital post, I would recommend taking up references as soon as the shortlist is agreed.

You need to decide whether only written references are to be requested on each shortlisted candidate or whether you also wish to speak to each referee. I would go as far as to say that you should not only obtain written references but that ideally the chair of the search committee should aim to meet each referee face-to-face to discuss the candidate. This is enormously time-consuming and difficult to achieve but immensely worthwhile. You will learn a great deal more about each final shortlisted candidate and have a much better understanding of their strengths and weaknesses. Referees are much more inclined to give a more rounded and full opinion in a face-to-face meeting then they are in a written reference or on the telephone. Either in the face-to-face meetings or on the telephone, you may wish to ask:

- 'If you were in my position, would you have any hesitation in appointing …. as chief executive?'
- If the person is not already a chief executive you may wish also to ask, 'Would you want to have him/her as your chief executive?'.
- It is worth asking, 'If …. is appointed, which professional development courses would you send him/her on during his/her first two years as chief executive?'

Referees who are reluctant to say anything negative will often answer this final question fully and give you an insight as to areas that need developing. Remember that we are all human and we all have our strengths and weaknesses – do not seek perfection but equally well do not ignore reservations expressed by a referee.

10.15 | References and verifying CVs and claims made by candidates continued

If you are using a recruitment consultant, the consultant should verify academic and other qualifications and should check that claims made by an applicant are genuine. Some candidates will claim achievements in which they have played only a very marginal role. If you are not using a recruitment consultant the search committee should probe by asking investigative questions such as: 'Who did you work with on this piece of work? What exactly was your involvement? How did you personally ensure its success?' Then move on to an earlier achievement and then the one before that. If the candidate has genuinely played an active part in these claimed achievements, the questions will be very easy to answer. It can get quite uncomfortable for some candidates and you should be able to tell how genuine the claims are. Those who have been liberal with the truth will usually bail out halfway through. However, occasionally one comes across an accomplished impostor. Face-to-face interviews with referees should help you to uncover him/her.

You may also wish to contact people who must know the candidate and who are not 'official' referees. This should be done with the consent of the candidate whenever possible. Comments made by an unofficial referee should not be used as justification for rejecting a candidate.

10.16 | Psychometric and other tests

People are generally either totally in favour of or totally against any form of psychometric or personality assessment when recruiting. Those in favour believe it provides information that is otherwise unavailable through CVs, references and interviews and helps selectors to get a much better picture of the individual's personality and provide insight into their decision-making ability and their leadership potential. Others believe that any process of personality measurement is deeply flawed and that the whole process is a waste of time and money. It is up to each board or each search committee to decide whether or not to use these tests. If you do, it is important to ask at interview whether each of the candidates felt that it was a true reflection of them. Their answers as a group will help you to decide how much weight, if any, to put on the results of these tests.

Usually headhunters will organise psychometric testing for you. There will be an additional charge for this. If you prefer you could go directly to companies that offer this service. Either way it helps to have some knowledge of the most commonly used psychometric tests. See Resource 10.3 for more information on the six most commonly used psychometric tests.

10.17 | The final screening

The final selection procedure needs careful planning. Questions you need to ask yourselves include:

Briefing visit to the charity

- When will each candidate have a chance of a one-to-one meeting with the chair of trustees? As it is essential that the chair can work with the chosen candidate, how will the chair feedback to the search committee his or her views on each candidate?
- How are you going to organise visits to the charity and who will the candidates meet? Who will show them around? What will they be shown?
- Who will have one-to-one sessions with each candidate (eg the current chief executive, some or all of the senior management team, a service user, a volunteer)?
- Will you want feedback from the people who have had one-to-one chats or from the people involved in showing the candidates round or both? How will you receive this feedback?

The final interview

- Will it be a fairly traditional interview only or do you also want a group discussion involving all candidates or do you want to send all shortlisted candidates to a management college for one or two days where they can be put through various screening and assessment exercises?
- If you are having final interviews, who will be on the interviewing panel – the search committee or the search committee with a few others or the whole board?
- If the whole board is not involved in the final interviews or even if they are, will you want to organise a reception or social event for the board and senior management team to meet the candidates informally?
- How are you going to pre-plan the areas of questioning and who will ask which questions? Will you want each interviewer to score each candidate or, through discussion, will the interview panel collectively grade each candidate?
- Who will keep notes: each interviewer; the chair of the interview panel or a person specifically brought in to take notes but not to interview?
- How will you structure the interviews?
- Will the interview involve a presentation? If so, what will the presentation be on? Will they be allowed to use PowerPoint? Will they be questioned about their presentation?
- Will you ask them to take part in a mock media interview or do we set up a group crisis management situation and see how they all cope or do neither?
- Will you ask them to respond in writing to an intray exercise?
- Will you have psychometric or other tests for each candidate?
- What other testing, if any, would we like to do?

Possible timetable and structure of the final interview:

5 mins	Welcome, introduction to panel and exchange of niceties to help the candidate relax
10 mins	Presentation
5 mins	Questions of clarification and amplification on the presentation
30 minutes	Core questions with any follow up questions
5 minutes	Opportunity for candidate to ask questions
	Chair concludes interview
At least 15 minutes	Panel discuss and complete their assessment of the candidate
At least 70-75 mins for each candidate	Total

Interviewing is a very exhausting exercise so make sure there are sufficient comfort breaks and there is ample food and drink for the interviewers. Do not forget to provide a fresh glass of water for each candidate.

The chair of the interview panel will need to set the tone and atmosphere of the interviews, and will need to ensure that interviews keep to time and achieve their objectives. A relaxed but business-like approach is likely to put candidates at their ease and you are more likely to get a glimpse of the 'real' person. This should not prevent you from asking challenging questions. It is important to put challenging questions in a non-aggressive way.

Be very clear to candidates as to when they are likely to hear the outcome. Err on the side of not being too optimistic about how quickly they will hear. This stage always takes longer than you expect. Do let candidates know if any offer is subject to a satisfactory checks (e.g CRB).

When making the final decision you must bear in mind all the information and the considerable evidence that you have gathered throughout the screening processes and not just performance at the final interview. Do not forget to record the reasons for your decision and what you will like to tell the unsuccessful candidates in their debrief.

You will also need to agree on a second choice in case the first choice candidate rejects the offer. Consider also, what you will recommend to the board if there is no second choice or if none of the candidates are strong enough. If the field is weak, search committees are tempted to appoint a very mediocre candidate who happens to be the best on the day. This is often because the thought of starting again fills them with dread or because they have not fully appreciated the weakness of the final shortlist. This appointment is too crucial for boards to appoint someone about whom they have reservations. Take calculated risks, if you feel this is appropriate, but if you have doubts, do not appoint.

10.18 | Post-selection

Making the offer and negotiating terms

Once you have identified your next chief executive, the process of negotiation begins. This is better handled by the recruitment consultant, if you are using one, or by the chair of the search committee or the chair of trustees. The board will have provided guidance on the negotiator's room for manoeuvre. If you have an exceptional candidate for whom a higher than planned salary can be justified, you should get clearance from the chair of trustees and the treasurer, who normally have delegated authority from the board to make these decisions in between board meetings. If they do not, the negotiator will have to go back to the board. However, do not let the chosen candidate 'have you over a barrel' during the negotiations. You cannot agree a remuneration package that the charity cannot afford or which cannot be justified to the Charity Commission or to major stakeholders.

Announcing the appointment

No announcement about the new chief executive should be made before the negotiations have been completed successfully and the post has both been offered and accepted in writing. Naturally, the chair of trustees needs to be kept fully informed at each critical stage of the negotiating process if he/she is not the negotiator.

It is vitally important that those most intimately involved in the charity hear about the appointment from the charity and not through someone else or the press. Staff will need to be informed as will other major stakeholders. People will want to know more than just the name of the next chief executive and his or her current post. You will need to provide a brief potted biography.

If the new chief executive is currently a chief executive elsewhere then both organisations will want to make the announcement on the same day so you will need to negotiate with them to identify a mutually convenient date.

You will need to decide whether press releases will be sent solely to the voluntary sector press or whether they should go out to the local press and/or to national newspapers. It is often a good idea to send a press release to your local radio and local television stations, especially if your chief executive designate or the charity may be of particular local interest.

Induction, support and future professional development

Work on the recruitment process does not end once the new chief executive has been announced. Possibly with the help of the search committee and certainly in discussion with the chief executive designate, it is now time for the chair of trustees to start planning the new chief executive's induction. The chair should seek advice from the current chief executive at this stage and should develop the induction programme in close collaboration with the person who has been appointed to take over.

If a handover period is seen to be necessary, when both the outgoing and incoming chief executives are employed simultaneously by the charity and actively involved, keep the handover period short: ideally about a week or a fortnight but never over a month. Lengthy handovers are enormously frustrating and unproductive for both the outgoing and incoming chief executives. Part of a handover period can be used to allow the chief executive designate to travel round the country visiting various parts of the charity and making him/herself known not just to staff, users and volunteers but also to major funders.

Induction should incorporate sessions with key people (including sessions with the senior management team, the chair of trustees, treasurer and other honorary officers) and key groups of people. It will incorporate visits to projects, branches and regions. Ideally, the chief executive designate should be invited by the chief executive to play a part in appointing senior staff and in decisions that will affect the charity after he/she has gone.

If the person appointed has never been a chief executive before, he or she should consider going on a course for new chief executives. Attending courses that are open to chief executives only will help to build up contacts and support networks. A course on governance and the chief executive's role in good governance is highly recommended[1].

Both new and experienced chief executives need mentors and various support networks. Most people, however busy or important, are usually enormously flattered by being asked to be a mentor. When selecting a mentor, it is essential that the chemistry is right between the two people concerned in the mentoring process and that both are within reasonable travelling distance of each other. Otherwise, at busy and stressful times, appointments to see each other are likely to be cancelled.

Agreement on first year's objectives and reviewing performance

Before the chief executive designate takes up the appointment, the chair of trustees needs to discuss arrangements for the chief executive's ongoing professional development and should ensure that funds are available for this are within the training budget.

Arrangements for chief executive performance reviews should be in place before the new chief executive takes up his/her post. The chair of trustees will need to explain the procedures to review the performance of the new chief executive during the first year, and specifically during the probationary period, and arrangements for ongoing performance reviews. If appraisal of the chief executive is already a well established process, the new chief executive is less likely to see the performance management system as a threat. For the same reason, reviewing the performance of the chief executive should be discussed before he/she takes up the post. Whatever you do, do not only introduce appraisal at the point when you have serious doubts about the way in which the new chief executive is performing.

After the chief executive has been in post for between six to eight weeks, the chair of trustees should arrange a meeting with the chief executive so that they can agree the chief executive's objectives for the first year. If you have appointed a dynamic chief executive who is really going to drive the organisation forward, these objectives will be challenging, so do not be surprised or disappointed if not all of them have been achieved in the first year. However, there should be significant progress towards most of them. As the chief executive settles in, some objectives will take on less importance while others that were not identified during the early stages, will become a priority and will need to be achieved or sufficiently progressed during the first year.

I do not agree with the advice that a chief executive should do little of significance in the first year except listen, learn and assess the charity. I agree that a new chief executive should not come into the post with too many preconceived, fixed ideas. I agree that he or she will, without doubt, be on a very steep learning curve for at least the first six months. Nevertheless, a new chief executive does need to make a positive and definite contribution to moving the organisation forward during his or her first year.

[4] www.civilsociety.co.uk

10.19 | Closing stages of the recruitment process

Lessons for the future and succession planning

While the chief executive recruitment process is still fresh in your minds the search committee and then the whole board, should spend some time reviewing the process and making notes of lessons learnt and ways in which the process could be improved. These notes will assist the board when it next has to appoint a new chief executive.

Even if the next search for a new chief executive seems a long time away, it is worth the board, if it has not done so already, developing a succession plan for all key people such as the chief executive, the chair of trustees and the treasurer.

Wishing farewell to the outgoing chief executive

How the charity bids farewell to the outgoing chief executive and welcomes the new is a forerunner of things to come. It is a good idea to establish a small group of people, ideally a mixture of trustees and staff and possibly service users, to plan the events to say farewell to the departing chief executive.

The incoming chief executive will need to be sensitive to the feelings of the outgoing chief executive and should not encroach, unless there is absolute certainty that it is the wish of the outgoing chief executive, on the various events organised to bid farewell to his/her predecessor.

People's significant contributions, employees and volunteers alike, should not be forgotten. We all depend on those who have gone before us and who have created the foundations upon which we build. Charities should remember them as the years go by and invite them to special and other charity events.

Advice to the new chief executive

The whole recruitment process is over and the new chief executive has just taken up the post. What advice should trustees give the new chief executive? From years of working closely with chief executives and having held chief executive roles, my advice would be:

- Make sure your personal ambitions are fully aligned with your trustees' and your ambitions for the charity that you now lead.
- Even if you are an experienced chief executive, make sure that an induction programme for you has been planned in advance, that you have agreement before you take up your post that the charity will invest in your professional development, and make sure you have appropriate mentors and support networks of other chief executives.
- Do not neglect your private life, family and friends. Even though you will have to work very hard, make sure that you get a proper work/life balance and make sure you get enough sleep. Keep yourself physically fit and maintain outside interests.
- Care for all your staff and get to understand them as people, not just as employees. On the other hand, remember to maintain a professional distance so that, if you have to carry out any disciplinary procedures, your professionalism and objectivity are never compromised.
- Do not surround yourself with clones of yourself or people who will always agree with you. You will need people who complement rather than duplicate your skills and personality, who see the world differently but who are equally committed to the work of the charity, who will give you an honest opinion and not be afraid to challenge you constructively.

- Build a strong professional relationship with your chair in which both of you understand your different but complementary roles. Nurture and cultivate all your trustees. However busy you are, make sure that you put time aside for building and developing these relationships. Remember their role is not to rubber stamp everything you want but to be a challenging friend and that they have ultimate responsibility for the charity. It is a key part of your role to ensure that they fulfil these responsibilities. Have sufficient confidence in yourself to give the board an accurate and balanced picture of what is going on. Give them both the good news and the bad news. If you have difficulties with your trustees, seek advice and help and do not try to turn the senior management team or other employees against them. Maintain high standards of professionalism throughout.
- However strong the finance director or your finance department is, always make sure you understand enough to keep your finger on the pulse of the current and predicted financial situation. You need to have some understanding of budgeting, balance sheets, depreciation, etc. You need to be able to put probing questions to your finance director.
- Make sure you have time to listen to others. Do not be afraid to admit mistakes or to ask for help when you need it. Your staff will feel empowered if you encourage them to come up with solutions and ideas rather than you always being the fount of all wisdom.
- Differentiate between what you must do and what you can safely delegate to others. Generally you should only be doing things that a chief executive can do. If someone else can do it, let them do it. This will allow you time to concentrate on planning strategically for the future and ensuring that the charity is on track to achieve its objectives.
- Be prepared to take calculated risks and follow hunches. Keep your trustees, especially your chair, fully informed about the risks you are taking and why you are taking them.

Resources for Chapter 10

Resource 10.1 Recruitment consultants and head-hunters

Executive Search and Recruitment Consultants

Recruitment consultants who work mainly but not exclusively in the not-for-profit sector

Cf Appointments Head Office
52-54 Gracechurch Street, London EC3V 0EH
Tel: 020 7220 0180
Email: enquiries@cfappointments.com
Web: http://www.cfappointments.com/contact.asp

Execucare
3 More London Riverside, London SE1 2RE
Tel: 0800 288 8677
Email: email@execucare.com
Web: http://www.execucare.com

NFP Resourcing
Executive Search Team, Midlands Farm, Duck Street, Chideock, Dorset DT6 6JR
Tel: 0845 0945 336
Email: info@nfp-resourcing.co.uk
Web: http://www.nfp-resourcing.co.uk/

Olga Johnson – HR and Career Management
40 Roseberry Avenue, London EC1R 4RX
Tel: 01892 532799
Email: olga@olgajohnson.co.uk
Web: http://www.olgajohnson.co.uk

People Unlimited
72 Borough High Street, London SE1 1XF
Tel: 020 7939 7439
Email: charities@peopleunlimited.co.uk
Web: http://www.charitypeople.co.uk/

Prospectus
20-22 Stukeley Street, London WC2B 5LR
Tel: 020 7691 1925
Web: http://www.prospect-us.co.uk/executive

TPP
52 Lime Street, London EC3M 7AF
Tel: 020 7198 6060
Fax: 020 7198 6100
Email: executive@tpp.co.uk
Web: http://www.tpp.co.uk/

Recruitment consultants who work mainly but not exclusively in the private and public sectors

Acertus Search and Selection
2nd Floor, Pages Court, St Peters Road, Petersfield, Hampshire GU32 3HX
Tel: 01730 266208
Email: enquiries@acertus.co.uk
Web: http://www.acertus.co.uk/

Executive Appointments – Charities Division
Financial Times
http://www.exec-appointments.com/sector/charity-jobs.ashx
Hanson Green, 110 Park Street, London W1K 6NX
Tel: 020 7493 0837
Email: info@hansongreen.co.uk
Web: http://www.hansongreen.co.uk

Harvey Nash
13 Bruton Street, London W1J 6QA
Tel: 020 7333 0033
Email: info@harveynash.com
Web: http://www.harveynash.com/uk/hnit/

Heidrick and Struggles- Educational and Social Enterprise Division
40 Argyll Street, London W1F 7EB
Tel: 020 70754000
Web:http://www.heidrick.com/ExecutiveSearch

Norman Broadbent
Public and Not for Profit Division,
12 St James's Square, Mayfair, London SW1Y 4LB
Tel: 020 7484 0000
Email: enquiries@normanbroadbent.com
Web: http://www.normanbroadbent.com/

Odgers Berndtson
11-13 Hanover Square, London W1S 1JJ
Tel: +44 (0)20 7529 1111
Email: info@odgersberndtson.co.uk
Web: http://www.odgersberndtson.co.uk/gb/home/

Penna
5 Fleet Place, London EC4M 7RD
Tel: +44 (0)20 7332 7777
Fax: +44 (0)20 7160 9332
Email: corporate@penna.com

Perrett Laver
44 Hertford Street, London W1J 7DP
Tel: +44 (0)20 7659 7900
Fax: +44 (0)20 7659 7901
Email: mail@perrettlaver.com

Robinson Keane – London
4th Floor, 27-35 Mortimer Street, London W1T 3BL
Tel: 0207 998 1801
Email: office@robinsonkeane.co.uk
Web: http://www.robinsonkeane.co.uk

Robinson Keane – Manchester
Century House, Regent Road, Altrincham,
Cheshire WA14 1RR
Tel: 0161 929 9123
Email: office@robinsonkeane.co.uk
Web: http://www.robinsonkeane.co.uk

Rockpools
1-6 Lombard Street, London EC3V 9AA
Tel: 0203 137 3450
Fax: 020 7017 0999
Email: kelly.rooke@rockpools.co.uk

Saxton Bampfylde
35 Old Queen Street, London SW1H 9JA
Tel: +44 (0)20 7227 0800
Email: clients@saxbam.com
Web: http://www.saxbam.com/

Stone Executive
London Office, 2nd Floor, Berkeley Square House,
Berkeley Square, London W1J 6BD
Tel: 01609 749102
Email: info@stoneexecutive.co.uk
Web: http://www.stoneexecutive.co.uk

Veredus
17 Rochester Row, London SW1P 1RP
Tel: 020 7932 4200.
Email: business.enquiries@veredus.co.uk.
Web: http://www.veredus.co.uk/practices/not_for_
profit

Resources for Chapter 10 continued

Resource 10.2 Questions for recruitment consultants

It is important to give time in advance to plan the questions that you wish to ask the recruitment consultants whom you are considering using. Listed below are a few questions that you may wish to ask.

- What recruitment process do you recommend when recruiting by advertisement alone, by search alone and by using a combination of advertising and search?
- How do you marry together candidates that come through search and candidates who respond to advertisements?
- What options do you offer and what are your fees for each option?
- What costs are not included in your fees and can you give us a rough idea of what these are likely to amount to?
- What is the ideal timescale for chief executive recruitment?
- If you are appointed by us, who will lead the process and who will work most closely with us/our search committee?
- Who else will be involved and what proportion of the work will be done by the lead person?
- In the last year how many charity chief executive appointments have you handled? How many were in the same sub-sector as us?
- Who is on your client list and who are you unable to approach as part of the search process?
- Can we speak to the chairs of at least two search committees that you have worked with recently?
- What steps do you take to test the integrity of each longlisted candidate's CV?
- How do you ascertain that achievements claimed by candidates are genuine and not highly exaggerated?
- What in your view is the most thorough way of taking up references? Do you take up references or do we? Do you take up references from people who are not named as referees but who know the candidate well?
- When the final candidate is selected, do you assist in negotiating the remuneration package?
- What happens if our first-choice candidate refuses the offer and we do not feel that any of the other final candidates are suitable?
- What do you do to ensure confidentiality?
- Do you have a diversity policy and a conflict of interest policy? May we have copies?

Resource 10.3 Some commonly used psychometric tests

Myers –Briggs™

This is based on the theories of Carl Jung, is probably the best known in the UK. It looks at how people:
- prefer to take in information (in the form of known facts and familiar terms or in the form of possibilities or new potential)
- prefer to make decisions (on the basis of logic and objective considerations or on the basis of personal values)
- use their energy (is it directed towards the outer world of activity and spoken word or to the inner world of thoughts and emotions)
- prefer to organise their life (in a structured way, making decisions and knowing where they stand or, in a flexible way, discovering life as they go along)

Myers-Briggs™ has 16 personality types

Belbin Team Role Theory™

The nine team roles Copyright © Belbin Associates, 2007-2011

The **"Plant"**. The role was so-called because one such individual was "planted" in each team. They tended to be highly creative and good at solving problems in unconventional ways.

The **Monitor Evaluator** was needed to provide a logical eye, make impartial judgements where required and to weigh up the team's options in a dispassionate way.

Co-ordinators were needed to focus on the team's objectives, draw out team members and delegate work appropriately.

When the team was at risk of becoming isolated and inwardly-focused, **Resource Investigators** provided inside knowledge on the opposition and made sure that the team's idea would carry to the world outside the team.

Implementers were needed to plan a practical, workable strategy and carry it out as efficiently as possible.

Completer Finishers were most effectively used at the end of a task, to "polish" and scrutinise the work for errors, subjecting it to the highest standards of quality control.

Teamworkers helped the team to gel, using their versatility to identify the work required and complete it on behalf of the team.

Challenging individuals, known as **Shapers**, provided the necessary drive to ensure that the team kept moving and did not lose focus or momentum.

The **"Specialist"**. An individual with in-depth knowledge of a key area. The Specialist also has a weakness: a tendency to focus narrowly on their own subject of choice, and to prioritise this over the team's progress.

Resources for Chapter 10 continued

16PF™ personality profile.

This test describes an individual's personality traits and how these traits relate to successful leadership ability, creativity and management performance.

The 16PF™ identifies 16 primary factors and 8 secondary factors

Primary factors

Warmth	Reasoning	Emotional stability	Dominance
Openness to change	Rule-consciousness	Social boldness	Sensitivity
Vigilance	Abstractedness	Privateness	Apprehension
Liveliness	Self-reliance	Perfectionism	Tension

Secondary factors

Extraversion	Anxiety	Tough-mindedness	Independence
Self-control	Self-esteem and adjustment	Social skills	Leadership and creativity

The California Psychological Inventory (CPI™)

The California Psychological Inventory assesses the personality characteristics of 'normal' individuals. It is also used to evaluate the candidate's general behaviour, as well as management potential, work orientation, leadership potential and creative potential.

As with most tests there are several versions. For example the CPI 260™ contains 260 carefully selected items that are used to measure more than two dozen scales in five areas:
- interpersonal behaviour
- social and personal values
- cognitive needs and performance
- personal characteristics
- work-related characteristics.

The SHL decision maker

SHL in partnership with Sheffield University undertook extensive research and developed the SHL Leadership model. It identifies four functions that are critical to leadership effectiveness:
- developing the vision
- sharing the goals
- gaining support
- delivering success.

These evolve into the SHL Great Eight Leadership Model. Four of the eight have a management focus and four a leadership focus.

Leadership function	Management focus (transactional)	Leadership focus (transformational)
Developing the vision	Analysing and interpreting	Creating and conceptualising
Sharing the goals	Interacting and presenting	Leading and deciding
Gaining support	Supporting and co-operating	Adapting and coping
Delivering success	Organising and executing	Enterprising and performing

This test is often used for senior civil service appointments.

The Prevue Assessment

The Prevue Assessment is an evaluation instrument designed to measure general abilities, interests/motivation, and personality. It provides four reports: an individual report, a hiring report, a coaching report, and a succession-planning report. Reports answer the key questions:

1. Can the person do the job?

2. Will the person do the job?

3. Does the person have the personality to enjoy the job?

4. Does the individual fit the job?

The occupational personality questionnaire

The occupational personality questionnaire provides information on 32 characteristics:

Relationships with people	Thinking style	Feelings and emotions
Persuasive	Data rational	Relaxed
Controlling	Evaluative	Worrying
Outspoken	Behavioural	Tough minded
Independent minded	Conventional	Optimistic
Outgoing	Conceptual	Trusting
Affiliate	Innovative	Emotionally controlled
Socially confident	Variety seeking	Vigorous
Modest	Adaptable	Competitive
Democratic	Forward thinking	Achieving
Caring	Detail conscious	Decisive
	Conscientious	
	Rule following	

Note: The descriptions of the psychometric tests above are précised versions of descriptions on their various websites where further information may be found.

Resources for Chapter 10 continued

Resource 10.4 Interview questions

A selection of chairs of trustees of larger charities were asked to contribute a question that they felt all aspiring chief executives should be asked during interview and, chief executives were invited to contribute questions they feel they should have been asked when they were being interviewed. Their questions are listed below.

Leadership and management

- What do you consider are the essential elements of effective leadership?
- What is the difference between leadership and management? When have you used one rather than the other? At which are you better?
- What does 'leadership' mean for you and how have you acted on this?
- If your colleagues in your current organisation were asked what they think of your management style – what do you imagine they would say?

Relationship with trustees, the board etc

- What are the strengths and weaknesses of the view that the chief executive should not be a member of the board?
- If appointed, how will you ensure that you can drive the organisation with the minimum involvement in day-to-day affairs from the trustees, who are usually volunteers who already have busy careers?
- If appointed, how do you plan to use the board of trustees collectively and individually?
- How do you perceive your relationship with the chair and the trustees and how will you establish it?
- What do you consider the role of the trustees to be?
- What added value do you believe a trustee body can contribute to the chief executive of a charity in helping him or her achieve their objectives?
- Describe the board environment which creates the atmosphere which extracts the best in you.
- How far do you believe it is important to work through the chair rather than to foster individual relationships with each and every board member?
- What should your role in board development be?
- How would you resolve a difference with your chair over the future strategic direction of the organisation?
- Trustees are responsible for the strategic direction of a charity and it is the chief executive's job to assist them to define and review it. How would you set about devising a new strategic plan and can you point to any experience of how you have undertaken a similar task before?

Change processes

- What approach will you take to ensure you change what needs to be changed but hold on to what is working well and is right for the organisation?
- How do you envisage the organisation changing over the next five years?

The wider voluntary sector

- What contribution do you think our organisation should make to the rest of the voluntary sector?
- Do you think more can be done to raise the profile of the voluntary sector as a whole, if so what would you do?

Beneficiaries and stakeholders

- How would you ensure that stakeholders and beneficiaries of services are fully engaged within the organisation including the board?

- Who are the real stakeholders of the organisation and why?
- What three things would you want to have achieved in your first six months to reassure key stakeholders that the organisation is in good hands?
- What are the main differences between managing staff and managing volunteers?

Miscellaneous

- How will you ensure that your personal ambitions are always in tune with the ambitions of the organisation?
- How will you ensure that the organisation will have an impact beyond its size and resources?
- Why do you want this job?
- Please describe two or three ways in which you think that this charity can and should make a difference.
- What do you look for when recruiting staff?
- If this was a job share, what should we be looking for in your partner?
- What do the annual report and accounts tell you about the health of the organisation and the challenges faced by its management over the next two or three years?
- What do you perceive as being the main people-related challenges of being a chief executive in the voluntary sector, as opposed to other sectors, and what evidence can you offer of your abilities to deal with such challenges?
- Given that central government is ever more reliant on public service delivery by charities, how do we ensure that our purpose remains to add value to government provision rather than replacing it?
- What have you learned from your past experience that you think would bring added value to our organisation?
- How far ahead do you think you could or should plan for this organisation?
- What do you think are the most important indicators of the current health of this organisation?
- What performance trends would you watch, over what period and why?
- Who should read the constitution or governing instrument of this organisation?
- If you're as good as your CV suggests, why aren't you making lots of money in the for-profit sector?
- What is unique about you and the contribution you can make?
- Why is this charity the one you would like to lead?
- How have you dealt with members of your staff who are brighter and more experienced than you?
- What is the single biggest difference you have made that has benefited the last organisation you worked in?
- Why do you care about the mission of this organisation and how do you demonstrate that care in your personal choices?
- If appointed, how would you plan to spend the first three months in post?
- What is the worst mistake you have ever made?
  What have you learned from this mistake?
- What drives you up the wall?
- You clearly have many strengths which would be a great asset to our organisation. What do you think you would find most challenging about this job, were you to join us, and how do you think would might respond to that?
- How would you ensure the charity will make a difference to people's lives?
- What is the role of the chief executive in safeguarding the organisation's reputation? How/what steps would they take to do this?
- Which of your strengths could become a weakness?
- Have you made a decision in your professional life which did not result in success and if so what did you learn from that?
- What personally motivates, inspires or challenges the chief executive to take on the job?

Resources for Chapter 10 continued

Resource 10.5 Chief executive competencies

The table below was originally developed by the civil service for senior civil servants and is very similar to competencies needed by charity chief executives.

DIRECTION	MANAGEMENT AND COMMUNICATION	PERSONAL CONTRIBUTION
Leadership • creates and conveys a clear vision • initiates and drives through change • is visible, approachable and earns respect. • inspires and shows loyalty • builds a high performing team • acts decisively having assessed the risks • takes final responsibility for the actions of the team • demonstrates the high standards of integrity, honesty and fairness expected	**Management of People** • establishes and communicates clear standards and expectations • gives recognition and helps all staff develop full potential • addresses poor performance • builds trust, good morale and cooperation within the team • delegates effectively, making best use of skills and resources within the team • seeks face to face contact and responds to feedback from staff • manages the change process perceptively • manages relationships with trustees and between staff and trustees	**Personal Effectiveness** • show resilience, stamina and reliability under heavy pressure • takes a firm stance when circumstances warrant • is aware of personal strengths and weaknesses and their impact on others • offers objective advice to trustees without fear or favour • pursues adopted strategies with energy and commitment • adapts quickly and flexibly to new demands and change • manages own time well to meet competing priorities
Strategic Thinking and Planning • identifies strategic aims, anticipating future demands, opportunities and constraints • demonstrates sensitivity to stakeholders' needs • makes choices between options which take into account their long term impact • translates strategic aims into practical and achievable plans • takes decisions on time, even in uncertain circumstances	**Communication** • negotiates effectively and can handle hostility • is concise and persuasive orally and in writing • listens to what is said and is sensitive to other's reactions • demonstrates presentational and media skills • chooses the methods of communication most likely to secure effective results	**Expertise** • earns credibility through depth of knowledge/experience • knows how to find and use other sources of expertise (including IT) • understands parliamentary and political processes and how to operate within them • applies best practice from other sectors and organisations • understands how policy impacts on operations, staff, users and volunteers

Trustees | CEO | Chairs

DIRECTION	MANAGEMENT AND COMMUNICATION	PERSONAL CONTRIBUTION
Delivery of Results • defines results taking account of users or other stakeholder's needs • delivers results on time, on budget and to agreed quality standards • demonstrates high level project and contract management skills • ensures that others organise their work to achieve objectives • knows when to step in and when not to • encourages feedback on performance and learns for the future	**Management of Financial and other Resources** • negotiates for the resources to do the job, in the light of wider priorities • commits and realigns resources to meet key priorities • leads initiatives for new and more efficient use of resources • ensures management information systems are used to monitor/control resources • manages contracts and relationships with suppliers effectively	**Intellect, Creativity and Judgement** • generates original ideas with practical application • homes in on key issues and principles • analyses ambiguous data and concepts rigorously • defends logic of own position robustly but responds positively to reasoned alternatives • encourages creative thinking in others • delegates decisions

Resources for Chapter 10 continued

Resource 10.6 Core competencies for New Zealand public service chief executives

The State Services Commission of New Zealand has developed a list of core competencies for public service chief executives and the personal attributes and skills that lie behind them. They also provide indicators of highly effective behaviour behind each competency as well as indicators of ineffective behaviour. These may be of interest to trustees although not all will be relevant to every charity. (ISBN 0-478-24403-7).

Only the basic competencies are given here:

Personal attributes	General management	Leadership
• Commitment to achievement • Honesty and integrity • Intellectual capability	• Management of people • Managerial expertise • Effective communication	• Building and sustaining relationships • Strategic leadership • Managing in political-cultural context

Resource 10.7 Draft letter of appointment for a chief executive of a voluntary organisation

Written by Bircham Dyson Bell, Solicitors & Parliamentary Agents, 50 Broadway, Westminster, London SW1H 0BL

[ON THE HEADED NOTEPAPER OF THE VOLUNTARY ORGANISATION]

Dear

I am writing further to your verbal acceptance of the offer of employment as Chief Executive of [VOLUNTARY ORGANISATION] ("the Organisation") on [DATE].

I am delighted that you have decided to accept the offer and I should be grateful if you could now formally confirm your acceptance in writing by signing and returning the duplicate copy of this letter in the envelope provided.

If formally accepted, your employment as Chief Executive will commence on [DATE] and will be **EITHER** [initially for a fixed-term of [PERIOD] subject always to a notice period of [insert period] **OR** [terminable thereafter upon [three (3)] months' notice by you or the Organisation].

I enclose a copy of the Service Agreement which you will be asked to sign upon joining but I summarise the main terms and conditions of employment below for your ease of reference. Where there is any conflict between the terms of the Service Agreement and this letter, the terms of the Service Agreement shall take precedence.

Main duties

Your main duties will be as set out below. However, this is a non-exhaustive list and you will be required to carry out such other general duties as may be required by a Chief Executive of a voluntary organisation.

[List Of Main Duties]

Place of work

Your main place of work will be [PLACE] but you may be required to work at any other location as the Board of Trustees ("the Board") may reasonably require. You are [not] required to travel outside the United Kingdom as part of your job.

Hours of work

Your normal hours of work will be [9.00 am to 5.30pm Monday to Friday] together with such additional hours as are necessary for the proper performance of your duties. **EITHER** You will not be paid overtime in respect of any additional hours worked outside your normal hours of work. **OR** No additional remuneration shall be payable for any additional hours worked by the you but you shall be entitled to request additional holiday entitlement you regularly work in excess of [NUMBER] hours per week over an average [13-week] period as set out in your service agreement.

Resources for Chapter 10 continued

Salary

You will initially receive an annual salary of £[AMOUNT] payable monthly in arrears in equal instalments into a bank or building society account of your choice. Your salary will be reviewed annually by the Board. Any salary increases will be at the absolute discretion of the Board and the fact that you may receive a salary increase in any particular year does not mean that you will be entitled to a salary increase in subsequent years.

You will also be reimbursed for expenses properly and reasonably incurred in the proper performance of your duties subject to provision of satisfactory receipts and to your compliance with any expenses guidelines or regulations (if any) issued by the Organisation from time to time.

Holidays

In addition to the normal bank and public holidays observed in England & Wales, you will be entitled to [25 days] paid holiday per annum. If you are joining or leaving the Organisation part way through the holiday year, this will be pro-rated accordingly for each completed calendar month of service. Holiday should be taken during the year in which it accrues since it generally cannot be carried forward without the consent of the Board.

Sick Pay

Subject to you complying with the Organisation's requirements for reporting and evidencing sickness, you will paid your normal salary during periods of sickness or incapacity for up to a maximum of [( )] working days' absence on medical grounds in any period of twelve (12) calendar months; or for the first [( )] working days' absence on medical grounds in any one continuous period of absence (or two or more linked periods as determined by the Social Security Contributions and Benefits Act 1992, as amended from time to time whichever is the lesser.

Any further sick pay will be at the absolute discretion of the Board.

Pension Arrangements

EITHER [There is no pension scheme applicable to your employment but the Organisation will facilitate your access to a Stakeholder Pension Scheme if it is legally required to do so.]

OR [The Organisation will pay contributions at the rate of an amount equivalent to [FIGURE]% of the Salary to an Inland Revenue approved personal pension scheme of your choice.]

OR [The Organisation has organised a [DETAILS OF TYPE OF SCHEME] with [PROVIDER] and it will contribute an amount equivalent to [AMOUNT]% of your basic annual salary provided that you make contributions to this scheme of an amount equivalent to [FIGURE]% of your basic annual salary.]

[Other benefits]

[You and your family will be entitled to membership of an appropriate private medical insurance subject to meeting eligibility criteria and to the rules of the scheme. You will also be entitled to participate in the Organisation's permanent health insurance and life assurance schemes, again subject to meeting eligibility criteria and to the rules of the relevant schemes.]

[You will also be provided with a car which you may use for private use subject to paying for private petrol and the cost of extending the insurance policy to cover private usage.]

As indicated above, please confirm your formal acceptance of your appointment by signing and returning the duplicate copy of this letter in the envelope provided. If, however, you have any questions, please do not hesitate to contact me.

Yours sincerely

[NAME]

I confirm that I agree to the terms and conditions set out in this letter and I hereby confirm my acceptance of the offer of employment as Chief Executive of [ORGANISATION] to commence on [DATE].

Signed:

_____

[CHIEF EXECUTIVE]

Date: /   /200

Resources for Chapter 10 continued

Resource 10.8 Draft contract (open-ended) for post of chief executive

Written by Bircham Dyson Bell, Solicitors & Parliamentary Agents, 50 Broadway, Westminster, London SW1H 0BL

NOTE: Boards of trustees should consult their legal advisers prior to finalising the contract.

AN AGREEMENT made on   201...

BETWEEN:-

1) *[VOLUNTARY ORGANISATION][1] [(a company limited by guarantee registered in England and Wales with registered number [NUMBER])] which has its registered office at [ADDRESS] ('the Organisation') and

2) *[NAME OF INDIVIDUAL] of [ADDRESS] ('the CE')

---

[1] Section 1 of the Employment Rights Act 1996 requires a statement of written particulars to be given to an employee not later than two months after the employment commences. Where there are no terms contained in the agreement regarding any of these particulars, this fact must be stated. This precedent Agreement is drafted to include the required particulars which are marked with an asterisk.

IT IS HEREBY AGREED as follows:

Definitions

In this Agreement unless the context otherwise requires the following expressions shall have the following respective meanings:

'the Act'	means the Employment Rights Act 1996;
'Associated Organisation'	means any organisation which is [wholly] owned by the Organisation;
'Board'	means the Board of Trustees or Board of Management of the Organisation from time to time and includes any committee or sub-committee appointed by it;
'Confidential Information'	Confidential Information shall include without limitation information relating to the Organisation's and/or any Associated Organisation's details of suppliers and their terms of business, details of members customers or clients and their requirements, the prices charged and terms of business with customers, financial information results and forecasts, details of employees and their remuneration, ideas, business methods, financial, marketing, development or manpower plans, sales agreements, computer systems and software know-how or trade secrets or other matters connected with the products or services manufactured, marketed, provided or obtained by the Organisation or any Associated Organisation and any information which has been given to the Organisation or any Associated Organisation in confidence by customers, suppliers or other persons;
'Effective Date'*	means [DATE];
'Employment'	means the employment by the Organisation of the CE as described in this Agreement;
'Intellectual Property Rights'	means all copyrights, patents, utility models, trademarks, rights in designs, database rights, goodwill, in each case whether registered or unregistered or the subject of a pending application for registration, all legal rights protecting the confidentiality of any information or materials and all other rights of a similar nature anywhere in the World in any work created by the CE in the course of the Employment;
'Pre-Contractual Statement'	any undertaking, promise, assurance, statement, representation, warranty or understanding (whether in writing or not) of any person (whether party to this Agreement or not) relating to the Director's employment under this Agreement which is not expressly set out in this Agreement [or any documents referred to in it;
'Salary'	means the salary payable to the CE pursuant to clause 7.1 as reviewed from time to time in accordance with clause 7.2;
'SSP'	means Statutory Sick Pay or any equivalent benefit under relevant legislation;

Any reference to a statutory provision shall be deemed to include a reference to any statutory modification or re-enactment.

References to clauses, paragraphs are references to clauses, paragraphs of this Agreement and references to sub-clauses are unless otherwise stated references to sub-clauses of the clause in which the reference appears.

The headings are inserted for convenience only and shall not affect the construction of this Agreement.

Resources for Chapter 10 continued

[Probationary Period

The CE's employment with the Organisation is subject to a probationary period of [(six)] [6] months.

During this period the CE's performance will be regularly reviewed and if the CE completes the period satisfactorily, the CE will be notified in writing of the CE's appointment to the Organisation's permanent staff.

If during or at the end of the CE's probationary period the Organisation is dissatisfied with the CE's performance, the Employment may be terminated by [one] [(1)] month's notice in writing from the Organisation subject to earlier termination as provided for below. If the CE wishes to terminate the Employment during the probationary period he/she must give the Organisation one month's notice in writing.

Subject to earlier termination as provided for below and once the CE has successfully completed the probationary period the Employment may be terminated in accordance with clause 3.1 of this Agreement.]

Term

*From the Effective Date the Organisation shall employ the CE in the capacity of CE of the Organisation on a [full/part] time basis.

*Subject to earlier termination [as provided for in the probationary period specified above or] as provided for below, the Employment shall continue unless and until terminated by either party giving to the other not less than [three] [(3)] calendar months' notice in writing.

The Organisation shall have the discretion to terminate the Employment lawfully without any notice or on notice less than that required by clause 3.1, by paying to the CE a sum equal to, but no more than, the Salary and the value of any contractual benefits in respect of that part of the period of notice in clause 3.1 which the Organisation has not given to the CE, less any appropriate tax, employee's National Insurance contributions, any other statutory deductions and any amounts which the CE may owe to the Organisation. Should the Organisation exercise its discretion to terminate the Employment in this way, all the CE's post termination obligations contained in this Agreement, including in particular the confidentiality provisions in clause 14, shall remain in full force and effect.

The CE represents and warrants that:-
- the CE is not bound by or subject to any court order, agreement, arrangement or undertaking which in any way restricts or prohibits the CE from entering into this Agreement or from performing the CE's duties under this Agreement;
- the CE is entitled to work in the United Kingdom and will continue to be so entitled throughout the Employment; and
- if the CE ceases to be entitled to work in the United Kingdom the CE will inform the Organisation of such fact as soon as the CE becomes aware of it.
- The CE warrants and represents to the Organisation that he/she will not be in breach of any existing or former terms of employment applicable to the CE, whether express or implied or of any other obligation binding on the CE by reason of the CE into this Agreement or performing any of his/her duties under it.

*For the purposes of the Act no previous period of employment shall count towards the CE's period of continuous employment with the Organisation which period will commence on the Effective Date.

*Duties

The CE agrees to perform such general duties as may be required of a chief executive of the Organisation and he/she shall also:-

- comply with the Organisation's and any Associated Organisation's Articles of Association;
- comply with such reasonable instructions directions and regulations as the Board shall from time to time issue including acting as a director or other officer or performing such services for any Associated Organisation for such period and on such basis as the Board may reasonably determine (and without any further remuneration);
- unless prevented by ill-health or unless agreement has been obtained in writing from the Board devote the whole of his/her time, attention and abilities to the Organisation's affairs during business hours between [9.00am and 5.30pm Monday to Friday] and such additional hours as may be reasonable for the proper performance of his/her duties;
- use his/her best endeavours to promote develop and extend the interests of the Organisation and any Associated Organisations; and
- keep the Board at all times promptly and fully informed (in writing if so requested) of his/her conduct of the business of the Organisation and any Associated Organisation and provide such explanations in that connection as the Board may require.

The CE shall report to the Board in terms of the general control and management of the Organisation.

The CE shall have direct access to the Board and shall have the right to submit items for the agenda of all meetings of the Board and shall have the right to receive notice of and to attend and speak at all such meetings but upon being given reasonable notice may be required by the Board to withdraw from any such meeting.

*Place of Work

The CE's normal place of work shall be at [LOCATION] or such other place or places within the United Kingdom as the Board may on reasonable notice require, notwithstanding that this may involve relocation for the CE on either a temporary or indefinite basis.

The CE may be required to travel on behalf of the Organisation anywhere within the World and may be required to perform his/her duties under this Agreement outside the United Kingdom.

EITHER [The CE is not required to work outside the United Kingdom for periods of more than one month.] **OR** [The CE shall be required to work EITHER [outside the United Kingdom] **OR** [in[COUNTRY] for a period of [PERIOD[1]] from [DATE] During this period the Salary shall be paid in [CURRENCY.] and during this period the CE will be entitled to [INSERT DETAILS OF ANY FURTHER REMUNERATION AND/OR BENEFITS THAT CE WILL RECEIVE WHILST OUTSIDE UK]

---

[1] Periods of more than one month only otherwise use the first option, i.e. that work outside the UK for periods of more than month is not required.

Resources for Chapter 10 continued

Working Time

*The CE's normal working hours shall be [9.00am and 5.30pm Monday to Friday] and such additional hours as may be reasonable for the proper performance of his/her duties. EITHER [No additional remuneration shall be payable for an additional hours worked by the CE.] OR [No additional remuneration shall be payable for any additional hours worked by the CE but he/she shall be entitled to request additional holiday entitlement pursuant to clause 10.5 if he/she regularly works in excess of [NUMBER] hours per week over an average [13-week] period.] Any such additional holiday must be agreed by the Board in accordance with clause 10.5.

The CE agrees that on account of the specific characteristics of his/her role and his/her responsibilities, the duration of his/her 'working life' (as such expression is defined by the Working Time Regulations) is not measured or predetermined. Accordingly the CE agrees that Regulations 4(1) and (2), 6(1), (2) and (7), 10(1), 11(1) and (2) and 12(1) of the Working Time Regulations do not apply.

While it is agreed by both parties that the unmeasured working time derogation will apply to the role and responsibilities of the CE as set out in clause 4 above, it is agreed that if the Working Time Regulations are found to apply to this Agreement the CE agrees that, the maximum average working time of 48 hours for each seven (7) day period which is contained in Regulation 4(1) of the Working Time Regulations shall not apply in relation to the CE's employment with the Organisation under the terms of this Agreement.

The CE may terminate his/her agreement to opt out of Regulation 4(1) of the Working Time Regulations pursuant to clause 6.3 above at any time by giving three (3) months' written notice to the Organisation of such termination. Upon such termination the other terms of the Employment under this Agreement will remain in force and shall not be affected.

*Remuneration

The CE will be entitled by way of remuneration to a fixed salary at the rate of   [   ] pounds (£[   ]) per annum. The Salary will accrue from day to day and be payable in arrears by equal monthly instalments by direct credit transfer to bank or building society account of the CE's choice.

The Salary shall be reviewed by the Board on [DATE] each year and the rate may be increased in its absolute discretion with effect from any such review date. The fact that the CE may receive a salary increase in any particular year does not mean that he/she will be entitled to a salary increase in subsequent years.. Any increases will not affect the other terms of this Agreement.

The Salary shall be inclusive of any fees to which the CE may be entitled as a director of the Organisation or any Associated Organisation.

The CE may with the prior written consent of the Board retain any fee received from a third party for work performed by him/her which is unconnected with his/her duties under this Agreement.

Payment of the Salary to the CE shall be made either by the Organisation or by an Associated Organisation and, if by more than one company, in such proportions as the Board may from time to time think fit.

Expenses

The Organisation shall reimburse to the CE [on a monthly basis] all travelling expenses, hotel, entertainment and other expenses reasonably and properly incurred by him/her in the proper performance of his/her duties subject to the CE complying with such guidelines or regulations (if any) issued by the Organisation from time to time in this respect and to the production by the CE to the Organisation of such vouchers or other evidence of actual payment of the expenses as the Organisation may reasonably require.

Where the Organisation issues an Organisation sponsored credit or charge card to the CE he/she shall use such card only for expenses reimbursable under clause 8.1 above, and shall return it to the Organisation at any time on demand and in all events forthwith on termination of the Employment.

[Following the successful completion of the CE's probationary period,] the Organisation will reimburse expenses which are incurred in respect of the cost of petrol consumed while driving his/her private vehicle on Organisation business **EITHER** at the HM Revenue & Customs approved mileage rate from time to time **OR** at the rate of [insert] pence per mile.] [DELETE IF BEING GIVEN A CAR]

Subject to a written approval from the Board, the Organisation will pay the reasonable cost of membership by the CE of any relevant professional organisation or body [provided that such cost shall not exceed the sum of £[   ].

*Pension Arrangements

EITHER [There is no pension scheme applicable to the Employment.] **OR** [The Organisation will pay contributions at the rate of an amount equivalent to [FIGURE]% of the Salary to an HM Revenue & Customs approved personal pension scheme of the CE's choice.] **OR** [The Organisation has organised a [DETAILS OF TYPE OF SCHEME] with [PROVIDER] and it will contribute an amount equivalent to [AMOUNT]% of the Salary provided that the CE makes contributions to this scheme of an amount equivalent to [FIGURE]% of the Salary.

EITHER [A] **OR** [No] contracting out certificate under the Pensions Scheme Act 1993 is in force in respect of the Employment.

The Organisation will facilitate access to a stakeholder pension scheme where it is legally obliged to do so.

Resources for Chapter 10 continued

*Holidays

The CE shall be entitled, in addition to all Bank and Public holidays normally observed in England, to [twenty five (25)] working days' paid holiday in each holiday year (being the period from [1 January] to [31 December]). The CE may take his/her holiday only at such times as are agreed with the Board.

In the respective holiday years in which the Employment commences or terminates, the CE's entitlement to holiday shall accrue on a pro rata basis for each completed calendar month of service during the relevant year.

If, on the termination of the Employment, the CE has exceeded his/her accrued holiday entitlement, the value of such excess, calculated by reference to clause 10.2 and the Salary, may be deducted by the Organisation from any sums due to him. If the CE has any unused holiday entitlement, the Organisation shall at its discretion either require the CE to take such unused holiday during any notice period or make a payment to him/her in lieu of it, calculated in accordance with this clause 10.3.

Holiday entitlement for one holiday year cannot be taken in subsequent holiday years unless otherwise agreed in writing by the Board. Failure to take holiday entitlement in the appropriate holiday year will lead to forfeiture of any accrued holiday not taken without any right to payment in lieu of it.

[The Board shall give reasonable consideration to any request by the CE for additional paid holiday pursuant to clause 6.1 provided that such additional paid holiday shall not exceed [NUMBER] days per holiday year.]

[Other Benefits

Subject to the health of the CE [and his/her spouse and children under the age of eighteen (18) years old [(including step-children)] not being such as to prevent the Organisation from obtaining cover on reasonable health grounds the Organisation shall during the Employment bear the cost of membership of the CE [and his/her spouse and children [(including step-children)] under the age of eighteen (18) years old] of an appropriate private medical insurance scheme. Membership of such scheme is subject to the rules of the scheme from time to time in force and of any related insurance policy. The Organisation reserves the right to change the provider with which the scheme is maintained and to change the rules of the scheme from time to time in force (including the basis of cover and the scale or level of benefit) or to withdraw the scheme altogether.

The CE shall be entitled to arrange temporary insurance cover to appropriate levels in respect of medical expenses which may be incurred by him whilst he/she is travelling outside the United Kingdom on the business of the Organisation or any Associated Organisation and the Organisation shall pay or reimburse to the CE the reasonable cost of such extra insurance cover upon the production by the CE to the Organisation of such vouchers or other evidence of actual payment of the expenses as the Organisation may reasonably require.

The CE is eligible to participate in the Organisation's life assurance scheme for the time being in force subject to the rules from time to time in force of the scheme or of any related policy of insurance and/or applicable Inland Revenue rules. The Organisation reserves the right to change the insurance company with which the scheme is maintained and to change the rules of the scheme from time to time in force (including the basis of cover and the scale or level of benefit) or to withdraw the scheme altogether).

Subject to the health of the CE not being such as to prevent the Organisation from obtaining cover on reasonable health grounds the CE is entitled to participate in the Organisation's permanent health insurance scheme from time to time in force. Membership of such scheme is subject to the rules of the scheme from time to time in force and of any related insurance policy. The Organisation reserves the right to change the insurance company with which the policy is maintained and to change the rules of the scheme from time to time in force (including the basis of cover and the scale or level of benefit) or to discontinue the permanent health insurance cover altogether [or to terminate any member's participation in the scheme]. The Organisation reserves the right to terminate the Employment whether or not the CE is in receipt of such benefit at any time [provided always that such termination will not prejudice the CE's right to receive benefits under the scheme.]]

[Provision of a Motor Vehicle

The Organisation shall provide the CE with a car of a make and model commensurate with his/her status for the purposes of performing his/her duties under this Agreement. The CE may use the car for private purposes [but the car must not be taken abroad without the prior written consent of the Board].

Subject to clause 12.3 the Organisation shall bear all standing and running expenses of the car except for fuel consumed during private use of the car and any additional insurance costs incurred to permit the CE to use the car for permitted private purposes.

The CE shall pay for or reimburse the Organisation for the cost of private petrol and any additional insurance costs incurred to permit the CE to use the car for permitted private purposes at the rate and in the manner as he/she shall agree with the Board from time to time.

The CE shall ensure that at all times the car is in a condition required by law and he/she shall always comply with all regulations laid down by the Organisation from time to time with respect to Organisation cars.

The Organisation may replace the car with a vehicle of an equivalent standard at the direction of the Board at any time during the Employment and in any event shall normally replace it not less than once every [NUMBER] years or after every [NUMBER] miles at its option unless there are circumstances which make such replacement not reasonably practicable.

The car provided to the CE in accordance with this clause 12 shall be and shall remain at all times the property of the Organisation and upon termination of the Employment for whatsoever reason the CE will immediately return the car to [ADDRESS]].

Resources for Chapter 10 continued

Other Business Interests

During the Employment the CE shall not (except with the Board's prior written permission) whether alone or on behalf of or in association with any other person directly or indirectly be employed, engaged, concerned or interested:

- in any other business or undertaking which is likely in the reasonable opinion of the Board to conflict with any of the objects of the Organisation or any Associated Organisation; or
- in any activity which the Board reasonably considers may be, or become, harmful to the interests of the Organisation or of any Associated Organisation or which might reasonably be considered to interfere with the performance of the CE's duties under this Agreement.

Clause 13.1 shall not apply:

- to the CE holding (directly or through nominees) investments listed on the Official List of the London Stock Exchange or in respect of which dealing takes place on the Alternative Investment Market or any other recognised stock exchange, as long as he/she does not hold more than 5 per cent of the issued shares or other securities of any class of any one company; or
- to any act undertaken by the CE with the prior written consent of the Board; or
- as the owner for investment of real property.

Confidential Information and Organisation Documents

Subject to clauses 14.2 and 23 the CE shall not during the Employment (except in its proper course) or at any time after its termination for any reason whatsoever (whether in breach of contract or otherwise) disclose, divulge or communicate to any person or persons whatsoever or otherwise make use of any trade secrets or Confidential Information which the CE has or may in the course of the Employment become possessed relating to the business affairs of the Organisation and/or any Associated Organisation.

The provisions of sub-clause 14.1 shall cease to apply to information which enters the public domain other than directly or indirectly by reason of the default of the CE or which the CE is required by law to disclose .

The CE acknowledges that all books, notes, memoranda, records, lists of customers, suppliers and employees, correspondence, documents, computer and other discs and tapes, data listings, codes, designs and drawings and other documents and material whatsoever (whether made or created by the CE or otherwise) relating to the business of the Organisation or any Associated Organisation (and any copies of the same):

- shall be and remain the property of the Organisation or the relevant Associated Organisation; and
- shall be handed over by the CE to the Organisation or to the relevant Associated Organisation on demand and in any event on the termination of the Employment and the CE shall certify that all such property has been handed over on request by the Board.

Assignment of Intellectual Property Rights

It is agreed that the CE is in a position of special responsibility and under a special obligation to further the interests of the Organisation. Accordingly any discovery, invention, secret process or improvement in procedure discovered, invented, developed or devised by the CE during the Employment (and whether or not in conjunction with a third party) and in the course of the CE's duties affecting or relating to the business of the Organisation or any Associated Organisation or capable of being used or adapted for use in it, shall immediately be disclosed by the CE to the Organisation and subject to such rights as the CE may have under the Patents Act 1977 will belong to and be the absolute property of the Organisation and shall not be disclosed to any other person, firm or company without the prior written consent of the Organisation.

The CE acknowledges that the Organisation is the sole owner of any and all Intellectual Property Rights and insofar as any of the Intellectual Property Rights are not vested in the Organisation and in consideration of the Salary payable to the CE under the terms of this Agreement, the CE assigns to the Organisation with full title guarantee the entire copyright (including future copyright) and all other rights and interests of whatsoever nature in and to the Intellectual Property Rights and any products of the Employment together with the right to take proceedings and recover damages and obtain all other remedies for past infringements in respect thereof throughout the World for the full period of copyright (and of any analogous rights) and all revivals renewals extensions and innovations thereof and thereafter (so far as possible) in perpetuity, together with the rights to the same in any manner and through any media as the Organisation shall in its absolute discretion decide.

The CE transfers to the Organisation all relevant lending and rental rights arising out of the Intellectual Property Rights throughout the World and the CE irrevocably and unconditionally confirms that the remuneration payable to the CE under the terms of this Agreement includes equitable remuneration for the right to exploit all rental rights.

The CE unconditionally and irrevocably waives all moral rights conferred by the Copyright Designs and Patents Act 1988 and all other moral and author's rights of a similar nature under the laws of any other jurisdiction.

The CE shall at the expense of the Organisation and upon its request (whether during or after the termination of the Employment) give and supply to the Organisation all such information data and drawings as may be required to enable the Organisation to exploit the Intellectual Property Rights to its best advantage and shall execute all such documents as may be necessary to vest such rights, title and interest in the Organisation.

The CE hereby irrevocably appoints the Organisation to be the CE's attorney in the CE's name and on the CE's behalf to execute and do any such instrument or thing and generally to use the CE's name for the purpose of giving to the Organisation the full benefit of this clause. In favour of any third party a certificate in writing signed by any director or by the secretary of the Organisation that any instrument or act falls within the authority conferred by this clause 15.6 shall be conclusive evidence that such is the case.

Resources for Chapter 10 continued

*Illness and Medical Reports

If the CE is unable to work through accident or illness the CE shall inform the Organisation immediately by telephone and keep it informed as to the CE's state of health throughout any period of absence;

Subject to clause 17 the Organisation shall continue to pay the Salary for:
- up to a maximum of [(   )] working days' absence on medical grounds in any period of twelve (12) calendar months; or
- for the first [(   )] working days' absence on medical grounds in any one continuous period of absence (or two or more linked periods as determined by the Social Security Contributions and Benefits Act 1992, as amended from time to time)

whichever is the lesser, provided that the CE shall from time to time if required:
- supply the Organisation with medical certificates covering any period of sickness or incapacity exceeding seven (7) days (including weekends); and
- undergo at the Organisation's expense, by a doctor appointed by the Organisation, any medical examination.

provided that the Board may at its absolute discretion pay additional sick pay.

Payment in respect of any other or further period of absence shall be at the Organisation's absolute discretion.

Any payment to the CE pursuant to clause 16.2 shall be subject to set off by the Organisation in respect of any SSP and any Social Security Sickness Benefit or other benefits to which the CE may be entitled.

Subject to clause 16.4, when all sick pay entitlement pursuant to clause 16.2 has been exhausted, no further salary will be payable by the Organisation to the CE until the CE has returned to active service of the Organisation.

If the CE's absence shall be occasioned by the actionable negligence of a third party in respect of which damages are recoverable, then the CE shall:
- notify the Organisation immediately of all the relevant circumstances and of any claim, compromise, settlement or judgment made or awarded in connection with it;
- give to the Organisation such information concerning the above matters as the Organisation may reasonably require; and
- if the Organisation so requires, refund to the Organisation any amount received by him/her from any such third party provided that the refund shall be no more than the amount which he/she has recovered in respect of remuneration.

The CE agrees that at the request of the Organisation he/she will submit him/herself to a medical examination by a registered medical practitioner nominated by the Organisation. The purpose of such examination shall be to determine whether there are any matters which might impair the CE's ability to perform his/her duties under this Agreement and accordingly the CE will give such authority as is required for the Organisation's nominated medical practitioner to disclose to the Organisation his/her findings.

Termination

This Agreement shall automatically terminate:-
- on the CE reaching his/her [65th] birthday subject to any statutory provisions to the contrary;
- if the CE resigns his/her office as a director of the Organisation;
- if the office of director of the Organisation held by the CE is vacated pursuant to the Organisation's Articles of Association save if the vacation shall be caused by sickness (including mental disorder) or injury;
- if the Organisation ceases to comply with the requirements of the Charity Commissioners.

The Organisation, without prejudice to any remedy which it may have against the CE for the breach or non-performance of any of the provisions of this Agreement may, by summary notice in writing, forthwith terminate the Employment if the CE:
- shall have committed any act of gross misconduct or any serious breach or repeats or continues (after written warning) any other material breach of the CE's obligations under this Agreement;
- is guilty of any conduct which in the reasonable opinion of the Board brings the CE, the Organisation or any Associated Organisation into disrepute;
- is convicted of any criminal offence carrying a custodial penalty;
- becomes or is declared insolvent or commits any act of bankruptcy or convenes a meeting of or makes or proposes to make any arrangement or composition with creditors;
- commits any act of dishonesty whether relating to the Organisation, any Associated Organisation, their employees or otherwise;
- has failed to perform the CE's duties to a satisfactory standard after having received a written warning from the Organisation;
- is disqualified from holding office or taking part in the management of the Organisation or in any other company by reason of any order made under the Company Directors Disqualification Act 1986 or any other enactment;
- becomes a patient under the Mental Health Act 1984.

Any delay by the Organisation in exercising such right of termination shall not constitute a waiver of it.

The expiry or termination of this agreement howsoever arising shall not operate to affect any of its provisions which are expressed to operate or have effect after the date of such expiry or termination and shall not prejudice the exercise of any right or remedy of either party which has previously accrued.

Deductions

For the purposes of the Act the CE authorises the Organisation at any time during the Employment, and in any event on termination howsoever arising, to deduct from the CE's remuneration under this Agreement any monies due from the CE to the Organisation including, but not limited to, any outstanding loans, advances, the cost of repairing any damage or loss of the Organisation's property caused by the CE (and of recovering it), excess holiday and any other monies owed by the CE to the Organisation.

Resources for Chapter 10 continued

Rights During Notice Period

The Organisation may require the CE to comply with the provisions of Clause 20 hereof during any period of notice prior to termination of the Employment.

Without prejudice to the rights of the CE to remuneration and other benefits and the CE's continuing obligations to the Organisation under this Agreement, the Organisation shall have a right at any time after either party has given notice to the other of termination of this Agreement under Clause 2.3 or 3.2 for the whole or any part of the CE's notice period, until the last day of the CE's employment;
- to require the CE not to attend any place of work [and the CE shall be excluded from any premises of any Group Organisation at such times as the Organisation, in its absolute discretion may determine]; and
- to restrict (in whole or in part) the powers, duties and work of the CE (in any manner the Organisation, in its absolute discretion, may determine)

and the Organisation shall be under no obligation to vest in or assign to the CE any powers or duties or to provide any work for the CE and shall have the right to suspend him.

The CE shall, at the written request of the Organisation, resign without prejudice to claim for compensation from any office held by him in the Organisation or in any other Associated Organisation and transfer (without compensation) to the Organisation or to its nominee any share held by the CE in trust on behalf of any Associated Organisation.

During the CE's notice period the Organisation may for the remainder of the notice period (or such lesser period as the Organisation may notify to the CE) require the CE to perform such duties as the Organisation may specify irrespective of whether these are consistent with the CE's position specified in clause 4.

Requirements After Termination

Upon any termination of the Employment, the CE:
- Shall not without the prior written consent of the Board at any time thereafter represent him/herself to be connected with the Organisation or any Associated Organisation;
- shall forthwith resign his/her directorship and any other position or office of the Organisation or any Associated Organisation and shall not be entitled to any compensation or other sum for so doing;
- appoints the Organisation as his/her attorney for the purpose of completing any resignation required under sub-clause 20.1(b) above or any other documents required to be signed under this Agreement by the CE on termination of the Agreement;
- shall deliver during normal working hours to the Organisation or as it may direct all materials within the scope of clause 14.3 and all original or copy materials, all records, documents, books, papers, accounts, credit cards, equipment and other property relating to the business operations or affairs of the Organisation or any Associated Organisation or its or their members clients or customers, including delivery of any property connected with this Agreement and shall give to it all reasonable information as to its affairs;
- if at the time at which notice is given by either party to terminate the Employment any licences are held by the CE on behalf of the Organisation and/or any Associated Organisation, shall at the request of the Board do all things necessary to transfer such licences to such person or persons as the Board may nominate; and
- shall continue to comply with the provisions of this Agreement including not by way of limitation the provisions of clause 14 which are expressed to apply following or notwithstanding termination of the Employment.

Grievance Procedure

Non-contractual grievance procedures are set out in [Employee Handbook/Organisation Intranet/Personnel Department], and while these shall not give rise to any legal rights or obligations of the CE or the Organisation, the CE should follow these procedures should any grievance matter arise in relation to the Employment.

The CE may apply to the Board when wishing to seek redress of any grievance relating to the Employment. The CE should do this by submitting to the Board, or if preferred to a specific member of the Board, a written description of the facts of the grievance and any suggestions that the CE may have for how the grievance may be resolved.

All further steps to be followed in the Organisation's grievance procedure are contained in [Employee Handbook/Organisation Intranet/Personnel Department].

Dismissal and Disciplinary Procedures

Non-contractual dismissal and disciplinary procedures are set out in [Employee Handbook/Organisation Intranet/Personnel Department], and while these shall not give rise to any legal rights or obligations of the CE or the Organisation, the Organisation will normally follow such procedures should any disciplinary matter arise in relation to the Employment.

If the CE is dissatisfied with any disciplinary decision that relates to him/her then the CE should raise this with the Organisation in accordance with the appeals procedure contained in the abovementioned disciplinary procedures. The CE may commence this process by advising the Board, or if preferred advising a specific member of the Board, of the CE's wish appeal against the disciplinary decision. This should be done in writing within five days of the CE receiving notice of the original disciplinary decision against which the CE wishes to appeal.

The Organisation may depart from the precise requirements of the dismissal and disciplinary procedures where it considers such steps to be reasonable and appropriate in the circumstances.

The Organisation reserves the right to suspend the CE on full pay during the investigation of any disciplinary matter relating to the CE for so long as may be necessary to carry out a proper investigation and (if applicable) hold a disciplinary hearing.

Public Interest Disclosure

For the avoidance of doubt clause 14 above shall not preclude the CE from making a disclosure of confidential information insofar as such disclosure is protected by the Public Interest Disclosure Act 1998.

The CE shall be under a duty to make full disclosure pursuant to the Public Interest Disclosure Act 1998 and report to the Organisation all matters which may be of concern to him/her in respect of the Organisation's conduct.

Resources for Chapter 10 continued

Previous Arrangements

The CE and the Organisation acknowledge and agree that:

This Agreement [together with any documents referred to in it] constitutes the entire agreement and understanding between the CE and the Organisation and supersedes any previous agreements between the CE and the Organisation, whether by way of letters of appointment, agreements or arrangements, whether written, oral or implied, relating to the employment of the CE, which shall be deemed to have been terminated by mutual consent as from the date of this Agreement and the CE acknowledges that he/she has no outstanding claims of any kind against the Organisation or any other Associated Organisation in respect of any such contract;

In entering into this Agreement neither the CE not the Organisation has relied on any Pre-Contractual Statement; and

The only remedy available to each party for breach of this Agreement shall be for breach of contract under the terms of this Agreement and neither party shall have any right of action against the other party in respect of any Pre-Contractual Statement.

Nothing in this Agreement shall, however, operate to limit or exclude any liability for fraud.

Interception of Communications

The CE hereby consents to the Organisation for business purposes from time to time to monitor and/or record the CE's use of e-mail, internet, fax and telephone and any other form of written or electronic communication received or sent by the CE at or from the premises of the Organisation.

Third Party

A person who is not a party to this Agreement has no right under the Contracts (Rights of Third Parties) Act 1999 to enforce any term of this Agreement but this does not affect any right or remedy of a third party which exists or is available apart from that Act.

Data Protection Act 1998

27.1 The CE consents pursuant to the Data Protection Act 1998 ("the DPA") to the "processing" by the Organisation of "personal data" including "sensitive personal data" relating to the CE for the purposes of the CE's employment (as such terms are defined by the DPA).

The Organisation's policy is to comply fully with the requirements of the Data Protection Act 1998. The CE shall therefore use his/her best endeavours to follow all rules and instructions on all aspects of data protection. Any misuse of any data on any of the Organisation's databases or unauthorised access to any databases or computerised data or any breach of the Organisation's rules on security by the CE may be regarded by the Organisation as gross misconduct.

*The Act

This Agreement sets out the additional particulars and information required to be given to the CE under the Act.

The CE is not required to work outside the United Kingdom during the course of the Employment for periods exceeding one month. [DELETE IF INCORRECT – ALSO SEE CLAUSE 5.3]

EITHER [There are no collective agreements that relate to the Employment.] **OR** [INSERT DETAILS OF COLLECTIVE AGREEMENTS INCLUDING, WHERE THE ORGANISATION IS NOT A PARTY, THE NAMES OF THE PERSONS BY WHOM SUCH AGREEMENTS WERE MADE]

English Law and Jurisdiction

This Agreement shall be governed and construed in accordance with English law and the parties to this Agreement shall submit to the exclusive jurisdiction of the English courts.

THIS AGREEMENT has been entered into by the parties on the date first above written

Executed and Delivered as a Deed   )
by [ORGANISATION]   )   _____
acting by:-   )   Director

                                                         _____
                                                         Secretary

Executed and Delivered as a Deed   )
by [CE]   )
in the presence of:-   )

Witness signature:

Name: _____

Address: _____

Occupation: _____

This draft contract was written by Bircham Dyson Bell, 50 Broadway, Westminster, London SW1H 0BL

Tel +44 (0)20 7227 7000 Fax +44 (0)20 7222 3480 www.bdb-law.co.uk

Chapter 11
Chief executive remuneration and expenses

By Tesse Akpeki (edited by Dorothy Dalton)

11.1 | Introduction

Many trustee boards find themselves in difficulties when faced with the issue of remunerating their chief executive. It is their duty to secure the best possible chief executive for their organisation. But, increasingly, getting the right person can be expensive. Voluntary organisations find themselves competing with the private and public sectors for skilled, experienced executives. To make life more difficult, there is growing public demand for transparency and accountability as far as executive remuneration packages are concerned.

Fortunately, this particular minefield can be made safe by adopting a systematic approach to chief executive remuneration. Rather than hiding their heads in the sand and letting consultants or executives effectively make their decisions for them, boards need to take charge, closing the accountability gap by assuming responsibility for setting chief executive pay.

Once upon a time, the story goes, charity chief executives devoted themselves to organisations out of the goodness of their hearts. They wanted to change the world, help others, make a difference, and to achieve these selfless aims they were happy to work for peanuts.

Those days, if they ever really existed, are gone for good. Chief executives may still be devoted to the organisations they direct but now they expect to be properly rewarded for their work.

At the same time, all organisations are coming under increasing scrutiny over senior staff remuneration. In the United States, a series of high-profile pay scandals involving non-profit executives has resulted in strict new regulations for voluntary organisations. In this country, the drive for greater accountability and transparency in executive remuneration has been lead by the private sector. First the Cadbury report (1991), then the Greenbury (1995), and, more recently, the UK Corporate Governance Code (June 2010) lay out guidelines for determining executive remuneration. Although these recommendations don't carry the weight of legislation, they set the standards for conduct in private, public and voluntary sectors alike.

11.2 | The challenge of remuneration

In this volatile climate, voluntary organisations must balance the public demand for low administrative and staff costs with the equally strong demand for accountability and high standards of management. The trustee board, in its role as organisational steward, must set chief executive remuneration at a competitive level, high enough to attract and retain good-quality staff with the skills and experience to manage the organisation effectively. At the same time, they must safeguard organisational interests by determining chief executive pay in a way that is rational, consistent and lawful – and they must be sure the organisation gets the best value for its money. This presents a challenge for trustees of large and small organisations alike.

This chapter is designed to help boards understand their role in setting chief executive remuneration and establish a logical, fair, and transparent remuneration review process for their organisation. It does not try to describe the wide variety of remuneration methods and pay refinements employed by voluntary organisations around the country. Rather, it provides a framework of good practice, which is adaptable to large, medium and small organisations regardless of their access to resources or specialist expertise.

The board's role

Why is senior executive remuneration the board's business? Many organisations, indeed many chief executives, don't think it is. Some find it expedient to circumvent the board and put pay decisions in the hands of executive committees or human resource professionals. Boards who allow this, however, may be failing to fulfil their duty of stewardship for two reasons.

First, it is the board's responsibility to hire the chief executive. When it does, it makes a strategic decision that shapes the future of the organisation. The character, skills and ability of the chief executive have an enormous influence, as does his or her working relationship with the board. In order to hire the right person with the right qualifications, the board needs to offer an attractive, well-structured remuneration package in keeping with the organisation's budget, culture and needs. In this sense, the chief executive remuneration scheme acts as strategic tool for the board to secure the best leadership their organisation can afford.

Secondly, in the eyes of regulators and the public, the board is ultimately accountable for the amount paid to its chief executive. Even when consultants or committees are used to conduct research and make payscale recommendations, the board, with its deciding vote, is responsible for any action the organisation finally takes. If the Charity Commission feels that a charity's remuneration is excessive, it will challenge the board to justify the arrangements – and take enforcement action if necessary. The press, members and other stakeholders may also call upon the board to justify the amount it pays its senior executive. For this reason, trustees need to understand the logic behind their remuneration decisions and be able to defend them in a public forum if need be.

Establishing a remuneration review process

To bring true accountability to the process of setting chief executive pay, trustee boards need to take charge of establishing a thorough, fair and efficient pay review and recommendation process. This process has three basic stages: research and fact-finding, recommendation, and board deliberation. The board's job is first to determine who will perform the initial research, then provide a detailed brief to the researchers, monitor their progress and finally receive and deliberate on their recommendations.

Your board may not fully understand its own role in making decisions about executive remuneration. Or it may have unrealistic expectations about what the chief executive should do or how much he or she should earn. Some trustees may think voluntary sector professionals should come cheap, while board members from the private sector may use their own, high salaries as a guide to what voluntary sector chief executives should be paid. A board away-day can provide an opportunity to uncover unexpressed assumptions that stand in the way of establishing the system your organisation needs.

Establishing a regular review cycle

Many organisations are suddenly faced with the question of remuneration when their serving chief executive departs. By setting up a system of regular pay review in advance for all top-level staff, including the chief executive, you can avoid being left in the lurch. Many boards establish a standing remuneration committee, which conducts an annual review, taking into account organisational development, industry standards, cost of living and other factors. Having such a system can also help keep remuneration packages fair and competitive throughout the organisation.

11.3 | Deciding who performs the research and makes recommendations

To set a fair, competitive remuneration package for your chief executive, your organisation will need up-to-date information and good advice. The board must decide who will be responsible for gathering the information and making recommendations to the board.

The whole board

In small organisations, the task of researching and developing a remuneration package may fall to the board at large. In such cases there still needs to be a clear, written brief (see Section 11.5) that sets goals and limits for the work. More tips for small organisations are detailed in Section 11.13.

A remuneration committee

Larger organisations with larger boards may find it more efficient to create a small remuneration committee charged with fact-finding and making recommendations to the entire body. The board must carefully define the committee's task and grant it sufficient resources and authority to carry out the task successfully. For more details, see Resource 11.1

Hiring consultants

Some organisations use consultants to help at the research and recommendation stages. If you can afford their services, a qualified consultant can save valuable time, serving as a neutral adviser and offering know-how gleaned from experience of many different organisations.

However, don't expect consultants to do all the work for you. The board still needs to do the initial groundwork of creating a role description for the chief executive and a detailed brief for the work to be done (see below). And then there's the challenge of choosing a qualified consultant, one with the expertise to design a remuneration package to suit the special needs of your organisation. A poor consultant, or one who works without adequate supervision or a clear brief, won't be able to come up with the right package for you. Finally, never forget that consultants are only hired advisers. The board is still responsible for evaluating their recommendations and taking the final decision.

Trustees   CEO   Chairs

11.4 | Creating a job description

Before the work of researching and recommendation begins, the board needs to come up with a detailed job description for the chief executive position if one doesn't already exist. Although trustees can certainly seek guidance from trained HR (human resources) professionals and staff members, only the board, in its capacity as strategic decision-maker, can determine the kind of leadership the organisation needs to assure its future.

To create a job description:
- review the existing job description for the chief executive
- speak to staff and, if appropriate, the departing chief executive, to find out if the current job description covers the chief executive's real day-to-day duties
- review your mission and organisational development goals
- decide what experience, skills, abilities and personal qualities would help your organisation achieve these goals
- gather several chief executive job descriptions from organisations similar to yours and compare them
- rewrite the chief executive job description that reflects the practical duties of the chief executive as well as his or her job in developing the organisation
- have a human resources (HR) professional review the new job description.

See Resource 3.1 for a model job description for a chief executive.

11.5 | Designing a brief, schedule and budget

The board needs to create a clear, detailed brief for its fact-finders. Even when the board is doing the work itself, a good brief helps ensure clarity of purpose and method.

The brief should:
- define the work precisely but be broad enough to allow researchers the latitude they need to get all the facts
- explicitly authorise researchers to seek expert advice if required
- give researchers the right to consult staff members and review organisational records regarding salaries, role descriptions and so on
- authorise researchers to call meetings
- require all the work to be systematically documented: all meetings and telephone conferences must have detailed minutes, all supplementary information, including consultants' reports, must be kept
- establish a realistic budget for the project, factoring in possible expenses such as staff time, travel, consultant salaries, IT resources, etc
- create a meaningful schedule, including milestones such as when the information collecting phase should be completed, when interim reports should be presented, and when final recommendations should be put before the board for deliberation.

11.6 | Selecting a remuneration committee

A Renumeration committee is an influential body. Its members must be capable, impartial, and responsible. The process of selecting the members must be fair, in keeping with organisational values and it should involve the board itself. In order to prevent standing committees from becoming too entrenched, many organisations limit the term of membership. Obviously, no chief executive or senior staff member with a stake in the outcome should sit on the committee or participate in the final decision in any way.

Ideally, the committee should include the board chair and other members of the board. It may also include non-board members, such as consultants or board members of other organisations. Organisations who have a human resources or legal counsel in-house may find their input invaluable. Those without such staff should look for individuals with HR experience and experience of setting pay levels.

11.7 | Checklist for boards

- Create a new job description for the chief executive or review and revise the existing job description.
- Design a working brief for the group responsible for doing the fact-finding and making recommendations to the board. Be sure the brief includes detailed instructions, a reasonable schedule and a budget.
- When forming the committee to do the research and recommendation, consider including board members from other organisations, board members from the organisations and non-board members with human resources, legal, financial or management experience.
- Monitor the fact-finding process, receiving interim reports from your committee, consultants and other advisers. Make sure the researchers keep to their schedule.
- As a board, receive the final recommendations of your researchers and advisers. Insist that your researchers demonstrate the reasoning behind their recommendations and disclose the sources for their information. Be sure that every trustee understands the rationale behind the remuneration package and its total cost to the organisation.
- Discuss the recommended package in light of overall organisational budget, mission and strategy.
- Vote on the package

The work of research and recommendation

Conducting a systematic remuneration review gives organisations the information they need to develop a chief executive remuneration package that's right for them. Whether the work is carried out by the board, a committee, a consultant or a combination of the three, the job of the researchers is to recommend a remuneration package that will attract the candidate that matches the role description supplied by the board.

Gathering industry salary information

Many factors drive the variations in voluntary sector chief executive remuneration, some easily measurable, others not. Budget size, number of employees, mission and geographic location all have an influence on how much the chief executive should be paid. Not surprisingly, an organisation which lacks knowledge of the voluntary sector marketplace is more likely to overpay or underpay its senior executive. By gathering as much data as possible, your remuneration researchers will develop a realistic sense of the market for top professionals.

Sources of information

- ACEVO publishes an annual survey of chief executive salaries in the voluntary sector.
- Consult consultants: they are an excellent source of information on who gets paid how much.
- Seek information from organisations like your own, ones similar in size and income who share your region or mission. Use only historic, publicly available information or you may fall foul of the Office of Fair Trading as some independent schools did.
- Examine advertisements for chief executive posts (mainly now online) but make sure you're comparing salaries in organisations that resemble your own in size, location, configuration etc.

Reviewing pay scales throughout the organisation

Even if the Charity Commission never challenges your remuneration arrangements, making bad choices can cost you dearly. Too large a gap between chief executive remuneration and that of other staff is bad for morale and lays the groundwork for a resentful working atmosphere.

If unpaid volunteers do much of your work, the perception that the chief executive is earning too much could cost you your workforce as well as the goodwill of your members and stakeholders.

Your chief executive remuneration scheme should form part of a rational organisation-wide remuneration structure. To guard against charges of inequity, some organisations have adopted a policy of paying their chief executive no more than three times the salary of the lowest-paid member of staff.

11.9 | Exploring innovative remuneration strategies

Salary is only one part of a complete remuneration package. A growing number of voluntary sector organisations are adopting innovative practices pioneered by the private sector which make bonuses, benefits, and incentive schemes an integral part of chief executive pay packages.

Benefits

Benefits are increasingly important to organisations trying to attract high-level staff.

When putting together a remuneration scheme, researchers should consider the advantages of offering benefits such as:

- training and professional development
- pension/retirement benefits
- sabbaticals after several years of service
- health insurance coverage
- life insurance
- daycare and childcare provision
- scholarships and education allowances
- company car, parking or travel allowances
- mobile phone
- personal computer and other IT equipment for the home
- housing allowance, housing maintenance and utilities
- severance provisions.

Many organisations already offer their top executives training and development opportunities as part of their remuneration packages. Building such opportunities into a remuneration package allows an organisation to constantly improve the quality of its leadership while attracting and retaining a well-motivated chief executive.

Perfect perks

Such creative benefit schemes can be a boon to voluntary organisations that may lack hard currency but have other resources to offer. However, boards should be aware of a few factors:

- The kind of benefits you offer should fit into your organisational ethos as well as your budget. Few would think it seemly for the head of a famine relief organisation to be swanning around in a private limousine!
- When remuneration packages get this complicated, the help of a trained human resources professional is a must.
- Whatever benefits you offer, they will come with a pricetag in the eyes of the regulators and the taxman. Their market value must be calculated into the sum total of any remuneration package.

Bonuses, incentive plans and performance-related pay

Bonuses, incentive plans and performance-related pay schemes, like so many innovations popularised by the private sector, have found their way into the remuneration strategies of voluntary sector organisations. The terms are used interchangeably to describe various kinds of schemes that offer extra pay for high performance. The schemes themselves are much misunderstood and, at least in the voluntary sector, their introduction has been fraught with controversy. However, any group charged with making remuneration recommendations needs to consider including a pay-for-performance component as a means of enhancing the chief executive remuneration package.

There are many ways of structuring a pay-for-performance scheme and the help of a qualified human resources professional is usually required. For remuneration researchers, however, the important thing is to clearly define the objectives of any such scheme.

Schemes can be designed to:
- act as an extra incentive to joining or staying with an organisation
- reward individual achievement of specified, pre-established tasks or targets
- recognise excellence in any pre-established area
- reward individual contribution to the overall performance of the organisation.

11.10 | Performance anxiety

Performance-related pay schemes come with a few caveats:

- Slaves of fashion: Don't allow yourselves to be swayed by the pay-for-performance trend. There is increasing evidence in the private sector to show that performance related pay doesn't always achieve what it was set up to achieve.

- Not every chief executive requires the carrot of an incentive scheme to get the job done really well.

- Fair's fair: Never use performance-related pay to artificially beef up an inadequate remuneration package. Your basic remuneration scheme should reward your chief executive fairly for doing the job he or she is hired to do. Use bonuses and other incentives to reward for true excellence, for achievement above and beyond the norm.

- No room for confusion: When setting up an incentive scheme, create clear written criteria against which chief executive performance will be measured. Make sure everyone, especially the chief executive and the board, understands what the criteria are, who will do the appraisal, when it will be conducted and how bonuses or extra pay will be rewarded. Targets should be objective, fair, easily measurable and distinct from those set forth in the chief executive's basic role description. Lack of clarity here causes bad feeling all around when pay expectations are disappointed.

- Serve the mission: Make sure that incentive targets directly serve the organisation's mission: Experience shows that goals linked directly to remuneration are the ones chief executives meet most readily. Don't place important issues on the back burner for your chief executive by failing to reward him or her for dealing with them.

- Punish not: Incentive pay is a carrot, not a stick. Although organisations can use pay-for-performance schemes to reward excellence they cannot use them to punish poor performance. By law (and in fairness) you cannot withhold promised payment if your chief executive meets pre-agreed, clearly-defined incentive targets, even when you may feel his or her performance in other areas is less than outstanding. By the same token, don't punish your chief executive for striving but not quite succeeding. Make sure honest effort is rewarded by building in an incremental scale that recognises different levels of achievement.

- Untangling appraisal: Don't confuse individual performance appraisal with the assessment that determines whether or not your chief executive gets paid extra for meeting specified incentive targets. Individual performance appraisal should take place on an annual basis and cover the chief executive's performance of his or her basic role (see chapter 9 for further details). It provides an opportunity to air differences and identify development needs. The pay-for-performance assessment is a more objective affair where only the pre-set performance goals are reviewed and extra pay or bonuses are awarded. Ideally, it should be held at a different time of year from the individual assessment, to avoid confusion.

11.11 | Considering tax and regulatory implications

Every benefit, bonus and perk comes with a bottom-line cost in the eyes of regulators. All must be taken into account, along with cash salaries, when doing your organisational books. Some offerings will cost you more in taxes than others. By careful structuring, certain schemes can improve overall cash flow. Be sure to run any remuneration scheme past your financial adviser in order to get a clear picture of its real cost to your organisation.

Remember that charities also need to disclose information about staff salaries over a certain level, currently £60,000 per year. Their accounts must show how many staff members earn salaries between £60,000–70,000, how many between £70,000–80,000 and so on. In this way, the Charity Commission monitors staff salaries and gathers the information it needs to take action against charities whose remuneration arrangements appear excessive.

Legal advice

All remuneration packages must adhere to the letter of the law. Have your legal adviser review any remuneration offer your organisation is planning to make. Formal contracts must of course always be prepared by a qualified legal professional.

11.12 | Making recommendations to the board

Once the researchers have gathered all relevant data, it's time to present findings to the board. The recommendations should come in the form of a coherent plan, which lays out salary, benefits and other remuneration components, giving an overall cost for the total package. Researchers must be prepared to discuss their process and back up their recommendations with a clear rationale, demonstrating how the package will attract the candidate described in the original chief executive role description. Then the floor should be thrown open to board discussion before a final vote is taken. Discussion, including dissenting opinions, should be carefully recorded in the minutes.

11.13 | Setting chief executive remuneration in small organisations

Small organisations with limited staff need a cost-effective way of determining chief executive remuneration. In such organisations, the board itself will probably do the research and recommendation work – and do it on a shoestring. If your board is faced with the challenge of wearing two hats, here are some tips to help the process work smoothly:

- Keep in mind that when the board acts as its own remuneration committee it takes on a much more limited and objective role. As remuneration advisers, your job is simply to come up with a fair, attractive and appropriate remuneration scheme for your organisation. To succeed, the group needs to stick to the task at hand and avoid dragging in larger organisational issues.
- Working as the board, write a clear, complete brief for the research and recommendation work, including a chief executive role description, just as you would if you were delegating the task. This will help your group keep on track.
- Make sure that no one involved in the research and recommendation has an interest in the outcome.
- Remember that committees can include non-board members. Invite individuals with HR and management experience to sit on your remuneration committee.
- Hold remuneration committee meetings at different times from your regular board meetings.
- Use personal contacts with other organisations and professionals to gather industry data; anecdotal information can be as useful to you as statistics in this case. Board members from other organisations can be a good source of advice.
- Consult with support organisations such as NCVO for help with legal and managerial issues.
- Keep your package simple: there's no need for fancy schemes when remuneration is fair and carefully thought out.
- Present your recommendations to yourselves as a board in written form. Now is the time to discuss broader organisational issues and thrash out compromises.

11.13 | Checklist for the remuneration research process

Use personal contacts to gather information about chief executive remuneration arrangements at other, similar organisations.

- Gather data on chief executive remuneration from official sources, such as surveys.
- Review the remuneration packages offered with chief executive job advertisements.
- Review remuneration levels throughout the organisation: chief executive remuneration should be in keeping with the remuneration levels for other staff.
- Hire consultants, if appropriate, or otherwise seek expert advice.
- Discuss the possibility of offering various benefits to make your remuneration package more attractive. Find out how much these would cost from a human resources professional or another organisation that offers similar benefits.
- If you are considering including a pay-for-performance component in your remuneration arrangements, determine the goals for the scheme. What specific tasks, targets or behaviours do you want to encourage? Seek the advice of an HR professional or an organisation experienced in administering a performance-related pay scheme.
- Determine the legal, tax and regulatory implications for your proposed scheme.
- Create a detailed recommendation to present to the board. This should include a full description of recommended remuneration arrangements, a figure for the total cost of the package and a clear rationale justifying the recommendation.

11.14 | Reviewing the remuneration of a serving chief executive

Remuneration review for a serving executive should take place as part of a regular organisation-wide programme of salary and benefits monitoring. Many organisations make such reviews an annual event, using them as an opportunity to regularly update their remuneration arrangements.

But what if your organisation lacks such a system? If this is the case and your chief executive is asking for an adjustment, then the process is similar to setting remuneration levels for a new chief executive.

- Establish a remuneration review committee and provide it with a brief. Your chief executive should naturally not serve on or otherwise influence such a committee.
- Review the chief executive role description, interviewing staff and the chief executive to discover if it still fits the bill. Revise if appropriate.
- Review the chief executive's most recent performance appraisal.
- Gather industry pay data to get a realistic sense of your chief executive's market value.

The remuneration committee should make recommendations based on industry standards, the role description and the chief executive's track record. The board should review these, taking into account the chief executive's own requests. Finally, the board should offer the chief executive the remuneration package it feels the organisation can justify and afford.

And if you can't meet your executive's demands? You may need to consider some of the more innovative benefit and pay-for-performance strategies to make your package more attractive. Sadly, if a chief executive asks for more than the board feels the organisation can legitimately afford, the board must let the chief executive go and seek another professional within its price range.

Resources for Chapter 11

Resource 11.1 The remuneration committee

by Dorothy Dalton

With greater quantities of public money coming to the voluntary sector (eg public service contracts), the media are taking a much closer interest in charities. 'Fat cat' articles are no longer confined to the private sector. It is therefore vitally important that professionally managed charities have a fair and open process for setting remuneration. If media interest falls on your charity's salaries, it is important that on these occasions the spokesperson for the charity is not the chief executive or the HR director but a member of the board of trustees, ideally the chair of trustees or the chair of the remuneration committee.

Details of sound, fair and objective processes for setting the remuneration packages of staff, especially senior executives, should be readily available to any interested member of the general public. Some boards of trustees may feel that the charitable sector should exhibit greater accountability and transparency by publishing more detailed information about the remuneration received by senior executives, and that the chair of trustees should be prepared to answer questions on senior executives' remuneration at the AGM.

Terms of reference for a remuneration committee

Approved by the board of trustees on ....20...

Composition, attendees, quorum and reporting

- The remuneration committee will consist of not less than ..... external, impartial members and not more than ..... trustees.
- Members of the remuneration committee should have a good knowledge of the charity, but have no financial or other interests in the remuneration decisions being taken. Take care to ensure that there is no cross membership of remuneration committees; for example the chief executives of two charities being on each others' remuneration committees.
- The board of trustees will appoint the chair of the remuneration committee. Ideally one of the external members of the remuneration committee will be appointed as chair.
- The chair will serve for not more than .....years.
- The chair shall, as and when necessary, require the chief executive, the finance director, the human resources director and such other members of staff to be in attendance.
- The remuneration committee will report to the board of trustees at least annually.
- Until otherwise determined by the board of trustees, a quorum shall consist of .... members of the committee.

Overall responsibility

With the best interests of the charity in mind and in accordance with current best practice:
- to make recommendations to the board on all aspects of the remuneration and terms and conditions of service of the chief executive and other key senior staff, maintaining an overview of policy in relation to other members of staff
- to ensure that remuneration is set at a level which is appropriate for a charity that wishes to pay sufficient, without paying more than is necessary, to attract, retain and motivate senior managers of the necessary quality and calibre to run the charity successfully in the long-term interests oResources and information.

Fundamental principles

1. Accountability
2. Transparency
3. Performance

These are the three fundamental principles recommended by the Greenbury Report (1995) and The Combined Code of Corporate Governance (2006) and accepted as good practice in the private sector.

It is our view that performance-related pay may not be appropriate for senior executives in every charity and that this must be a policy decision taken by the board of trustees based on the advice of the remuneration committee.

Main duties

1. Make recommendations to the board on the broad policy framework for senior management remuneration and its cost.

2. Determine on behalf of the board, the contractual terms and total remuneration package for each member of the senior management team.

3. Take advice from the chief executive, human resources director, finance director and independent consultants, as appropriate, on the discharge of the above responsibilities.

1. Make recommendations to the board on the broad policy framework for senior management remuneration and its cost:

- to develop a remuneration policy that supports the objects, vision, mission and strategic priorities of the charity.
- to consider as part of the policy framework, whether or not it is in the interests of the charity for remuneration of senior managers to be linked to (individual and/or team) performance.
- if remuneration is linked to performance, to advise on the broad policy issues of how performance can be measured against the achievement of strategic objectives and targets, the range and levels of performance and the corresponding levels of performance pay, ensuring that targets are achievable and that rewards are worthwhile, consistent and affordable.
- to recommend to the board the level of investment in the professional development and growth of the chief executive and other members of the senior management team ensuring these recommendations are compatible with the training policy of the charity and are timed to feed in to the budget planning cycle.
- to ensure that the remuneration policy, names of members of the remuneration committee and outline details of remuneration are available to the general public through publications such as the annual report.

Resources for Chapter 11 continued

2. Determine on behalf of the board, the contractual terms and total remuneration package for each member of the senior management team:

- to recommend to the board the various elements of the remuneration package eg level of pension contribution, provision of company car, mobile phone, laptop computer, etc, provision of insurance cover (for example, permanent health insurance, medical insurance, death in service), payment of fees for membership of professional bodies
- to recommend to the board the outline terms and conditions of employment for the chief executive and key senior executives including
  - length of probationary period, whether appointments should be permanent, rolling or fixed term
  - period of notice for termination of contract;
  - opportunities for paid sabbaticals
  - amount of annual paid holiday
  - levels of paid or unpaid study leave
  - levels of paid, partially paid or unpaid sick leave
  - disciplinary, grievance and appeals procedures, etc
- to ensure there are adequate processes for reviewing the work of the chief executive and other members of the senior management team (note: the remuneration committee is not expected to carry out these reviews but to ensure these processes are in place).
- to ensure that these terms and conditions will support the achievement of the strategic objectives; conform to the values and philosophy of the charity, and are compatible with the terms and conditions of other employees.

3. Take advice from the chief executive, human resources director, finance director and independent consultants, as appropriate, on the discharge of the above responsibilities:

- to commission (either from internal professionals or external specialists) and consider regularly data gathered on salaries for comparable senior posts in similar organisation in the voluntary and other sectors
- to take professional advice on employment issues as and when necessary
- to obtain advice from the chief executive (especially in relation to terms and conditions of the senior management team and the levels of their remuneration packages), human resources director and the finance director prior to finalising recommendations to the board.

Further Information and Support

Resources and information

A CEO's Guide to Board Development, Acevo
http://www.acevo.org.uk

Essential Guide to Recruiting a Chief Executive, Chair and Trustee, Acevo
http://www.acevo.org.uk/Page.aspx?pid=1040

The Essential Trustee, The Charity Commission (CC3)
http://www.charity-commission.gov.uk/Publications/cc3.aspx

Finding new trustees- what charities need to know, (CC30) the Charity Commission
http://www.charity-commission.gov.uk/Publications/cc30.aspx

Good Governance: A Code for the Voluntary and Community Sector
http://www.ncvo-vol.org.uk/codeofgovernance

The Good Guide to Employment, NCVO
http://www.ncvo-vol.org.uk/products-services/publications/good-guide-to-employment

The Good Practice in Trustee Recruitment Toolkit
http://www.ncvo-vol.org.uk/toolkit-downloads-good-practice-trustee-recruitment-toolkit

The Good Trustee Guide, NCVO
http://www.ncvo-vol.org.uk/products-services/publications/good-trustee-guide

Governance: essential information for effective trustees Magazine and online newsletter edited by Dorothy Dalton
http://www.civilsociety.co.uk/shop/product/11/governance_magazine/

Guidance on the legal status of Charity Chief Executives, Acevo
http://www.acevo.org.uk

The Hallmarks of an Effective Charity (CC10), the Charity Commission
http://www.charity-commission.gov.uk/Publications/cc10.aspx

Learning to Lead, Third Sector Leadership Centre
http://www.ncvo-vol.org.uk/products-services/publications/learning-to-lead

Lost in Translation, NCVO
http://www.ncvo-vol.org.uk/products-services/publications/lost-in-translation

National Occupational Standards for Trustees, Skills Third Sector
http://www.skills-thirdsector.org.uk/national_occupational_standards/trusteenos/

NCVO Trustee and Governance information centre, NCVO
http://www.ncvo-vol.org.uk/advice-support/trustee-governance

Reducing the Risks, NCVO
http://www.ncvo-vol.org.uk/products-services/publications/reducing-the-risks

Reward for the Chief Executive and Senior Management, Acevo, 2009
http://www.skills-thirdsector.org.uk/national_occupational_standards/trusteenos/

Trustee Recruitment for Small Organisations
http://www.ncvo-vol.org.uk/trusteerecruitmentforsmallorganisations

Your Chair and Board - a survival guide and toolkit for CEOs, Acevo
http://www.acevo.org.uk